Cinema
Speculation

Also by Quentin Tarantino

Once Upon a Time in Hollywood

Cinema
Speculation

Quentin Tarantino

HARPER
An Imprint of HarperCollins*Publishers*

HarperCollins books may be purchased for educational, business, or sales promotional use. For information, please email the Special Markets Department at SPsales@harpercollins.com.

Excerpts on pp. 152–154 from "A Look at '50s, Flatbush Style," "Violence Bared in 'Supervixens,'" "Corman Gang Spoofs Itself," "Teen-age Hijinks in 'Pom Pom Girls,'" "'Thunder' Lets Bloodbath Roll," and "'Malibu High': A Study in Obsession" by Kevin Thomas. Copyright © 1974, 1975, 1976, 1977, 1979 *Los Angeles Times*. Used with permission.

Excerpts on pp. 206–208 from "The True Facts Behind Lugosi's Tragic Drug Addiction" by Barry Brown, *Castle of Frankenstein* #10, 1966. Used with permission of Castle of Frankenstein®, mymoviemonsters.com.

FIRST EDITION

Designed by Nancy Singer

Library of Congress Cataloging-in-Publication Data has been applied for.

ISBN 978-0-06-311258-2

22 23 24 25 26 LBC 7 6 5 4 3

Cinema
Speculation

Little Q Watching
Big Movies

In the late sixties and early seventies, the Tiffany Theater owned certain cultural real estate that made it stand out from the other big cinemas in Hollywood. For one, it wasn't located on Hollywood Boulevard. With the exception of Pacific's Cinerama Dome, which sat proudly by itself on the corner of Sunset and Vine, the other big houses all existed on Old Hollywood's last refuge to the tourists—Hollywood Boulevard.

During the day tourists could still be seen walking down the boulevard, going to the Hollywood Wax Museum, looking down at their feet and reading the names on the Walk of Fame ("*Look Marge, Eddie Cantor*"). People were drawn to Hollywood Boulevard for its world-famous theatres (Grauman's Chinese Theatre, the Egyptian, the Paramount, the Pantages, the Vogue). However, once the sun went down and the tourists went back to their Holiday Inn's, Hollywood Boulevard was taken over by the people of the night and transformed into *Hollyweird*.

But the Tiffany wasn't just on Sunset Boulevard, it was Sunset Boulevard west of La Brea, officially making its location *the Sunset Strip*.

What difference does that make?

Quite a difference.

During that period, huge nostalgia for all things *Old Holly-wood* was taking place. Pictures, paintings, and murals of Laurel and Hardy, W. C. Fields, Charlie Chaplin, Karloff's Frankenstein, King Kong, Harlow, and Bogart were everywhere you looked (this was the time of the famous psychedelic posters by Elaine Have-lock). Especially in Hollywood proper (i.e., east of La Brea). But once you drove past La Brea on Sunset, the boulevard turned into *the Strip* and Old Hollywood as defined by the movies melted away, and Hollywood as the home of hippie nightclubs and the youth culture took over. The Sunset Strip was famous for its rock clubs (the Whisky a Go Go, the London Fog, Pandora's Box).*

And right there among the rock clubs and across the street from Ben Frank's Coffee Shop sat the Tiffany Theater.

The Tiffany didn't show films like *Oliver!*, *Airport*, *Goodbye, Mr. Chips*, *Chitty Chitty Bang Bang*, *The Love Bug*, or even *Thunderball*. The Tiffany was the home of *Woodstock*, *Gimme Shelter*, *Yellow Submarine*, *Alice's Restaurant*, *Andy Warhol's Trash*, *Andy Warhol's Frankenstein*, and Robert Downey's *Pound*.

These were the movies that the Tiffany played. And while the Tiffany wasn't the first theatre in Los Angeles to play *The Rocky Horror Picture Show* or even the first one to have regular midnight screenings, in terms of the legend the film would become it was the first cinema engagement where much of what constituted the Rocky Horror phenomenon really exploded—coming in costume, shadow cast performing, callbacks, theme nights, etc. Throughout the seventies the Tiffany would continue to be the counterculture home for *head flicks*. Some successful (Frank Zappa's *200 Motels*),

---

*Dean Martin's smirking face, drawn in neon, out in front of his nightclub Dino's was the only Old Hollywood holdout to be found on *the Strip*.

some not (Freddie Francis' *Son of Dracula* with Harry Nilsson and Ringo Starr). The counterculture films from 1968–71, whether or not they were good, were exciting. And they demanded to be seen in a crowd, preferably stoned. Soon, the Tiffany would be far less of a scene than it was, because the head movies that came out from 1972 on were more afterthoughts of a niche market.

But if the Tiffany had a year, it was 1970.

That same year, at the age of seven, I first attended a show at the Tiffany when my mother (Connie) and my stepfather (Curt) took me to see a double feature: John G. Avildsen's *Joe* and Carl Reiner's *Where's Poppa?*

Wait a minute, you saw a double feature of Joe and Where's Poppa? at seven?

You bet I did.

And while that was a memorable screening, hence I'm writing about it now, for me at the time, it was hardly culture shock. If we go by author Mark Harris' timeline, the beginning of the New Hollywood revolution was 1967. Then my first years of going to see movies at the theatre (I was born in '63) coincided with the beginning of the revolution ('67), the cinematic revolutionary war ('68–'69), and the year the revolutionary war was won ('70). Which was the year New Hollywood became *the* Hollywood.

Avildsen's *Joe* made quite a splash when it was released in 1970 (it was an undeniable influence on *Taxi Driver*). Unfortunately, in the last fifty years this powder keg of a picture has kind of faded away. The film tells the story of a distraught upper middle-class father (played by Dennis Patrick) who loses his daughter (Susan Sarandon, in her motion picture debut) to the hippie drug culture of the era.

While visiting the disgusting pad his daughter shares with her scumbag junkie boyfriend, Patrick ends up bashing his head in (she's not there at the time). While sitting in a tavern, trying to come to grips with both the violence and the crime he committed, he meets a racist loudmouth blue-collar hard hat worker named *Joe* (played, in a star-making performance, by Peter Boyle). Joe is sitting at the bar, drinking his beer after work, carrying on a pro-fanity filled "*America Love It or Leave It*" rant about hippies, black folks, and society circa 1970 in general. Nobody in the working-class tavern is paying attention to him (the bartender even tells him, obviously not for the first time, "*Joe, gives us all a break*").

Joe's diatribe ends with the sentiment that somebody oughta kill 'em all (the hippies). Well, Patrick just did and, in an unguarded moment, makes a barroom confession that only Joe hears.

What follows is the strangely antagonistic, yet symbiotic, rela-tionship between the two different men from two different classes. They're not exactly friends (Joe's practically blackmailing the an-guished father), but in a black-comic twisted way they do become compadres. The distinguished middle-class man of the executive class has enacted the fascistic rants of this low-class blue-collar loudmouth slob.

By blackmailing Patrick into a sort of alliance, Joe shares both the murderer's dark secret and, to some degree, the culpability of the murder. This dynamic unleashes the desires and inhibitions of the blue-collar blowhard and buries the cultured man's guilt, replac-ing it with a sense of purpose and righteousness. Till the two men, armed with automatic rifles, are executing hippies at a commune. And in a tragic, ironic *freeze-frame*, the father ends up executing his own daughter.

Pretty strong stuff? You bet.

But what that synopsis can't begin to convey is how fucking funny the film is.

As harsh, and ugly, and violent as the movie *Joe* is, at its heart it's a kettle-black comedy about class in America, bordering on satire, while also being savagely vicious. Blue-collar, upper middle class, and youth cultures are represented by their worst surrogates (every male character in the film is a loathsome cretin).

Today it might be controversial to even refer to *Joe* as a black comedy. But it sure wasn't when it was first released. At the time I saw *Joe* it was easily the ugliest movie I'd ever seen (a spot it held till four years later when I saw *The Last House on the Left*). Frankly it was the squalor of the apartment the two junkies at the beginning lived in that creeped me out the most. In fact, it made me a little sick to my stomach (even the rendering of the junkie apartment in the *Mad Magazine* spoof made me a little ill). And the audience at the Tiffany Theater in 1970 watched the early section of the film in silence.

But once Dennis Patrick enters the tavern, and Peter Boyle's Joe enters the movie, the audience started laughing. And in no time at all the adult audience went from repulsed repose to outright hilarity. I remember they laughed at pretty much every fucking thing Joe said. It was a superior laugh; they were laughing *at* Joe. But they were laughing *with* Peter Boyle, who enters the movie like a force of nature. And the talented screenwriter Norman Wexler gives him a bunch of outrageous lines. Boyle's comedic performance alleviates the picture's one-note ugliness.

It doesn't make Joe likable, but it does make him sort of enjoyable.

Avildsen, by combining Peter Boyle's bravura comic performance with this grim trash-o-logue, produces a cocktail mixed with piss that's disturbingly tasty.

Joe saying fucked up shit is a crack up. Like with *Freebie and the Bean* a few years later, audiences might feel guilty for laughing, but I'm here to tell you, laugh they did. Even seven-year-old little me laughed. Not because I understood what Joe was saying or was appreciating Norman Wexler's dialogue. I laughed for three reasons. One, the room full of adults were laughing. Two, even I was able to plug into the comic vibe of Boyle's performance. And three, because Joe cursed all the time and there's few things funnier to a little kid than a funny guy cussing up a storm. I remember just as it seemed the laughter in the tavern scene had started to calm down, Joe gets up from the barstool and moves over to the jukebox to drop some coins in. And as soon as he gets a look at all the (I assume) *soul music* on the jukebox's playlist, he yells out, "*Christ, they even fucked up the goddamn music!*" The audience of the Tiffany Theater burst out laughing even harder than before.

But after the bar scene was over, and sometime after Dennis Patrick and his wife go over to Joe's house for dinner, I fell asleep. So I missed the whole scene where Joe and his newfound acolyte go on a hippie-hunting murder spree. A fact my mother was thankful for.

On the ride home that night, I remember my mother telling Curt: "*I'm glad Quint fell asleep before the end. I wouldn't have wanted him to see that ending.*"

In the back seat I asked, "*What happened?*"

Curt filled me in on what I missed. "*Well, Joe and the father ended up shooting a bunch of hippies. And in the mess, the father ended up shooting his daughter.*"

"*The girl hippie from the beginning?*" I asked.

"*Yes.*"

"*Why did he shoot her?*" I asked.

"*Well, he didn't mean to shoot her,*" he told me.

Then I asked, "*Was he sad?*"

And my mother said, "*Yes, Quentin, he was very sad.*"

Well, I might have slept through the second half of *Joe*, but once the movie was over and the lights came on, I woke up. And in no time at all the second movie on the Tiffany double feature started, the more overtly comedic *Where's Poppa?*

And right from the get-go when George Segal puts on a gorilla suit and Ruth Gordon punches him in the nuts, this movie had me.

At that age, the height of comedy was a guy in a gorilla suit, and the only thing funnier than that was a guy getting punched in the nuts. So a guy in a gorilla suit getting punched in the nuts was the absolute *pinnacle* of comedy. No doubt, this movie was going to be hysterical. As late as it was, I was going to watch this movie all the way to the end.

I've never seen *Where's Poppa?* all the way through since that screening. But so many visual moments have remained burned into my brain, whether I understood them then or not.

Ron Leibman, as George Segal's brother, being chased by the black muggers through Central Park.

Ron naked in the elevator with the crying woman.

And of course, the shocking moment for me, but to gauge from the reaction of the auditorium, everybody else as well, the moment when Ruth Gordon bites George Segal on the ass.

I remember asking my mother as the muggers were chasing Ron through the park:

"Why are the Negroes chasing him?"

"Because they were robbing him," she said.

"Why were they robbing him?" I asked.

And then she said, *"Because it's a comedy and they were just making fun of things."*

And in that moment the concept of *satire* was explained to me.

My young parents went to a lot of movies around this time, and usually brought me along. I'm sure they could have found somebody to pawn me off on (my Grandmother Dorothy was usually game), but instead they allowed me to tag along. But part of the reason I was allowed to tag along was because I knew how to keep my mouth shut.

During the daytime I was allowed to be a normal (annoying) kid. Ask dumb questions, be childish, be selfish, you know, like most children. But if they took me out at night, to a nice restaurant, or a bar (which they sometimes did because Curt was a piano bar musician), or a nightclub (which they also did from time to time), or the movies, or even on a double date with another couple, I knew this was *adult time*. If I wanted to be allowed to hang around during *adult time*, my little ass better be fucking cool. Which basically meant don't ask dumb questions, don't think the evening's about you (it's not). The adults are there to talk to each other and laugh and joke. It was my job to shut up and let them, without constant childish interruption. I knew no one truly cared (unless it was *cute*) about any observation I had about the movie we saw, or the evening itself. It's not like if I broke these rules I was treated harshly. But I was encouraged to act mature and well behaved. Because *if* I acted like a childish pain in the ass, I'd be left at home with a babysitter, while they went out and had a good time. I didn't want to stay at home! I wanted to go out with them! I wanted to be part of *adult time*!

In some ways I was like a child version of *Grizzly Man*, able to observe grown-ups at night in their natural habitat. It was in my best interest to keep my mouth shut and my eyes and ears open.

This is what adults did when they weren't around children.

This is how adults socialized.

This is what they talked about when they were with each other.

This is the shit they liked to do.

This is the shit they found funny.

I don't know if it was my mother's intention or not, but they were teaching me how adults socialized with each other.

When they took me to the movies, it was my job to sit and watch the movie, whether I liked it or not.

Yes, some of those adult movies were fucking amazing!

MASH, the Dollars Trilogy, *Where Eagles Dare*, *The Godfather*, *Dirty Harry*, *The French Connection*, *The Owl and the Pussycat*, and *Bullitt*. And some, to an eight- or nine-year-old, were fucking boring. *Carnal Knowledge? The Fox? Isadora? Sunday Bloody Sunday? Klute? Goodbye, Columbus? Model Shop? Diary of a Mad Housewife?*

But I knew, while they were watching the movie, no one cared whether or not *I* was having a good time.

I'm sure early on, at some point, I must've said something like, *Hey Mom, this is boring.* And I'm sure she said back, *Look, Quentin, if you're going to be a pain in the ass when we take you out for an evening, next time we'll leave you at home [with a babysitter]. If you'd rather stay at home and watch TV, while me and your father go out and have a good time—fine—that's what we'll do next time. You decide.*

Well, I decided. I wanted to go out with them.

And the first rule, *don't be a pain in the ass.*

The second rule, during the movie, *don't ask stupid questions.*

Maybe one or two, at the beginning of the movie, but after that, I was on my own. Any other questions would have to wait till the movie was over. And, for the most part, I was able to follow this rule. Though there were some exceptions. My mom would recount with her friends about the time they took me to see *Carnal Knowledge.* Art Garfunkel is trying to talk Candice Bergen into sex. And their dialogue back and forth was something like, *C'mon let's do it? I don't want to do it. You promised you'd do it? I don't want to do it. Everybody else is doing it.*

And apparently, in my squeakiest nine-year-old voice, I asked loudly, "*What do they want to do, Mom?*" Which, according to my mother, made the theatre full of adults burst out laughing.

Also, I found the iconic *freeze-frame* ending of *Butch Cassidy and the Sundance Kid* too obscure.

"*What happened?*" I remember asking.

"*They died,*" my mom informed me.

"*They died?*" I yelped.

"*Yes, Quentin, they died,*" my mother assured me.

"*How do you know?*" I shrewdly asked.

"*Because when it froze, that was what that was meant to imply,*" she patiently replied.

Again I asked, "*How do you know?*"

"*I just know,*" was her unsatisfying answer.

"*Why didn't they show it?*" I asked, almost indignant.

Then, clearly losing her patience, she snapped, "*Because they didn't want to!*"

Then I grumbled under my breath, "*They shoulda shown it.*"

And despite how iconic that image has become, I still agree with me, "*They shoulda shown it.*"

But usually, I knew enough to know while my mom and dad were watching the movie wasn't the time to bombard them with questions. I knew I was watching adult movies and some things I wouldn't understand. But me understanding the lesbian relationship between Sandy Dennis and Anne Heywood in *The Fox* wasn't what was important. My parents having a good time, and me spending time with them when they went out for the evening, *that* was what was important. I also knew the time to ask questions was on the drive home, *after* the movie was over.

When a child reads an adult book, there's going to be words they don't understand. But depending on the context, and the paragraph surrounding the sentence, sometimes they can figure it out. Same thing when a kid watches an adult movie.

Now obviously, some things that go over your head, your parents *want* to go over your head. But some things, even if I didn't *exactly* know what they meant, I got the gist.

Especially jokes that made the room full of adults laugh. It was fucking thrilling to be the only child in a packed room of adults watching an adult movie and hearing the room laugh at (usually) something I knew was probably *naughty*. And sometimes even when I didn't *get it, I got it.*

Even though I didn't really know what a *rubber* was, by the way the audience laughed, I still more or less got the idea during the scene between Hermie and the druggist in *Summer of '42*. Same thing with most of the sex jokes in *The Owl and the Pussycat*. I laughed at that movie with the adult audience from beginning to end (the *"bombs away"* line brought the fucking house down).

But when it came to the movies I just mentioned, there was something else about the adults' reaction I couldn't have pinpointed at the time, but I realize now. If you show children a movie with a guy cursing in a funny way, or a poop joke, or a fart joke, usually they giggle. And when they get a little older you show them a movie with a sex joke, they'll giggle at that. But the type of laugh they do is a naughty laugh. They know this is inappropriate, and they know *maybe* they shouldn't be hearing or seeing this. And the laugh reveals that they feel a touch naughty partaking in the exchange.

Well, in 1970 and 1971 that's how adult audiences responded to the sexual humor in films like *Where's Poppa?*, *The Owl and the Pussycat*, *MASH*, *Summer of '42*, *Pretty Maids All in a Row*, and *Bob & Carol & Ted & Alice*. Or the pot brownies scene in *I Love You, Alice B. Toklas!* Or when the football players smoked a joint on the bench in *MASH*. Or scenes that had a comic sting but wouldn't have been possible a year or two years earlier. Like *Joe*'s introduction scene or Popeye Doyle's bar roust in *The French Connection*, the laughter from the grown-ups had a similar naughty vibe. Which in retrospect makes sense. Because these adults weren't used to seeing this type of material. These were the first couple of years of *New Hollywood*. These audiences had grown up on movies from the fifties and sixties. They were used to peekaboo, insinuation, double entendres, and word play (before 1968, in *Goldfinger*, Honor Blackman's character name *Pussy Galore* was the most explicit sex joke ever uttered in a big commercial film).

So, in a strange way, the adults and I were sort of on the same page. But naughty giggles weren't the only thing I heard coming from the grown-up audiences. Gay characters were constantly laughed at. And yes, sometimes those characters were presented as comedic cannon fodder (*Diamonds Are Forever* and *Vanishing Point*).

But not always.

Sometimes it revealed a real ugliness in the audience.

In 1971, the same year as *Diamonds Are Forever* and *Vanishing Point*, I sat in a movie theatre watching *Dirty Harry* with my parents.

On screen Scorpio (Andy Robinson), the film's surrogate for the real-life Zodiac Killer, stood on a rooftop in San Francisco holding a high-powered sniper rifle pointing it down at the city park. In the scope sight of Scorpio's rifle was a gay black man wearing a flamboyant purple poncho. What's memorable about the tableau is the scene itself we see play out inside Scorpio's rifle sight. Purple Poncho is on a date with a hippie-like cowboy type with a black mustache, who looks a helluva lot like Dennis Hopper's character from *Easy Rider*. In the movie, we get a pretty clear idea of what's going on. They don't appear to be a couple; the two men are definitely on a date. The cowboy has just bought Purple Poncho a vanilla ice cream cone. And without any physical contact between them, and played completely silently, we can tell the date is going pretty well.

We can tell Purple Poncho is having a good time, and the Dennis Hopper–type cowboy is charmed by him. This silent scene might be one of the most nonjudgmental depictions of gay male courtship ever presented in a Hollywood studio film up to that time.

Yet, at the same time, we watch it all through the scope sight of Scorpio's rifle, with the crosshairs aimed directly at Purple Poncho. But, when I was a little boy, how did I know the fella in the purple poncho was gay? Because at least five patrons laughingly said out loud, "*It's a faggot!*" Including my stepfather Curt. And they laughed at his antics, even though their only view of him was through the rifle site of a vicious killer, while Lalo Schifrin's eerie killer's-got-a-victim-in-his-sights music accompanied the visual on the soundtrack. But I felt something else in that theatre full of grown-ups. As opposed to the other victims in the film, I didn't really feel the audience of adults had a tremendous amount of concern for Purple Poncho. In fact, I'd say a few filmgoers were rooting for Scorpio to shoot him.*

On the ride home, even if I didn't have questions, my parents would talk about the movie we had just seen. These are some of my fondest memories. Sometimes they liked the movie and sometimes they didn't, but I was usually a little surprised how thoughtful they were about it. And it was interesting to review the movie I had just seen from the perspective of their analysis.

Both parents liked *Patton,* but the whole discussion driving home revolved around their admiration for George C. Scott's performance.

Neither liked Roger Vadim's *Pretty Maids All in a Row* for reasons I'm not sure of. Most of the sexually oriented stuff they took me to bored the shit out of me. But *Pretty Maids All in a Row* had a genuine liveliness about it that caught my attention and kept it. As did Rock Hudson's cool *savoir faire,* which wasn't lost on an eight-year-old. Naturally, my stepfather made homophobic slurs against Rock Hudson the whole car ride home, but I remember my mother sticking up for Mr. Hudson ("*Well, if he is a homosexual, that just shows what a great actor he is*"). I remember *Airport* being a big hit with my family in 1970. Mainly due to the surprise of Van Heflin's bomb going off. The moment the bomb exploded on board the aircraft was one of the most shocking moments in any Hollywood movie up to that time. As Curt said on the ride home, "*I thought Dean Martin was going to talk the guy out of it,*" subtextually

---

*In the *Mad Magazine* spoof, "Filthy Harry," when Harry spots Scorpio on the roof with the rifle aiming his gun at the homosexual, Harry arrests the homosexual.

remarking on how a Dean Martin movie of 1964 or 1965 would have played out, compared to a film—even a relatively *old-fashioned* one—of 1970.

And the scene that followed—the hole in the aircraft sucking people out—was the most intense cinematic set piece I had ever experienced. But in that year of 1970, I saw a lot of intense shit.

The eagle-claws-through-the-chest initiation rite in *A Man Called Horse* blew my fucking mind. As did Barnabas Collins' blood-squirting slow-motion wooden-stake evisceration in *House of Dark Shadows*. I remember, during both moments, staring at the screen with my mouth wide open, not quite believing a movie could do that. On those nights, I'm sure *I* was the most vocal one on the car ride home (I thought those movies were *incredible*).

At the Dorothy Chandler Pavilion on April 15, 1971 (not long after my eighth birthday), the Academy Awards for the films of 1970 were held. The five films up for best picture were *Patton*, *MASH*, *Five Easy Pieces*, *Airport*, and *Love Story*. By the night of the Oscars, I had seen all five (obviously at the theatre). And the film I was rooting for, *MASH*, I saw three times. I saw practically every big movie that year. The only two I missed were *Ryan's Daughter* and *Nicholas and Alexandra*, which I didn't mind missing. Besides, I saw the trailers so many times for both I felt like I *did* see them (okay, I didn't see *Duck, You Sucker!* because Curt thought the title sounded stupid. Same thing for *Two Mules for Sister Sara*).

My two other favorite movies that year were *A Man Called Horse* and, probably, *Kelly's Heroes*. To illustrate how these movies were molding my taste, in 1968 my favorite movie was *The Love Bug*. In 1969 my favorite movie was *Butch Cassidy and the Sundance Kid*. But by 1970, my favorite movie was *MASH*, an anarchist-themed military sex comedy.

That didn't mean I didn't like Disney movies anymore. The two big Disney movies that year were *The Aristocats* and *The Boatniks*, and I saw and liked them both. But nothing made me laugh harder than Hot Lips (Sally Kellerman) being exposed in the shower. Or Radar (Gary Burghoff) placing the microphone under the bed as Hot Lips and Frank Burns fucked, then Trapper John (Elliott Gould) broadcasting it throughout the camp. (However, the whole middle section with Painless, the camp dentist, going through homosexual panic never meant anything to me. Of course not, it's the lousiest part of the film.)

Again, while I really enjoyed *MASH*, part of the delight I had watching it was sitting in a cinema full of adults laughing hysterically, all getting off on their own naughtiness. Not to mention the fun I had going back to school and describing those scenes to the other kids in my class who could never dream of seeing a movie like *MASH* or *The French Connection* or *The Godfather* or *The Wild Bunch* or *Deliverance* (there was usually *one* other kid allowed to see some of the wild shit I saw).

Because I was allowed to see things the other kids weren't, I appeared sophisticated to my classmates. And because I was watching the most challenging movies of the greatest movie-making era in the history of Hollywood, they were right, I was.

At some point, when I realized I was seeing movies other parents weren't letting their children see, I asked my mom about it.

She said, *"Quentin, I worry more about you watching the news. A movie's not going to hurt you."*

Right fucking on, Connie!

After being exposed to all these images, did any of them disturb me? Of course, some did! But that didn't mean I didn't *like* the movie.

When they removed the naked dead girl out of the hole in *Dirty Harry*, it was totally disturbing. But I understood it.

Scorpio's inhumanity was beyond the beyond. All the better for Harry to blast him with the most powerful handgun in the world.

Yes, it was disturbing to see a woman in hysterical agony being dragged through the street and whipped by the villagers after she'd been condemned for being a witch in the Vincent Price movie *Cry of the Banshee,* which I saw on a double feature with the great Spanish horror film *The House That Screamed.* What a great night!

Just making a list of the wild violent images I witnessed from 1970 to 1972 would appall most readers. Whether it was James Caan being machine-gunned to death at the toll booth, or Moe Greene being shot in the eye in *The Godfather.* That guy cut in half by the airplane propeller in *Catch-22.* Stacy Keach's wild ride on the side of the car in *The New Centurions.* Or Don Stroud shooting himself in the face with a tommy gun in *Bloody Mama.* But just listing grotesque moments—out of context of the movies they were in—isn't entirely fair to the films in question. And my mother's point of view—that she later explained to me—was always a question of context. In those films, I could handle the imagery, because I understood the story.

However, one of the earlier sequences I saw that genuinely disturbed me was when Vanessa Redgrave, as Isadora Duncan, was strangled by her scarf getting caught in the wheel of a roadster in *Isadora.* I guess I was so affected by that ending because I was so utterly bored by everything that preceded it. On the drive home that night I was full of questions about the dangers of accidentally dying by getting your scarf caught in the wheel of your car. My mom assured me I had nothing to worry about. She'd never allow me to wear a long flowing scarf in a convertible roadster.

One of the most terrifying things I witnessed in a film at that time wasn't some act of cinematic violence. It was the depiction of the Black Plague in James Clavell's *The Last Valley.* And after the movie was over, my stepfather's historical description of it had my hair standing straight up.

Some of the most intense experiences I had at the cinema weren't even the movies themselves. It was the trailers.

Hands down the most terrifying movie I saw as a child wasn't any of the horror films I watched. It was the trailer for *Wait Until Dark.*

Before I even knew what homosexuality was, I watched the male sex scene between Peter Finch and Murray Head in *Sunday Bloody Sunday.* I wasn't shocked, I was confused. But I *was* shocked by the naked wrestling match by the fireplace between Alan Bates and Oliver Reed in the trailer for Ken Russell's *Women in Love.* I also got the gist of the terrifying implications of male subjugation in the trailer for the prison drama *Fortune and Men's Eyes.* And for some reason I found the trippy trailer for Frank Zappa's *200 Motels* frightening.

Was there any movie back then I couldn't handle?

Yes.

Bambi.

Bambi getting lost from his mother, her being shot by the hunter, and that horrifying forest fire upset me like nothing else I saw in the movies. It wasn't until 1974 when I saw Wes Craven's *The Last House on the Left* that anything came close. Now those sequences in *Bambi* have been fucking up children for decades. But I'm pretty sure I know the reason why *Bambi* affected me so traumatically. Of course, Bambi losing his mother hits every kid right where they live. But I think even more than the psychological dynamics of the story, it was the shock that the film turned so unexpectedly tragic that hit me so hard. The TV spots really didn't emphasize the film's true nature. Instead they concentrated on the cute Bambi and Thumper antics. Nothing prepared me for the harrowing turn of events to come. I remember my little brain screaming the five-year-old version of *"What the fuck's happening?"* If I had been more prepared for what I was going to see, I think I might have processed it differently.

There was, however, one night my parents went to the movies when they didn't take me along. It was a double feature of

Melvin Van Peebles' *Sweet Sweetback* and Robert Altman's *Brewster McCloud.*

They went with my mom's younger brother Roger, who had just returned from Vietnam and was casually dating my babysitter Robin, a nice young middle-class red-haired girl who lived down the street.

The evening was not a success.

Not only did they not like the two movies, my stepfather and uncle proceeded to bitch about them for days after. *Brewster Mc-Cloud* is one of the worst movies to ever carry a studio logo, and that's fully acknowledging Altman also made *Quintet* for a studio as well. *Quintet* is just terrible, boring, and pointless. But *Brewster Mc-Cloud* is the cinematic equivalent of a bird shitting on your head. Nevertheless, it's kind of amusing imagining my parents, and my young uncle, and my seventeen-year-old babysitter buying a ticket to *Brewster McCloud* expecting to see a *real movie.*

They were just baffled (my uncle, especially).

However, the Altman film was the lower half of the double bill. The film they paid to see was *Sweet Sweetback.*

Now the reason I didn't attend that screening was because since it was rated X (*"by an all-white jury!"*), I couldn't. I'm sure Curt, Uncle Roger, and Robin didn't know what to make of Melvin Van Peebles' howling cry of black empowerment any more than they did *Brewster McCloud.* But while I'm sure they couldn't fathom why anyone would bother to make Altman's malarkey, the Van Peebles film was *something.*

Something they didn't understand.

Something they couldn't grasp (which made them mad).

Something that wasn't for them (after *it* rejected them, they rejected *it*), but unlike *Brewster McCloud, something* they couldn't deny.

The interesting part of my memory was the only reason they saw it was due to my mom. I doubt, other than her, any of them had ever heard of it (she hipped them to it). Also, mom never used the short version of the film's title. Always referring to it by its full soul title, *Sweet Sweetback's Baadasssss Song.* And while I remember the men coming home complaining about the movie (for days), my mother didn't say much. She didn't defend the picture, but she also didn't join in on the diatribe. She remained (strangely for her) quiet on the subject.

Less than a year later she would leave Curt and exclusively date black men for the next three years.

During that time my mom and I went to fewer movies together, because she was going to more movies on dates. And on these dates she saw some of the early films of the *Blaxploitation genre.* One of those movies was *Super Fly.*

Now, I knew of *Super Fly* because she already owned the smash hit soundtrack album, and it was played constantly in the apartment. The movie was also advertised heavily on *Soul Train.* And in our apartment, come Saturday, we never missed *Soul Train.* By this point I was living with my mother in a pretty hip apartment building that she shared with two cocktail waitresses that were her best friends at the time, Jackie (black) and Lillian (Mexican).

All three were young, hip, good-looking women in the funky seventies, with a penchant for dating athletes. Three sexy women (at the time my mother looked like a cross between Cher and Barbara Steele), one white, one black, one Mexican, sharing an apartment with the white one's ten-year-old son: we were practically a sitcom.

My mother's verdict on *Super Fly?* She thought it was a bit amateurish. But she thought the bathtub scene between Ron O'Neal and Sheila Frazier was one of the sexiest scenes she had ever seen.

Another Blaxploitation film she told me about was a movie called *Melinda,* starring Calvin Lockhart (again, heavily advertised on *Soul Train*). Many years later I saw the film myself. It's alright (it's sort of a Blaxploitation version of the film noir *Laura,* with a bunch of kung fu fights at the end). My mother really liked it. And I told her I wanted to see it too. But this time she told me I couldn't. Now she didn't say that often (the only other two movies she said I couldn't see were *The Exorcist* and *Andy Warhol's Frankenstein*). So, I asked her why. And while the film *Melinda* wasn't memorable, her answer to my question, I've never forgotten.

She said, "*Well, Quentin, it's very violent. Not that I necessarily have a problem with that. But you wouldn't understand what the story was about. So since you wouldn't understand the context in which the violence was taking place, you would just be watching violence for violence's sake. And that I don't want you to do.*"

Considering this would be a conversation I would have for the rest of my life, I've never heard it articulated better than that. However, it's not like I understood the confusing plot machinations of *The French Connection*, other than the cops were after the French guy with the beard. But as far as my mom was concerned, I suppose that was enough.

During this time my mother was dating a professional football player named Reggie. So, in an effort to score points with her, Reggie asked to hang out with me.

Being a football player, he asked her, *Does he like football?*

She told him, *No, he likes movies.*

Well, as luck would have it, so did Reggie. And, apparently, he saw every Blaxploitation flick that came out. So late one Saturday afternoon, Reggie (who I never met before) dropped by the apartment, picked me up, and took me to the movies. He took me to a part of town I had never been before. I had been to the big movie theatre districts in Hollywood and Westwood. But this place was different. This theatre row had huge cinemas on both sides of the street, which went down for about eight blocks (I realized, when I got older, Reggie took me to the theatre district in Downtown Los

Angeles located on Broadway Boulevard, which included, among others, the *Orpheum*, the *State*, the *Los Angeles*, the *Million Dollar Theatre*, and the *Tower*). Not only were all the cinemas big, with large marquees out front, they also had giant (what to me looked like twenty-foot-tall) paintings of the movie poster towering above the marquee. And, with the exceptions of the chop-socky classic *Five Fingers of Death* and (strangely) *My Fair Lady*, all of them were Blaxploitation films. Films I had never seen, but was aware of from either seeing the TV spots (especially on *Soul Train*), hearing the radio ads on 1580 KDay—the soul music radio station of Los Angeles—or reading the exciting and graphic-looking movie ads in the *Los Angeles Times* Calendar section.

The sun was beginning to set and the flashy colorful marquees started turning on their buzzing neon. My new friend told me I could pick any movie I wanted to see (except *My Fair Lady*). Playing on that street that Saturday night were *Hit Man* with Bernie Casey (a black remake of the British film *Get Carter*) and the soon-to-be classic *The Mack*, starring Max Julien and Richard Pryor. "*How about The Mack?*" I asked.

"*Well, I've already seen The Mack,*" he informed me.

"*Is it any good?*" I asked.

"*It's sensational!*" he told me. "*And if you really want to see that I can watch The Mack again, but let's keep looking.*"

Also playing was *Super Fly*, *Trouble Man*, *Cool Breeze* (a black remake of *The Asphalt Jungle*), and *Come Back Charleston Blue* (a sequel to *Cotton Comes to Harlem*), all of which he'd seen. But the new movie on Broadway, having opened just last Wednesday, was Blaxploitation superstar Jim Brown's new motion picture, *Black Gunn*. I had seen the TV spots a lot that week, and it looked really exciting. I even remember the radio spots proclaiming, "*Jim Brown's gonna git the mutha who killed his brotha.*"

Well, *Black Gunn* was definitely the movie Reggie wanted to see. One, being the connoisseur that he apparently was, it was the only one of the movies playing he *hadn't* seen. Also, it was pretty fucking obvious he dug Jim Brown.

I asked him who his favorite actors were. He said Jim Brown, Max Julien, Richard Roundtree, Charles Bronson, and Lee Van Cleef.

He asked me who my favorite actor was.

I said, "*Robert Preston.*"

"*Who's Robert Preston?*"

"*He's The Music Man!*" (I was a big fan of *The Music Man* at the time.)

This being the Saturday night showing of the brand-new Jim Brown movie, the huge auditorium (there were probably 1,400 seats) wasn't exactly packed, but it was definitely busy, and buzzing with anticipation.

My little face was the only white one in the audience.

This was to be my *first* movie in an (except for me) all black movie theatre in a black neighborhood. This was 1972. By 1976 I would be venturing on my own to a mostly black theatre called *the Carson Twin Cinema* in Carson, California, which is where I would catch up on all the Blaxploitation and kung fu film classics I'd missed in the earlier part of the decade (*Coffy*, *The Mack*, *Foxy Brown*, *J.D.'s Revenge*, *Cooley High*, *Cornbread, Earl and Me*, *The Watts Monster*, *Five Fingers of Death*, *Lady Kung Fu*, *The Chinese Connection*) as well as all the other exploitation films that came out around that time. And by the early eighties, I found my way back to that theatre row on Broadway. Though by that time, the neighborhood was far more Mexican than black, and the 35mm film prints they showed usually contained Spanish subtitles.

Also, later in the seventies, I'd often spend the weekend at Jackie's house (remember my mother's old roommate?) who lived in Compton. By this time Jackie was like my second mother, her daughter Nikki (who was four years older than me) was like my sister, and Jackie's brother Don (we called him *Big D*) was like my uncle.

And Nikki and her girlfriends would take me to the movies in Compton where I saw *Mahogany*, *Let's Do It Again*, *A Piece of the Action*, and *Adiós Amigo (*we didn't just see black movies, we also saw *Airport 1975* and *Foul Play)*. Nikki and one of her girlfriends also took me (when I was fourteen) to the Pussycat Theatre on Hollywood Boulevard to see my first porno movie: the classic double bill that played at that theatre for eight years, *Deep Throat* and *The Devil in Miss Jones*. (We didn't understand what all the fuss was about *Deep Throat*. But *The Devil in Miss Jones* we thought was a pretty good movie.)

How did I get in at fourteen?

One, I was kind of tall. Only my squeaky voice would have given me away. So, I just let Nikki do all the talking.

Two, the theatre was open all night. So, we showed up at two in the morning. I don't think any woman buying a ticket at two in the morning was ever denied admission to the Pussycat Theatre.

Later, when I became sixteen, I got a job as an usher at the Pussycat Theatre in Torrance.

But back to me, Reggie, and Jim Brown.

Black Gunn was playing at the Tower Theatre on a double feature with another film. Some amateurish black-themed social drama called *The Bus Is Coming*.

We entered the theatre with about forty-five minutes left before *The Bus Is Coming* was finished. As I have demonstrated, when it comes to a little kid watching challenging films with adult audiences, I was pretty sophisticated. I had watched many different adult audiences react to many different types of movies. And I had even experienced audiences turn against a movie and jeer it off the screen (that happened to a Crown International film I saw called *The Young Graduates*). But I had never experienced anything like *this* audience's reaction to *The Bus Is Coming*.

They fucking hated it.

And they proceeded to constantly yell profanities at the screen for the remaining forty-five minutes of the movie. The first time in my life I ever heard the expression *Suck my dick!* was when one of my fellow audience members screamed it at a character on screen. Since I had never experienced anything like this before, at first, I didn't know how to take it. But their insults to the characters just got dirtier and dirtier, and every minute the movie unspooled, the audience seemed to find a deeper level of contempt for it, and the funnier their insults became. Until I began to giggle. And then pretty soon I was giggling uncontrollably. I'm sure my reaction and the uninhibited giggling of my squeaky nine-year-old voice must've tickled the football player with me as much as the audience was tickling me.

"*You havin' a good time, Q?*" he asked.

"*These guys are so funny,*" I said, not meaning the movie.

He smiled at me and patted my shoulder with his huge hand. "*You're a cool kid, Q.*"

And then I felt emboldened to join in. So, I screamed something at the screen. And quickly checked to see if it was okay with a side glance at Reggie. But Reggie just giggled at the fact I felt comfortable enough to join in. So, join in I did. And I even yelled out at the screen my new favorite expression, "*Suck my dick!*"

And that cracked up Reggie and a few other older guys sitting by us.

Wow! What an evening.

But the night had just begun.

The last thing I remember about *The Bus Is Coming* is at the end of the movie, the twelve-year-old black kid who's waiting the whole film for the bus (I think the bus was supposed to be a metaphor), starts repeatedly screaming the line that gives the film its title when the bus finally arrives. At which point somebody in the audience yelled back, "*Yeah well get on it, and go fuck yourself!*"

I was wiping tears of laughter from my eyes as the lights came up in the massive auditorium. I started figuring out, because of my mother, Reggie was trying to get in good with me. So, I asked him could I get a Coke and some candy at the snack bar. But instead of taking me to the concession stand, he just dug out his wallet, whipped out a twenty-dollar bill and said, *"Get anything you want."*

As far as I was concerned, mom could marry this cat.

So, in a huge movie theatre that was practically the size of the Metropolitan Opera House, I made my way to the snack bar. Then, loaded down with ten dollars' worth of junk, found my way back to my seat as the lights began to dim. Then, on a *Downtown Saturday Night*, Jim Brown's new movie, *Black Gunn*, began flickering through the film projector's shutter gate for an extremely excited audience of about eight hundred and fifty black folks, eight hundred of them male.

And frankly, I've never been the same.

To one degree or another I've spent my entire life since both attending movies and making them, trying to re-create the experience of watching a brand-new Jim Brown film, on a Saturday night, in a black cinema in 1972. The closest thing to *that* experience I had prior was the year before, when I saw my first James Bond film, *Diamonds Are Forever*, with the way the audience knowingly responded to every quip Sean Connery made. And I'd probably add the way the audience had responded to Clint Eastwood as *Dirty Harry* as well.

Still . . . there was no comparison.

When Jim Brown sat behind his desk, and Bruce Glover (Crispin's father) and his other white gangster henchmen threaten him, and Gunn hits a button under the desk and a sawed-off shotgun dropped in his lap . . . the massive theatre full of black males cheered in a way the nine-year-old little me had never experienced in a movie theatre before. At the time—living with a single mother—it was probably *the most masculine experience* I'd ever been part of.

And when the movie ended with a freeze-frame of Jim Brown as *Gunn*, the guy behind Reggie and me proclaimed out loud, "*Now that's a movie about a bad motherfucker!*"*

Sadly, after that night, I never saw Reggie again. And to this day I have no idea what happened to him. From time to time I'd ask my mom, "*Whatever happened to Reggie?*"

She'd just shrug her shoulders and say, "*Oh, he's around.*"

---

*And no, *Black Gunn* today doesn't live up to that experience in 1972. But the sawed-off shotgun under the desk bit is still pretty cool, and Jim Brown is *still* "a bad motherfucker."

Bullitt

(1968)

Along with Paul Newman and Warren Beatty, Steve McQueen was the biggest of the younger male movie stars of the sixties. The UK had its share of exciting young leading men like Michael Caine, Sean Connery, Albert Finney, and Terence Stamp, but of the young sexy guys in America—that were also genuine movie stars—it was McQueen, Newman, and Beatty. On the next level down was James Garner, George Peppard, and James Coburn. But for the most part, anytime one of them got a picture, it was because one of the top three turned it down. Producers wanted Newman or McQueen, they settled for George Peppard. They wanted McQueen, they settled for James Coburn. They wanted Beatty, they settled for George Hamilton. James Garner was actually popular enough to get scripts from time to time that weren't covered with the top three's fingerprints, but not often.

The next level down was up and coming leading men like Robert Redford, George Segal, and George Maharis, and pop stars like Pat Boone and Bobby Darin (who in the sixties actually had legit movie careers). In fact, if he had ever taken his movie career seriously, the young movie star leading man who could have truly given the three actors at the top a run for their money was Elvis Presley. But Elvis was a prisoner of both Col. Tom Parker and his own success. Elvis made two movies a year and none of them ever lost money. Now, not all those Elvis movies were bad. Some were better than others. But it's safe to say they weren't real movies, they were "Elvis Presley movies."*

But one of the things that made Steve McQueen so popular in the sixties, along with his *king of cool* persona and his undeniable charisma, was that of the top three actors (Newman, McQueen, and Beatty), McQueen did better movies.

Once McQueen became a movie star with *The Great Escape*, he made a string of movies that were all pretty damn good. In the sixties the only real dud in his filmography post–*The Great Escape* is *Baby the Rain Must Fall*. And that's mostly due to the ridiculous sight of Steve trying to play a folk singer. Whereas Paul Newman for his whole career did an incredible amount of lousy movies mixed in with some iconic ones. I mean, some of the movies Newman agreed to do over the years are really baffling. I suspect he just wanted to get out of the house. After *Splendor in the Grass*, none of Beatty's films are worth a damn before *Bonnie and Clyde* (okay, maybe *Lilith*). But the material McQueen chose to do—compared to the other two—was consistently of a higher quality.

But the reason McQueen's material was superior wasn't due to the fact that the actor was poring over all the material available and demonstrating his uncanny ability to choose projects. McQueen didn't like reading. It's doubtful he ever read a book of his own volition. He probably never read a newspaper unless there was a story about *him* in it. And he only read scripts when he had to. It wasn't

---

*After McQueen dropped out of the role of the Sundance Kid, before Redford, it was offered to Warren Beatty. Naturally, if Beatty did it he wanted to play Butch Cassidy (a nonstarter because that role had always been Newman's). But if they had gone for it, Beatty wanted to do it with Elvis Presley as Sundance.

that he *couldn't* read. He wasn't illiterate. Neile McQueen, his first wife, told me, "*He read car magazines.*"

And it wasn't that he wasn't smart. He could talk to you about engine displacement, how to break apart the carburetor of a motorcycle, or discuss armaments until you couldn't listen anymore.

He just didn't like reading.

So who read the material?

Neile McQueen.

The importance of Neile McQueen to Steve's success as a movie star can't be overemphasized.

It was Neile who read the scripts. It was Neile who narrowed down the material. It was Neile who was good at choosing material that would be best for Steve. Steve's agent, Stan Kamen, would read ten scripts that were being offered, then narrow that down to five and send those off to Neile. She'd read those five scripts, write a synopsis on the material, narrow it down to the two she liked best, and then tell Steve the stories and explain her reasons why she liked them for him. Which would usually end up in him reading the one Neile liked the most.* Now of course the director was important, how much they were paying him, the location they were shooting the film at—all of these things were important. But so was Neile weighing in. Naturally, directors who worked with Steve before— that he liked—got preferential treatment. But if Neile didn't like the script, it was an uphill battle. And it was thanks to Neile's good taste and her keen understanding of both her husband's ability and his iconic persona that she steered her husband, starting with *The Cincinnati Kid*, into the biggest winning streak of the second half of the sixties (a Neile McQueen is what Elvis needed).

Neile was also aware of something that action director maestro

---

*McQueen hated reading material so much, later in his career, he charged studios a million dollars for just reading a script.

Walter Hill told me about McQueen. Hill worked twice as 2nd AD with Steve on both *The Thomas Crown Affair* and *Bullitt* and then later when he was a screenwriter he wrote *The Getaway.*

Hill told me, *"Quentin, one of the things you would have liked about Steve is that while Steve was a good actor, he didn't see himself as just an actor.* Steve saw himself as a MOVIE STAR. It was one of the most charming characteristics about Steve. He knew what he was good at. He knew what the audience liked about him and that's what he wanted to give them."

Walter said, *"I really admired Steve. He was the last of the true movie stars."*

And it's true, McQueen didn't want to bury himself under layers of characterization, or wear false beards that changed his appearance (a la Paul Newman in *The Life and Times of Judge Roy Bean* or Robert Redford in *Jeremiah Johnson*). When he did movies, he wanted to do cool movie star things in these movies. He didn't want to do movies where anybody else had a better role than him. He didn't want to share the screen, and he always wanted to come out on top. McQueen knew his audience, and he knew they paid to see him win.

I asked Neile McQueen how the film *Bullitt* came about. She told me Steve had just made a deal with Warner Bros.-Seven Arts to back his film production company, *Solar Productions.* And that was their project that Warner's wanted to start the association with. Neile wanted Steve to do *Bullitt* too. *Bullitt* was coming after Steve's biggest hit, *The Thomas Crown Affair,* and Neile thought, *"It would be a good change of pace for him. In Thomas Crown he was a robber. Now he'll be a cop."*

---

*As opposed to Paul Newman, who thought of himself as a New York stage actor.

Everybody wanted McQueen to do it but McQueen. "*It took him forever to say yes. He took so long agreeing to do it,*" Neile said. "*Jack Warner would call up the house and scream into the phone in my ear. And then I'd scream at Steve 'Just do the damn thing!'*"

McQueen was famous for taking a long time to commit to projects, but the reason for his trepidation on the cop picture was his embrace of the flower-child counterculture. The actor started sporting love beads around his neck and wearing more hippie-inspired clothing. As Neile chuckled, "*Steve had been practicing free love for years. So now it was a philosophy, he was all for it.*"

She explained, "*Steve wanted to be one with the flower children. And they hated the cops. He said, they call the cops 'pigs.' I can't play a 'pig.'*"

Walter Hill also described this to me: "*Steve felt a mysterious kind of connection with his audience. He felt they were younger and hipper than the normal movie star's. He knew they cared about the clothes he wore and the things he did in a movie. The exact cut of his blue jeans. He thought his audience was into these kind of cool details.*"

And Neile remembered Steve saying: "*If I make this movie as a cop, my fans' heads would spin.*"

In the book *Steve McQueen: Star on Wheels*, author William Nolan related that Steve's daughter Terry gave him a string of hippie love beads as a birthday gift. Nolan wrote, "*He liked them so much he actually considered using the beads in a trade ad for Bullitt.*" Love beads and a gun. A symbol of the hip detective.

Eventually McQueen put *Bullitt* into production as a Solar picture with Warner Bros.-Seven Arts handling distribution. The end result was not only Steve McQueen's biggest hit, but a zeitgeist smash, and finally McQueen surpassing his greatest rival, Paul Newman. The way *Dirty Harry* (which Steve later passed on) took the already iconic Clint Eastwood and gave him a new level of Clint-specific iconography, is what the chic cool-dude, slow-boil, fast-driving *Frank Bullitt* did for McQueen.

Bullitt also changed the cop film genre, and later cop shows on TV for good. Thanks to James Bond, it was secret agents that were the cool cats. Even private eyes, like Paul Newman as *Harper*, Frank Sinatra as *Tony Rome*, Ralph Meeker in *Kiss Me Deadly*, and George Peppard as *P.J.*, were allowed to dress better, live in swankier digs, and generally have fun. But movies about cops were all very somber, serious, and frankly a drag. The movies were all the same, the cops were all the same, and they all dressed the same in their cheap dark suits and ties, with their porkpie hats and their trench- or raincoats. Frank Sinatra in *The Detective*, Sidney Poitier in *They Call Me Mister Tibbs!*, Richard Widmark in *Madigan*, and George Peppard in *Pendulum* were literally interchangeable. They all could have jumped ship on their films and taken over the lead on any of the other ones without anybody noticing the difference.

Maybe Poitier playing Madigan might have drawn some attention—due to the actor's nice-guy image—but that's why it could have been interesting, rather than snarling Widmark giving another in his never-ending line of snarling performances. But everything about those movies was the same. They all could have been costumed by the same costume designer, they could have rented the cars from the same garage, the supporting actors (Ralph Meeker, Harry Guardino, Jeff Corey, Jack Klugman, James Whitmore, Richard Kiley) could have all swapped parts with each other, and the scripts could have been written by the same screenwriter and adapted from the same book. The cases they were involved in all dealt badly with something considered provocative in the late sixties. And they all struggled to have slightly more roughsounding street dialogue (a struggle they'd lose). And almost comically, all these sourpuss cops seemingly had the same dissatisfied wife at home (Inger Stevens, Lee Remick, Barbara McNair, and Jean Seberg).

Enter Steve McQueen's *Frank Bullitt*.

Bullitt is introduced to the audience waking up in the morning—having gone to bed at five—in snazzy pajamas he could have borrowed from Hugh Hefner. Bullitt doesn't have a dissatisfied wife, he has a very satisfied hot-piece-of-ass girlfriend in the guise of Jacqueline Bisset. When you see the police detective officially on the job—meeting with Robert Vaughn—he too is wearing a suit and tie, but a suit and tie that actually fit. And throughout the rest of the movie, Bullitt's wardrobe consists of one chic outfit after another.*

Neile said, "*Steve had fabulous taste. If he wore a pair of jeans in a movie, he'd have those jeans washed a hundred times.*"

Peter Yates' film doesn't quite have the same zeitgeist position it enjoyed through the last decades of the twentieth century. While a lot of people born since 2000 may have heard of it, and they probably have heard about its famous car chase, that doesn't mean they've seen it. I'm old enough to have actually seen *Bullitt* at the cinema when it came out. Which means I saw it at six. I don't remember the movie. I remember the car chase. And that's what most people usually remember about *Bullitt*. But they also remember how cool Steve McQueen was as Frank Bullitt, his cool clothes, his cool haircut, and his cool Ford Mustang. If they had a sense of the movie, they also might remember Lalo Schifrin's terrific jazzy score (the type of score Quincy Jones tried to do for years and always failed miserably at). The one thing they don't remember is the story. *Bullitt* does *have* a story. But it's not a memorable story, nor does it have anything to do with what you respond to in the movie.

---

*On television really only David Soul as *Dave Hutchinson* on *Starsky and Hutch*, in his black turtlenecks under tan-brown leather jacket, was able to channel McQueen's chic-looking cool cat.

So for most people who haven't seen the movie in five or six years, even though they've seen it a few times before, if you asked them to describe the plot of *Bullitt*, they couldn't do it. The comedian Robert Wuhl once told me, "*I've seen Bullitt four times and I couldn't tell you what the plot's about. All I know is it has something to do with Robert Vaughn.*"

But strangely, in the case of the film Peter Yates made, this isn't a negative observation. In fact a case could be made it's a mark of the film's inner integrity. All those other cop pictures I mentioned spend *all* their time telling us boring stories nobody in the audience gives two shits about. They populate their boring movies with dull characters that are meant to add depth but create only apathy. They bore us with scene after scene that illustrates the lead cop's dismal life, or one plot exposition scene after another about a murder nobody gives a fuck about.

We don't give a shit who killed the homosexual in *The Detective*, we don't care who killed the hooker in *They Call Me Mister Tibbs!*, we don't give a flying fuck what happens to *Madigan*'s gun, and we know *exactly* who killed Peppard's wife in *Pendulum*, and we can't believe it takes the movie as long as it does to figure it out.

Yet since Yates cares so little about the crime story at the center of *Bullitt*, it suggests he knows we don't care either, and *that* suggests a bohemian hipness that was unusual in a Hollywood crime movie. A light Hitchcockian thriller could ultimately be laissez-faire about the McGuffin the film's characters chase one another over, but not a violent-bloody-cop picture.

For the record, the plot, taken loosely from Robert L. Pike's novel *Mute Witness*, deals with San Francisco cop *Frank Bullitt* (Steve McQueen) and his partner *Delgetti* (Steve's pal Don Gordon), who are given an assignment by the smarmy assistant district attorney named *Chalmers* (a deliciously oily Robert Vaughn) to guard his witness, *Johnny Ross* (Walter Hill regular Felice Orlandi), for the weekend. Chalmers wants Ross to testify at a big commission against organized crime Monday morning. In fact he's the publicity-seeking A.D.A.'s big star witness. So a lot of emphasis is put on keeping him alive through the weekend. But the location that was chosen to stash Ross is compromised. While one of Bullitt's men sits in the hotel room guarding Ross, two hit men, one with a shotgun, appear at the door and blast the cop and the witness. The witness soon dies in the hospital. But Bullitt covers up his death—spiriting his corpse away from the hospital—to convince the killers that Ross is still alive so that they'll try again before the weekend's out. Meanwhile he has to dodge Vaughn's D.A. Chalmers and his powerful friends in the department who want Bullitt to produce the witness they think is still alive. Now just me writing that out sounds like a pretty nifty plot. And it is. But I just took more time explaining it than Yates does in telling the story of the movie.

I'm exaggerating. But only a little.

Even Neile McQueen laughed about how confusing the script was. She said both Steve and Robert Vaughn were tearing pages out of the script when they were shooting. "*At times they were writing the script on the street.*"

The story itself is more or less simple to follow. What's unclear, especially during the middle section, is exactly what Bullitt's up to, or why he does half the things he does. And if you think about it later, some of the things he does don't make sense. At least not narrative sense. But as you watch—as you follow him breezing through San Francisco—it makes emotional movie-sense. One of the producers of the film, Philip D'Antoni, would also make *The French Connection* a few years later. And he followed the same narrative strategy in that film as well. The audience doesn't know what's going on half the time in *The French Connection* either. We know Popeye Doyle's after the French guy with the gray beard, but none of the procedural shit means anything to us. It's just lively, busy, and sort of exciting . . . like Yates' film.

Bullitt is filled with weird moments and conveniences, but they don't matter, because Yates, D'Antoni, and McQueen know we don't give a fuck as long as the movie's cool and doesn't get dumb.

If *Bullitt* was going to change action films (I'd say *create* the modern action film), it first had to break the back of the police procedural. The snazzy opening credit sequence with Lalo Schifrin's score and Pablo Ferro's stylishly designed titles sets the audience up for the whole movie. We don't really have any idea what's going on. But the characters on screen seem to know what's going on. And we don't really care, because it's groovy to watch.

Instead of wasting time trying to explain a mystery, it's the first urban action movie to go from one expertly executed set piece to another (you could make the case that *Goldfinger* was the first modern movie to do that. But the fantastical nature of the story allowed for it more than a modern-day cop/crime picture). And it's not just the car chase. The scene where the killer (John Aprea) is loose in the hospital—and Bullitt and Delgetti are after him—is terrific as well (when you see how well Yates does that scene you have to wonder how he managed to so badly stumble his way through the suspense scenes in his anemic 1981 thriller *Eyewitness*).

Bullitt is about action, atmosphere, San Francisco, Yates' great location photography, Lalo Schifrin's jazzy score, and Steve McQueen, his haircut and wardrobe.

Nothing else matters.

Aside from the opening credit sequence, the other scene that sets up the movie is early on when Frank takes his girlfriend out to dinner. They go to a restaurant called Coffee Cantata. And we watch them have a good time and eat dinner. Yet, we don't hear a fucking thing they say. Other than demonstrating they like each other and that Frank is capable of having a good time, nothing personal is revealed about the couple during the whole sequence. What Yates feels is important is the jazz band performing at the restaurant, the sound of jazzy music, the hip vibe of the establishment, the San Francisco atmosphere, and the spot-on looking extras that surround McQueen and Bisset.

The scene tells us nothing narratively. But we dig it. It was cool being in the Coffee Cantata. It was cool watching McQueen and Bisset vibe with each other in the San Francisco surroundings.★

It *both* didn't tell us anything *and* told us everything.

Don Siegel did terrific location photography in his career, and he would do a good job shooting San Francisco three years later in *Dirty Harry* (even though half the movie would be shot on the Universal back lot). But nobody had ever shot San Francisco as great as Peter Yates did or ever will again. The way he utilizes location to such a dynamic degree suggests a master cinematic stylist. One of the reasons he did such a dynamite job was he went thirty days over schedule. Yates was shooting a movie, not a schedule. While Yates would do good work many times again—*Breaking Away*, *The Hot Rock*, *The Friends of Eddie Coyle* (overrated), *The Deep*, and *Mother, Juggs & Speed* (underrated)—he would never demonstrate the cinematic style and confidence he does in *Bullitt*. If he had? If he managed to do what he did in *Bullitt* four more times? He would have been the greatest action filmmaker (save for Steven Spielberg and Sam Peckinpah) of the seventies. I mentioned that to film critic Elvis Mitchell and he said, "*If he did it even one more time he would have been a pantheon director.*"†

★The British film critic Dilys Powell noted of Yates' film, "*Outside the work of Antonioni, I haven't seen such effective narrative and emotional use of an urban background.*"

†While Yates never really employed this style again, other filmmakers did. William Friedkin in *The French Connection*, *Cruising*, and *To Live and Die in*

And then there's Steve McQueen as Frank Bullitt.

The reason why we're here.

The reason we're watching.

The reason the whole fucking thing works.

Rarely in the entire history of Hollywood movie stars being movie stars has a movie star done less and accomplished more than McQueen with this role in this movie. The part is nothing and yet he makes it a great role. He *practically* does nothing, but nobody in the history of movies did *nothing* like Steve McQueen.

As great as McQueen could be, this is the role he needs to be remembered by. Because it's in this role he demonstrates what he could do that Newman and Beatty couldn't.

Which is just *be.*

Just fill the frame with *him.*★

I'm not saying McQueen was playing himself. Steve McQueen in real life was decidedly *not* like Frank Bullitt. Frank Bullitt was a McQueen creation.

But what makes it such an achievement is how minimalistic the creation was, and how the minimalism was key to the performance's success. In real life everything suggests Steve McQueen could be a real hothead. In Don Siegel's autobiography he relates that a few times during the making of *Hell Is for Heroes* the two men almost came to blows. Apparently McQueen and his costar on

---

L.A., Gordon Parks in *Shaft,* the people behind *Puppet on a Chain* (which plays like Frank Bullitt goes to Amsterdam), and Douglas Hickox's shooting and staging of *Sitting Target.*

★ Eastwood tried to give a McQueen-like performance in *Thunderbolt and Lightfoot,* and he didn't pull it off. But McQueen would never do *Thunderbolt and Lightfoot* because he was honestly and refreshingly selfish. Why spend four months shooting a film just to get Jeff Bridges an Oscar nomination?

that film, Bobby Darin, also couldn't stand each other. When the fat Hollywood hack James Bacon once mentioned to the Sicilian-tempered Darin that McQueen was his own worst enemy, Bobby replied, *"Not while I'm alive."*

But McQueen's Lt. Frank Bullitt is no hothead. He is the epitome of cool.

And when I say *cool*, I don't mean just the charismatic he-man bad-boy cool McQueen was famous for (though he does have that too).

I mean, emotionally, Frank Bullitt is as cool as a reptile.

Nothing makes him get hot.

Nothing makes him *lose* his cool.

When Robert Vaughn's ambitious D.A. Chalmers bitches out Bullitt in the hospital, accusing him of incompetence and threatening his career, Bullitt says nothing.

No blowup.

No, *Look, Chalmers, I have a wounded man in there fighting for his life because of you and your assignment!*

Bullitt just looks at him.

He doesn't quietly seethe behind the eyes.

When Chalmers leaves, he doesn't even roll his eyes. He doesn't make a face or say to himself a 1968 version of *"What a prick."*

And when Bullitt's back with his partner Delgetti, he doesn't make comments about *"that asshole Chalmers."*

He just doesn't engage.

Lt. Frank Bullitt doesn't engage with anything that would upset him. And he possesses a Herculean power to *not* get upset. His one conflict with girlfriend Jacqueline Bisset is over how the crime, and the death, and the murder he witnesses in his job *don't* affect him. When he misses the killer at the hospital, yeah, he's a little frustrated, but he doesn't go on a tear about how they had him and he slipped through their fingers.

He just goes back to work.

When he shows up Chalmers and the police brass, he offers no sarcasm (like Dirty Harry would).

He just exits the room.

And after the climax at the airport, there's no sense of satisfaction or vindication on Bullitt's part.

It's just done.

Interestingly, the climax at the airport does play different than the other action scenes in the movie. Because *finally* we know what's going on and what Frank is trying to do. There's a sense of urgency to this sequence that isn't in the others.

I wondered how much this minimalist design of the character was in the script. I asked Neile McQueen—since she was one of the first people to read the material—how different was that first script compared to the finished film. She told me it was "*vastly different.*" She implied the original script by Harry Kleiner was much more of a straight adaptation of Pike's novel. She described the original script as "*almost genteel.*" But then McQueen and his partner at Solar Productions, Robert E. Relyea, brought on *Thomas Crown Affair* screenwriter Alan Trustman and they just built a movie around Steve.

But Yates doesn't employ the old movie-star trick of having everybody else overact, while the lead underacts so he comes across as cooler and more in control. The ham and phony dramatics that always accompanied the supporting players in their stock roles in cop movies were stripped away by Yates. Robert Vaughn, in his own way, is as effective in his role as McQueen. Vaughn never overplays his smarmy oily act. He never makes a meal out of his provoking dialogue. Like McQueen as Bullitt, he finds his own register, his own monotone, and never veers off course. In his entertaining study of the actor's career, *Robert Vaughn: A Critical Study*, author John B. Murray described Vaughn's sneaky Chalmers: "*He works so well within the scheme of the film because his style here is unobtrusive yet too dynamic and compulsive not to make one fascinated by the character.*

Audience feeling towards Chalmers remains at all times rather ambiva-lent, recognizing how despicable he is yet unable to conquer a grudging but substantial admiration."

On one hand, even though he's just a functionary obstacle, he comes across as the film's main villain (you halfway expect him to be part of the conspiracy at the climax), which is a testament to Vaughn's performance. But also by the end, as he walks away from the airport, facing a Monday morning hearing that will fizzle when it was promised to pop, you feel a little bad for him (you wouldn't be surprised to find out Vaughn's assistant district attorney in *Bullitt* becomes Vaughn's senator in *The Towering Inferno*). Simon Oakland also turns in a strong, low-key performance as Bullitt's boss. For once in Oakland's career he plays his signature role without any bluster. On Oakland's TV series, *Kolchak: The Night Stalker*, as *Carl Kolchak*'s (Darren McGavin) harried newspaper editor *Tony Vincenzo*, he screamed his dialogue in every scene he ever appeared in. In *Bullitt* you could mistake him for a completely different actor. Bill Hickman and John Aprea as the two shotgun-wielding killers—and Bullitt's racing opponents through the streets of San Francisco—are effective in a uniquely uncliched way (they're not cast for their ugly faces). And the shotgun-wielding member of the duo, Aprea, with his thinning white hair and his long tan trench coat, has a surprisingly soft and appealing voice when he's in the hospital inquiring to the staff about where Johnny Ross is (so he can finish the job). And this stripped-down level of playing even extends to Don Gordon, as Bullitt's partner Delgetti. I've never liked Don Gordon. I don't care if it's his dirty cop in *The Mack*, as Jim Brown's goofy sidekick in *Slaughter*, or Dennis Hopper's side-kick in *The Last Movie*, or any of the parade of seventies cop shows he guested on. But this built-for-speed version of Don Gordon is very effective. He's actually perfect as Bullitt's partner. And the fact that McQueen and Gordon liked each other in real life is felt in the movie.

As Frank Bullitt, Steve McQueen has more lines than he would in *Le Mans*. But not *much* more. In *Le Mans* the lack of lines is self-conscious. When Eastwood as *Frank Morris* in *Escape from Alcatraz* doesn't speak for the first fifteen minutes, it's self-conscious too (it's also cool and effective). But *Bullitt*'s lack of dialogue is never self-conscious. Because it's a physical performance. Bullitt doesn't explain to the audience or other characters what he's doing or thinking. He just does them and we watch. When I mentioned to Neile McQueen how little Bullitt spoke, she said, "*That was all Steve. He really didn't like to talk too much in movies. He would just rip out pages of dialogue. He'd do scenes with Don Gordon and say, 'Give those lines to Don.' Then Don would say, 'Who cares who says it, the camera's still gonna be on you.' And Steve smiled and said, 'That's right, baby.'"*

Walter Hill said the same thing. "*Steve would say, 'Let him say that. I'll be over here peeling an apple.'*"

Steve McQueen plays the role the way Peter Yates directs the picture. Neither man seems to have any narrative or dramatic concerns whatsoever.

Steve McQueen as Frank Bullitt keeps moving forward, Yates as the director follows him, and we the audience sit back and let them do our thinking for us. As *pure cinema*, it's one of the best directed movies ever made.

Dirty Harry

(1971)

D on Siegel started his career at Warner Bros. in the Montage Department working closely alongside great Warner directors such as Raoul Walsh, Anatole Litvak, and the man who was to become Don's mentor, Michael Curtiz. Siegel shot and designed montages for *Yankee Doodle Dandy*, *They Drive by Night*, *Confessions of a Nazi Spy*, and *The Roaring Twenties*, some of the most iconic and re-created montages ever made (Don told Peter Bogdanovich in his book, *Who the Devil Made It*, "*The strangest things about the pictures I do: I bend over backwards not to do montages.*" The exceptions are his excellent montages in *Escape from Alcatraz*). After graduating out of the Montage Department he started directing second unit for some of the biggest pictures on the Warner lot. Before director Byron Haskin made *The War of the Worlds*, *Robinson Crusoe on Mars*, and *The Naked Jungle* he was Siegel's boss in the Warner Bros. Special Effects Department.

In Stuart Kaminsky's book, *Don Siegel: Director*, Haskin said, "*We spent whole days doing things like having guys take punches, dropping masts on sailors, throwing people through roofs, cracking boats in half and sinking them.*

"*Most directors didn't know and most still don't know what to do with a fight or a piece of action.*

"What this did for Don was orient him towards cinematic violence."

From the very beginning of Siegel's filmography he could shoot a fistfight, or a chase, or crosscut a shoot-out like damn few. There was no Hollywood director in the fifties *better* at shooting action than Don Siegel. What made his action sequences stand out was a combination of technique and tone. Coming from a montage background, in order to achieve the desired pace in the editing room, he filmed the action with a mind to be able to crosscut the shots. This wasn't really the common practice of the day. A lot of action scenes were shot in big masters, where you'd watch two stuntmen (filling in for the stars) punch each other and break furniture for five minutes or until the stuntmen got tired.

Siegel told director Curtis Hanson (back when he went by the name Curtis Lee Hanson) in the 1968 issue of the film magazine *Cinema*, *"I'm extremely conscious of editing when I'm shooting. Because I work with limited time, very short schedules, I plan everything as I think it's going to be cut."* Then he added, *"It doesn't necessarily follow that because you're a good editor, you'll be a good director. But I do think that to be a good director you have to be a good editor."*

There was another aspect to Siegel's action scenes that made them stand out from his contemporaries. Most other genre directors shot fistfights and shoot-outs, but when they did, it was *action.* When Siegel shot those same conventions, it was *violence.* The violent sequences in New Hollywood cinema like *The French Connection, Busting, Dillinger, The Mechanic, Coffy, Straw Dogs, Point Blank,* and *Rolling Thunder* were played out one and two decades earlier in Siegel pictures like *The Duel at Silver Creek, Riot in Cell Block 11, Baby Face Nelson, Private Hell 36, The Lineup, Flaming Star,* and *The Killers.*

Neville Brand, star of *Riot in Cell Block 11* (and killer of many men in World War Two), said, *"Don is like Peckinpah. They both dig violence and are two of the least violent guys I've ever met. It takes that type of guy to understand violence."*

When it came to directing violence you could call Don Siegel *the Surgeon.* But in his early days, shooting second unit on somebody else's film or directing his own tightly budgeted short scheduled flicks, he would be better described as a *combat surgeon.*

But after he made *Dirty Harry,* he was the combat surgeon who goes on to become the dean of Harvard Medical School.

After years of crafting montages and shooting second unit action scenes for other directors, when Warner Bros. finally gave Siegel a chance to direct his own feature, it was with an extremely clever potboiler titled *The Verdict* (not to be confused with the Paul Newman/Sidney Lumet film with the same name). The film was a star vehicle for the audience-favorite odd couple Sydney Greenstreet and Peter Lorre. From any perspective the film is entertaining (it's a really strong first film). But, coming from an auteurist perspective, it's kind of amazing. Since the picture was obviously an assignment, it's almost comical how it predates so many of the characteristics that Siegel would later become known for. Primarily, it's a mystery plot that completely hinges on Siegel's exciting narrative facility for *audience misdirection.* It's a narrative device he employed often (*The Duel at Silver Creek, Flaming Star, The Lineup*), always to the betterment of the picture, reaching its apex with *Charley Varrick.* And audience misdirection is just as crucial to *The Verdict* as it would later be to *Charley Varrick.* But the even more amazing prototype to his later work would be the similarity of the picture's lead protagonist, Sydney Greenstreet's *Superintendent Grodman* of Scotland Yard, to both Clint Eastwood's Inspector Harry Callahan of the San Francisco police force and Richard Widmark's Detective Dan Madigan of the NYPD. At the film's start, Greenstreet's Grodman sends a man to the gallows for murder, only it's discovered later that the man was actually innocent. The superintendent's error wasn't due to malice or faulty detective work, but because the man's alibi couldn't be corroborated until after the execution (like *Madigan*, it's a mistake the lawman makes at the beginning of the picture that instigates the story to follow).

Grodman is forced to resign his position in disgrace and watch a despised underling assume the mantle of superintendent of Scotland Yard. Yet a new murder occurs of the impossible-to-accomplish-locked-room type that allows the former top cop to prove both his mental superiority to his inferior former colleagues and, in a poetic touch, bring the original, real murderer of the earlier crime to justice. However, like Eastwood's Harry Callahan and Richard Widmark's Dan Madigan, to accomplish this Greenstreet's Grodman eschews all recognized legal procedure to follow his *own* self-declared brand of justice. The film's similarity to the director's most popular success is so uncanny it's surprising that Siegel never mentions it in his autobiography (instead he berates *The Verdict* as "*dull.*" It does have a stagey, studio look, maybe why Siegel hated it).

But the rogue law enforcement officer, at odds with their superiors, who operates independently to get their man and enforce their *own self-determined version of justice,* is practically the quintessential Siegel protagonist. Not only *Dirty Harry, Madigan,* and *The Verdict*'s Grodman, but Eastwood's Coogan in *Coogan's Bluff,* Michael Parks' Vinny McKay in *Stranger on the Run,* as well as David Niven's comical Scotland Yard Inspector in *Rough Cut* (even in Siegel's two espionage films, *The Black Windmill* and *Telefon,* his protagonists, secret agents working for MI6, the KGB, and the CIA, all end up going rogue inside their own agencies). Even his criminals go rogue. Mickey Rooney's *Baby Face Nelson* stands in direct contrast to Leo Gordon's *Dillinger,* and both Walter Matthau's *Charley Varrick* and Burt Reynolds' cat burglar in *Rough Cut* execute secret schemes under the noses of their partners (Andy Robinson and Lesley-Anne Down, respectively). Michael Parks' sheriff in *Stranger on the Run* is at odds with his deputies, Steve McQueen's soldier in *Hell Is for Heroes* is at odds with his company, and Elvis' half-breed Indian Pacer in *Flaming Star* is at odds with the white community of his father, his mother's tribe, and finally even the father and brother who love him. This iconoclasm seems to resemble Don Siegel's relationship with his producers and the studio heads he worked for.

Bogdanovich asked him was he consciously attracted to that kind of antisocial character.

Siegel told him, "*I think I AM that Character. Certainly I am at the studios!*"

That's what McQueen got wrong in the actor's initial assessment of the director as a "company man" or "studio hack." He might have done the assignments the bosses wanted—that was his job—but he didn't do them the *way* the bosses wanted. Like his cop characters, Siegel did them *his* way. He usually did what *he* thought was right, oftentimes at odds with the producers and under the noses of his studio bosses. And if his (slightly self-aggrandizing) autobiography is to be believed, he was quick to sarcastically point out how stupid or impractical the ideas of the people he worked for were—like Harry Callahan.

If Siegel *did* have a stylistic edge over his action filmmaking elders (Hawks, Ford, Walsh, Curtiz, Gordon Douglas) or his contemporaries (Aldrich, Karlson, Witney, Jack Arnold, J. Lee Thompson), it came from his penchant for shocking explosions of brutal violence inside his films, often when the viewer least expects it. No other filmmaker in Andrew Sarris' *The American Cinema* accumulated more scenes of cinematic brutality throughout their filmography than Siegel.

Henry Hathaway rolls an old lady down the stairs. Fritz Lang throws hot coffee in a woman's face. Critics have chronicled these individual instances of screen violence for decades. Yet Siegel's filmography contains sequence after sequence—incident after incident—of this type of screen brutality. I could write out a laundry list of incidents, but that would only diminish their power. They need to be experienced in context.

Even after Sam Peckinpah rocked the world and the industry with his powder keg *The Wild Bunch*, Siegel didn't abdicate his throne.

Peckinpah's violence is more *explicit* (i.e., *bloody*) then Siegel's ever was or would be (though the wet red blood hit in the back of the female pool swimmer at the beginning of *Dirty Harry*, once seen, is never forgotten).

Siegel's violence was more about *brutality* then explicit bloodshed (I know I'm overusing the word *brutal*, but you try and describe Don Siegel's stock-in-trade without overusing the word).

D*irty Harry* was Siegel and Eastwood's fourth collaboration and the film both men would be most known for. It was with *Dirty Harry* that Eastwood would establish himself outside of cowboy pictures and dethrone John Wayne as America's number one action star (remarkably Wayne was still going pretty strong into 1970). *Dirty Harry* would make Siegel, along with Sam Peckinpah, Hollywood's premier director of action cinema, and its most expert practitioner of cinematic violence. Along with *The French Connection*, *Dirty Harry* would facilitate the move from westerns to cop films that took place in that decade both on screen and television. And it would become the most imitated action film of the next two decades, as well as being the first real official entry into the popular subgenre of serial killer movies.

It was also Siegel's most *political* film since his earlier masterpiece, *Invasion of the Body Snatchers*. With *Body Snatchers*, the liberal-leaning Siegel was able to have his cake and eat it too. On one hand, it can be read as a subtextual attack on McCarthyism (its most popular reading). But on the other hand, the film also plays into the *Red Nightmare* paranoia of the fifties. The Pod People's society seems like a socialist utopia that these hysterical humans (Americans) are blindly reacting against.* In many of Siegel's stories

---

*I've always had an alternative reading of the *Body Snatchers* movies (Siegel's, Kaufman's, and Ferrara's). Each movie presents the *Pod People* in a sinister light. Yet really, *almost* nothing they do on screen really bears out this sinister interpretation. If you're one who believes that your *soul* is what makes you *you*, then I suppose the Pod People are murdering the Earthlings they duplicate and replace. However, if you're more of the mind that it is your *intellect* and your *consciousness* that make you who you are, then the Pod People transformation is closer to a *rebirth* than a murder. You're reborn as straight intellect, with a complete possession of your past and your abilities, but unburdened by messy human emotions. You also possess a complete fidelity to your fellow beings and a total commitment to the survival of your species. Are they *inhuman*? Of course, they're vegetables. But the movies try to present their lack of humanity (they don't have a sense of humor, they're unmoved when a dog is hit by a car) as evidence of some deep-seated sinisterness. That's a rather species-centric point of view. As human beings it may be our emotions that make us human, but it's a stretch to say it's what makes us great. Along with those positive emotions—love, joy, happiness, amusement—come negative emotions—hate, selfishness, racism, depression, violence, and rage.

For instance, with all the havoc that Donald Sutherland causes in the Kaufman version, including the murder of various Pod People, there never is a thought of punishment or vengeance on the Pod People's part, even though he's obviously proven himself to be a threat.

They just want him to become one of *them*.

Imagine in the fifties, when the Siegel film was made, that instead of some little town in Northern California (Santa Mira) that the aliens took root in, it was a horribly racist, segregated Ku Klux Klan stronghold in the heart of Mississippi.

Within weeks the color lines would disappear. Blacks and whites would be working together (in genuine *brotherhood*) towards a common goal. And *humanity* would be represented by one of the racist Kluxers whose investigative

working for producers and studio executives he didn't respect, the director referred to them as *Pod People.* Even referring once to Elvis' obedience to Col. Tom Parker as a *"pod person."*

But in the seventies cop thriller, the subtextual attack is of a much different political bent. *Dirty Harry* tells the story of the quintessential Siegel protagonist taken to its logical extreme. Eastwood's Harry Callahan is the baddest-ass cop on the San Francisco police force. In a different era he'd be portrayed as a by-the-book type. Except in the era and location the movie takes place (San Francisco in the early seventies), in Callahan's opinion, the book has been rewritten in favor of the scum.

Society is screaming police brutality.

The public is siding with the crooks.

And the gutless police brass, local government, and the courts are cowed into compliance with an increasingly permissive social order that favors lawbreakers over law enforcement.

Now this point of view would not be shared by some kid sitting in jail for three years for carrying a bag of weed. But it *is* Harry's point of view. The genius of the film is it takes that transgressive character and pits him up against a fictionalized version of San Francisco's real-life *"Zodiac Killer"* (this fictionalized version, *"Scorpio,"* is a calculated mastermind as well as being batshit crazy).

And in the process, the film creates the first cops-after-a-serial-killer thriller. Most cops in seventies action movies were busy busting dope rings or Mafia Mister Bigs. But from the eighties to today, cops after serial killers is the main occupation of the movie police. *Cruising, 10 to Midnight, Manhunter, Silence of the*

---

gaze notices formerly like-minded white folks seemingly enter into a conspiracy with some members of the county's black community. Now picture *his* hysterical reaction to it (*"Those people are coming after me! They're not human! You're next! You're next!"*).

Lambs, Seven (and every other David Fincher film) are the children of Siegel's *Dirty Harry*.

As in most seminal films, there are prototypes. In the case of *Dirty Harry* the most obvious example is 1969's *Pendulum*, with George Peppard playing a violent rule-breaking cop hell-bent on bringing down overacting sicko Robert F. Lyons.

The soon-to-be Warner Bros. legacy title started life at Universal, where Jennings Lang offered *Dirty Harry* to Paul Newman (probably sometime soon after *Harper*). Newman turned it down. According to Lang, "*[Newman said he] thought it was too tough a role, that he couldn't play that type of character.*" Universal sold the script by Harry Julian Fink and R. M. Fink to Warner Bros., where it was going to be made with Frank Sinatra playing Harry and directed by Irv Kirshner. Then Sinatra sprained his wrist, seriously limiting his ability to wield Callahan's .44 Magnum. Warner offered it to Eastwood, who agreed on the condition that he could bring Don Siegel over from Universal to direct. Siegel came on and brought over not only his cinematographer (Bruce Surtees) and his editor (Carl Pingitore), but also more importantly his go-to screenwriter, Dean Riesner. It was Riesner's rewrite that turned the script into the *Dirty Harry* movie we know and love. Because it was Riesner's rewrite that turned the killer from a lone sniper to a surrogate for the Zodiac Killer (later John Milius would do one of the more famous dialogue polishes in Hollywood history when he added the "*I know what you're thinking. Did he fire six shots or only five?*" speech).

Before the script took that interesting turn, in fact while Siegel was reading it after he'd been offered the job, he had a truly intriguing casting idea. He was on an airplane, and it just so happened so was Audie Murphy. Siegel had earlier directed two pictures starring Murphy (*The Duel at Silver Creek* and *The Gun Runners*), and the two men were happy to see each other again. And as they talked and got reacquainted, it suddenly came to the director, "*My god, I'm looking for a killer and here's the killer of all time, a war hero who killed over 250 people. He was a killer though he didn't look like it. I thought it might be interesting. He had never really played a killer.*" The executives at Universal weren't convinced Murphy could handle the acting demands (though Siegel, apparently, was). But Murphy perished in a plane crash before the idea could be fully explored. And then Siegel and Riesner started to rethink the role. Frankly, the idea of *Dirty Harry* without Andy Robinson is even more un-thinkable than *Dirty Harry* without Eastwood. Nevertheless, the Audie Murphy idea is still incredibly intriguing.

The skill Siegel demonstrates in *Dirty Harry* is remarkable. In a filmography studded with diamonds (*Riot in Cell Block 11, Invasion of the Body Snatchers, Baby Face Nelson, Flaming Star, Hound-Dog Man, Coogan's Bluff, Escape from Alcatraz*) *Dirty Harry* is unquestionably the best of his career. It belongs on a list of other audience-enthralling films of the seventies like *Jaws, Carrie, Annie Hall,* and *The Exorcist* that in retrospect seem like *perfect films.* Siegel's technique, along with all of his strengths, blend together in complete harmony. The director's handling of the film's hero and villain. His career-constant affinity for location photography. The director's ability to *shock* audiences with brutality (the naked corpse of the fourteen-year-old victim removed from its hole, Scorpio paying to get his face bashed in, that first bloody bullet hit of the woman in the swimming pool, Scorpio smacking the terrified child on the bus), and also *thrill* with crowd-pleasing action set pieces (hot dog eating Harry firing his Magnum at the bank robbers, the phone-booth-to-phone-booth ransom drop, the school bus climax). The Siegel humor that punctuates, what is in essence a grisly thriller. It's the humor and Eastwood's flair when it came to delivering Harry's quips that went a long way in both getting the audience on Harry's side, and as even Pauline Kael had to admit, "*turning the audience on*" (the other great serial killer films put the audience through a wringer. But in 1971 packed auditoriums loved *Dirty Harry* because it was fun). It also included Siegel's biggest flaw, his penchant for labored symbolism such as the broken peace sign belt buckle that Scorpio sports around his trousers.

But what made *Dirty Harry* a political film wasn't just its cinematic flirtation with what Roger Ebert described as "*a fascist moral position.*" It was the way Siegel so skillfully tailored the film for its intended audience: frustrated older Americans who by 1971— when they looked out their car door windows, and read their daily newspapers, and watched the evening news—didn't recognize their country anymore.

One of the most memorable tag lines for a modern movie at that time was the one that sold Dennis Hopper's *Easy Rider.* "*A man went looking for America, and he couldn't find it anywhere.*"

A great line, but it wasn't true. If you responded to Hopper's Billy the Kid or Fonda's Captain America rather than the ugly rednecks in the cafe, you didn't have to seek out representation. It was all over music, movies, TV, and magazines.

On the other hand, the generation that fought World War Two in the forties and bought homes in the suburbs in the fifties were the ones who went looking for *their* America and "*couldn't find it anywhere.*"

What Richard Nixon called the "*silent majority*" were frightened. Frightened of an America they didn't recognize and a society they couldn't understand.

Youth culture had taken over pop culture.

If you were under thirty-five, that was a good thing.

But if you were older, maybe not.

Many people back then watched the news in abject horror. Hippies, militant black power groups, killer cults that brainwashed suburban kids to drop acid and rise up and kill their parents, young men (the sons of veterans) burning their draft cards or fleeing to Canada, *your* children calling *your* policemen *pigs*, violent street crime, the emergence of the serial killer phenomenon, drug culture, free love, the nudity, violence, and profanity of the films of New Hollywood, Woodstock, Altamont, Stonewall, Cielo Drive.

To many Americans it was a mosaic that scared the shit out of them.

This was the audience that *Dirty Harry* was made for.

To frustrated Americans, Harry Callahan represented a solution to the shocking violence that they were suddenly forced to adjust to. Eastwood's rogue cop in *Dirty Harry* and Charles Bronson's vigilante *Paul Kersey* in *Death Wish* stood in a showdown stance on one side of the cultural divide. While Tom Laughlin's hippie-loving barefoot face-womping *Billy Jack* and Richard Roundtree's superbad, super-chic black private dick who's a sex machine to all the chicks *John Shaft* stood on the other.

There's been a lot of speculation over the years whether or not Harry Callahan is a racist character or *Dirty Harry* is a racist film, or both. In Charles Higham's book *Celebrity Circus*, the author interviewed both Eastwood and Siegel on the set of *Dirty Harry*. Siegel described Eastwood's character as "*a racist son of a bitch . . . who blames everything on the blacks and the Hispanics.*" Well, the character Siegel's describing is not the character in the movie he made. In the film, Harry may be politically incorrect, but he's not "*a racist son of a bitch.*"

The film would be better—or at least more serious—if he was. But then it would be *Taxi Driver.* Which, even more than the *Cobra* clones to follow, is the real bastard stepchild of *Dirty Harry* and *Death Wish.* But it's doubtful if *Dirty Harry* could ever work as potently as it does if it dared challenge its genre to that degree. The artistry of Siegel's picture is in its creative, provocative effectiveness. Harry's a great character, Scorpio's a great character, the story really works (it's a movie you really can watch a dozen times), but it's the sleek execution of a genre master that makes it sing. If

Steven Spielberg's *Jaws* is one of the greatest movies ever made, because one of the most talented filmmakers who ever lived, when he was young, got his hands on the right material, knew what he had, and killed himself to deliver the best version of that movie he could, then *Dirty Harry* is its opposite number, from a salty dog genre master, with twenty-seven films under his belt at that point—in his fourth collaboration with his greatest star partner—delivering the goods so beautifully it becomes a powerhouse work of art.

If *Dirty Harry* were a boxer it would be Mike Tyson in his knockout prime.

I challenge you to program a double feature of practically any of the great films from the seventies and put them against a double feature with Siegel's picture.

Dirty Harry will wipe them off the screen and knock them the fuck out!

Boom!

But as opposed to all the *Dirty Harry* wannabes (and that includes all the *Dirty Harry* sequels) there remains a disturbing quality to Siegel's creation. Both the film *and* the character of Callahan.

While *Dirty Harry* isn't a racist film, or quite the fascist film its critics at the time claimed, it *is* reactionary.

Aggressively reactionary.

And it promotes a reactionary view, sometimes as subtext and sometimes as text. Because the audience the film sought to excite held a view of the rapidly changing society around them that was bordering on *future shock*.

Dirty Harry gave voice to their fears, told them they were right to feel that way, and gave them a .44 caliber hero who would fight for them. This element would disappear from the Harry sequels. Because while this element was why it connected so well with its audience, it's also what put the film in the crosshairs of social commentators.

It's this reactionary element the very violent Ted Post–directed sequel *Magnum Force* not only avoided, but tried to reverse.

The entire premise of the movie, Harry uncovering a black leather-jacketed death squad of killer motorcycle cops executing criminals that the courts can't, seems to be a rather rare Hollywood occurrence. The counterpoint argument sequel.

I know what we should do. Let's downplay everything about the first movie that really struck a nerve, and make both the film, and Harry himself, preach against that type of thinking.

Death Wish ended up being the movie audiences wanted *Magnum Force* to be (a much better movie with the same premise as *Magnum Force* was an *ABC Movie of the Week, The Death Squad*, with Robert Forster, Melvyn Douglas, and Claude Akins).

The cornucopia of Callahan clones that came out after Siegel's success would ape the hard-ass do-things-his-own-way rule-book-be-damned no-mercy-for-the-wicked posture of Eastwood's creation. But these other films bent over backwards not to touch that type of real-world nerve. The object of ire of these other hard-asses was usually generic movie bad guys, syndicate Mr. Biggs (Allen Garfield in *Busting*, Jack Kruschen in *Freebie and the Bean*, Vittorio Gassman in *Sharky's Machine*), or else so outlandishly unreal that the only level they can exist on is that of a comic book. The motorcycle-riding cult army in *Cobra* looks and acts more like a post-apocalyptic gang of marauders in an Italian *Mad Max* rip-off. The one significant exception to this rule is Charles Bronson's contribution, J. Lee Thompson's *10 to Midnight*, which like *Dirty Harry* has a real-life inspired serial killer at its center. Gene Davis' killer is a surrogate for nursing student murderer Richard Speck, and the intensely violent and sickening restaging of those murders is pretty strong stuff.

But normally the formula is as by-rote as a *Jaws* or *Alien* rip-off. The characterization of the Dirty Harry dude is the same, his quips sound similar, his harassed screaming boss looks, sounds, and dresses the same, and the hammy bad actors who play the villainous creeps in actual Dirty Harry movies like *The Enforcer* and *Sudden Impact* aren't any different from the crap actors in straight to video junk usually starring ex-football players like John Matuszak or Brian Bosworth.

Where the others aimed for generalities, Siegel's film was specific about its reactionary vision.

Nowhere is this point illustrated more clearly than in what has become one of the film's most remembered set pieces. The famous scene where Callahan foils a bank robbery in progress with his big-ass .44 Magnum, while continuing to chew a hot dog.

What makes that scene *political* is the casting of three black men to play the bank robbers. If the robbers had been played by three white actors the scene wouldn't have had a political context. Harry would just be a cop who came across a bank robbery and stopped it. Just like Superman has done in about a thousand issues of his comic book. If the robbers had been white they would have been viewed (more or less) as professional criminals (Willie Sutton, Richard Stark's Parker, Jim Thompson's Doc McCoy). Since we've had professional criminals robbing banks since we've had banks, nothing in the scene would have been indicative of societal change. But let's try on some other racial or ethnic groups for size. Could the bank robbers be Asian? Well, yes, of course they *could be*. But unless the bank was in San Francisco's Chinatown, it would seem odd. The viewer would notice it and think to themselves, *Why are they Asian?* In fact they'd expect it to become a plot point later ("*It's the Teddy Wong Gang, Harry. A Chinese street gang started robbing banks in Chinatown, now they broke out and are robbing banks all over the city.*"). Same thing if they were Hispanic. Yeah, you could explain to the audience how the *Latin Kings* have started robbing banks all over San Francisco, but it would require some sort of explanation. The reason it would play odd is because the nightly news isn't full of stories of Latin or Asian bank robbery crews looting banks across America. But then neither is bank robbery a crime associated with black Americans.

That is except for—at that particular time—one subsection of Black America: militant black revolutionaries who robbed banks to buy weapons. And just one look at the robbers in *Dirty Harry* and you can tell they got their wardrobe in the Black Panther section of the Warner Bros. costume department. For many older white Americans, angry black militants scared them more than the Manson "Family," the Zodiac Killer, and the Boston Strangler combined. The hippies disgusted them. Because the hippies were their children, and they were disgusted with their children. Hippies burning the American flag in protest of the Vietnam War made them livid with anger. But black militants scared the fuck out of them. The anger, the rhetoric, the agenda, the uniform, the posing for pictures with automatic weapons, their hatred of the police, the dismissal of white America (white folks can never comprehend a situation where they *can't* be forgiven for past transgressions).

Yet, there was Harry Callahan.

He wasn't scared.

Not only was he not scared, as he approached a shotgun wielding stand-in for a Black Panther, he couldn't even be bothered to stop chewing his hot dog. He shoots down three black men during the robbery without an iota of fear (he doesn't even seek cover), and even faces one down with an empty weapon, complete with smart-mouthed cracker cop talk meant to antagonize ("*Do you feel lucky? Well . . . do you, punk?*" With the word "*punk*," [at least] replacing the word "*boy*").

These qualities give Siegel's film a dubious morality and a faintly disturbing undercurrent, as opposed to "superhero Harry," which is what he would become in the shoddy sequels.

Siegel's Harry Callahan is both a troubled and troubling character.

Well, that makes him a classic *Siegelini-hero* (the director's self-mocking name for his auteur persona). The director has always confronted the audience with lead characters you're drawn to despite on-screen evidence of their troubling nature, and deeds. Lead protagonists he makes it difficult to root for, but, ultimately, you root for them nonetheless. Which goes to prove what I've always believed, *"It takes a magnificent filmmaker to thoroughly corrupt an audience."* Greenstreet's Grodman in *The Verdict*, McQueen's Reese in *Hell Is for Heroes*, Elvis' Pacer in *Flaming Star*, Widmark's *Madigan*, Matthau's *Charley Varrick*, the two crooked cops (Steve Cochran and Howard Duff) in *Private Hell 36*, the convicts in *Riot in Cell Block 11* (what, are you rooting for the warden?), John Cassavetes' violent street punk in *Crime in the Streets*. Eli Wallach and Robert Keith's two killers in *The Lineup* are by far more involving than the colorless cops from the TV series, same with Lee Marvin and Clu Gulager's sunglasses-wearing hit men in *The Killers*, who are far more compelling than John Cassavetes' milquetoast race car–driving Johnny North. In *Stranger on the Run* you may feel sorry for Henry Fonda's innocent patsy, but it's the story of Michael Parks' compromised lawman Vinny McKay that grips you. Whichever side you take in *The Beguiled*, Eastwood's manipulative, conniving wounded soldier or the murdering, conspiring, vindictive ladies, you're tainted. Even when Siegel bends over backwards to present a character as loathsome, like he does with the brutish, vulgar gambler Rip Torn in the director's final film, *Jinxed!*, how can you not be on his side during his all-or-nothing takedown of the blackjack table (were we *actually* supposed to be on the side of the casino?).

And sure enough, once Rip Torn exits the picture, he takes any viewer's interest with him.

The *New York Times*, Pauline Kael, and Roger Ebert all labeled *Dirty Harry* as *fascist*. And implied (to the point of self-parody) that the film is somewhat politically dangerous, if not outright irresponsible in what they claim is its perpetration of a social fraud (while Ebert claimed the film had a *"fascist moral position"* he attributed it to the times and not moral bankruptcy on the filmmakers' part). While Eastwood would be irked about this for years, none of this came as a surprise to Siegel. In Peter Bogdanovich's book *Who the Devil Made It*, he recalls seeing an industry screening of *Dirty Harry* and Siegel worrying that all his liberal friends would disown him. But Don, as an old genre filmmaker, was apolitical. His job was to thrill audiences by any means necessary. And if he could do that by bringing into question America's criminal justice system or a suspect's Miranda rights, fair enough. If pressed for a defense, I'm sure old Don would just crinkle his eyes, smile, and point at the grosses.

But in Siegel's *Dirty Harry*, almost comically, the skill of the filmmaking was so evident that it was impossible for even the movie's harshest critics to deny. Kael even went so far as to write, *"It would be stupid to deny that Dirty Harry is a stunningly well-made genre piece, and it certainly turns an audience on."* Then in a later piece wrote, *"There's an aesthetic pleasure one gets from highly developed technique; certain action sequences make you feel exhilarated just because they're so cleverly done—even if, as in the case of Siegel's Dirty Harry, you're disgusted by the picture."*

Even Siegel's friend Sam Peckinpah expressed the same opinion as Pauline: *"I loved Dirty Harry, even though I was appalled by it. A terrible piece of trash that Don Siegel really made something out of. Hated what it was saying, but the day I saw it the audience was cheering."*

The point of the film's detractors was crystal clear. It was *Dirty Harry*'s embrace of a fascist ideology, not its quality, that was in question. But this so-called fascist element to the film was overstated by the critics of the daily newspapers and weekly magazines. Fifty years later, Siegel's film stands as a towering achievement of genre filmmaking. The audiences that have thrilled to the movie these last five decades *haven't* been reactionary. Nor have they had to embrace a *"fascist moral position"* in order to enjoy it.

Because frankly, it's the critics' response to it in its day that strikes one as reactionary.

Does anything in the movie that Harry does depict outright fascism? No.

When he fires on the black bank robbers in the hot dog scene, they *were* running from a bank, alarm blaring, and jumping into a speeding car with both money and pump action shotguns in their hands.

Even all of his efforts towards Scorpio don't strike anybody as excessive today. He keeps him under surveillance when he's not supposed to? They know he's *Scorpio*! It's not a question. He's the fucking guy! Kael's strongest jab at the movie is her calling horseshit on the ridiculous Josef Sommer scene, where they know Scorpio's killed all these people and they refuse to let Callahan keep him under surveillance. This scene is guilty of presenting the liberal argument as dumbfoundingly absurd. But it's the scene itself that plays as dumbfoundingly absurd. The only sequence that truly qualifies as *fascist* is when Callahan tortures Scorpio to find the whereabouts of the kidnapped fourteen-year-old girl.

Really, would Billy Jack do any less?

One of the big reasons *Dirty Harry* fails to outrage anymore is Siegel's film had another agenda that the critics chose to ignore but the public got right away. As much as *Dirty Harry* is a white western fantasy played out against a modern-day San Francisco backdrop, it is also a plea for *New Laws for New Crimes.*

The serial killer phenom to be exact.

And one of the reasons *Dirty Harry* ages well is when it comes to catching and stopping Scorpio, what the film preaches is pretty much what society ended up doing in regard to that type of crime.

At the same time, our familiarity with the genre—a genre that this film officially started—dates it in terms of the techniques of the investigation. It would appear that Callahan and his (rookie) partner Gonzales are the only two investigators on the case of a madman who's terrorizing the entire city.

When you watch it today you can't help but ask yourself, *Where's the task force? Where's the FBI? Where's Will Graham? Where's the BAU?* Without these societal advantages we now employ against this type of crime, *nothing* Harry does seems unjustified. Since 1971 we've become so adjusted to a world that includes serial killers in it, we can have a television series like *Criminal Minds* that presented for three hundred twenty-three episodes a new deranged serial killer every week for fifteen years.

But back in 1971 both Andy Robinson's bravura performance and his character's methods were from a new-to-movies villain. There had never been a movie fiend quite like Scorpio before, or a performance quite like Robinson's. It's why, after *Dirty Harry*, Eastwood's career was assured, but Robinson's was nipped in the bud (until fifteen years later, when an older Robinson shows up in *Hellraiser*). I'm here to testify, as unfair and unjust as it may have been, whenever Andy showed up in a movie, all I saw was Scorpio. Andy Robinson scared viewers in a way no movie monster ever had or ever would again (we would never again be as innocent as we were when we first witnessed Scorpio sow his sick oats). And forty years of movie serial killers haven't diminished Robinson's performance one iota (it's the single best performance *ever* in a Don Siegel picture).

I remember sitting in the cinema at age nine, feeling the *exact* same thing the adults around me were feeling. Terrifying disbelief that Scorpio could be so sick and depraved. In Pauline Kael's review in the *New Yorker* she never refers to the character or the actor by name. Nor does she write one word regarding his performance.

Instead she refers to the film's antagonist by a plethora of sarcastic bogeyman names (*"hippie maniac," "the many-sided evil one," "super-evil dragon"*).

Her point was, in order for the audience to be on Harry's side, the filmmakers needed to contrive a bogeyman of such evil dimensions that *anything* Harry does seems justified.

Well, despite the Boston Strangler, Richard Speck, the Manson "Family," and of course Zodiac, we may once have looked at Scorpio's sickness with disbelief.

But we don't anymore.

We know *exactly* how sick and evil people can be.

Many real-life individuals have demonstrated Scorpio's depravity as anything but a fantasy. Yes, Ms. Kael was right about the filmmakers' motives. They did create a *"super-evil dragon"* for Harry's .44 caliber Siegfried to slay. What she was wrong about was writing off Robinson's character as just a monster in a monster movie.

In *Dirty Harry* Siegel, Riesner, and especially Robinson gave us a forward-looking glance at what would replace the monsters of old in the collective nightmare of a society to come. During its initial engagement, every audience member of *Dirty Harry* entered the cinema with an innocent view. An innocence we would soon lose.

Deliverance

(1972)

At a very young age, I saw my fair share of powerful double features, and even a few triple features.

The aforementioned *Joe* & *Where's Poppa?*

The Owl and the Pussycat & *Diary of a Mad Housewife.*

Cry of the Banshee & *The House That Screamed (La Residencia).*

Trog & *When Dinosaurs Ruled the Earth.*

Equinox & *Beneath the Planet of the Apes.*

Soylent Green & *The Omega Man.*

The Abominable Dr. Phibes & *The House That Dripped Blood* (my favorite double feature of my childhood).

I saw *The French Connection* on a double feature with *Vanishing Point*, when Twentieth Century Fox rereleased both pictures together in a citywide car-chasing engagement (Fox would do the same thing with *The Seven-Ups*, pairing it with *The French Connection*. Then later get a ton of high-octane mileage by doubling up *Vanishing Point* with *Dirty Mary Crazy Larry*).

I first saw *The Good, the Bad and the Ugly* on a double feature with *For a Few Dollars More.*

My first official James Bond movie (a seminal moment in a young boy's life) was in '71 when Curt took me to see *Diamonds Are Forever* during its premiere engagement at the Grauman's Chinese

Theatre (we stood for an hour and a half in a line that wrapped around the huge parking lot and down the block).

And a year later, Curt and my Uncle Roger took me to a James Bond triple feature that was playing at the Loyola cinema, *From Russia with Love*, *Dr. No*, and *Goldfinger*. After the nonstop excitement of *Diamonds Are Forever*, I found both *From Russia with Love* and *Dr. No* dull as hell (*these* boring movies are James Bond movies?). But as soon as *Goldfinger* started, I thought "that's more like it."

My first Woody Allen movie was *Take the Money and Run*. Even though I was too young to understand what was being parodied (crime films and television true crime documentaries), I thought it was one of the funniest things I had ever seen. When Woody Allen carves a gun out of soap to make his prison getaway (a la John Dillinger) and escapes into the rain, only to reveal a handful of soap suds, I still think that's one of the great all-time sight gags. But because my mom didn't like Woody Allen, I didn't see any more of his movies for years.

So no *Bananas*, no *Everything You Always Wanted to Know About Sex (But Were Afraid to Ask)*, no *Sleeper*. Then my Uncle Roger was dating his soon-to-be first wife, a lovely English girl named Jill, and they took me on their date to see *Play It Again, Sam*.

Again, I couldn't believe a guy could be so funny. I laughed from the beginning of that picture to the end. I kind of knew who Bogart was, though I doubt I had ever sat down and watched a full Humphrey Bogart movie (actually Curt showed me *The African Queen* on TV, but except for the part with the leeches, I didn't dig it). And I know, at that time, I had never heard of *Casablanca*. But it didn't matter. I got the gist. When Bogart said his funniest joke in the movie, "*You're as nervous as Lizabeth Scott was just before I blew her brains out*," did I know who Lizabeth Scott was? Of course not. Could I figure out at twelve that she was probably some old-time actress that Bogart did pictures with? Of course.

But later when I watched Elvis in *Loving You*, during one of the nineteen times NBC showed it on prime time network television, I went, "*Oh, that's Lizabeth Scott.*" So, if you're reading this cinema book, hopefully to learn a little something about cinema, and your head is swimming from all the names you don't recognize, congratulations, you're learning something.

But I digress.

Suddenly, one week, United Artists did a citywide rerelease of three Woody Allen movies! *Bananas, Everything You Always Wanted to Know About Sex*, and *Sleeper*. I begged my mom to take me to see it, and shockingly, she agreed (on a school night, no less). So, naturally, the next day at school, I regaled the other children with stories about the movie I saw the night before, which had a giant monster boob terrorizing the countryside ("*Be careful, honey.*" "*Don't worry, baby. I know how to handle tits.*").

But of all the double features I saw back then, none was as powerful, nor as controversial, as the time my mother took me with her on a date to see a double feature of *The Wild Bunch* and *Deliverance*.

That particular double feature was controversial when I told people about it then. And it's controversial when I tell people about it now. Some parents didn't even want me playing with their children at school because of the wild movies I saw and talked about. I guess they were afraid I'd give their kids ideas, or spill the goods on the taboo images I witnessed. But make no mistake, when I tell the story of seeing *The Wild Bunch* and *Deliverance* at eleven—then and now—I'm fucking bragging!

The Wild Bunch was released in 1969. And we didn't go see it then. Maybe the age of six might have been a *little* too young for Peckinpah's masterpiece (though a year later I did see *House of Dark Shadows*, which had very similar imagery). But even though I didn't see it, I definitely heard of it. My favorite uncle, Cliff, saw it and told us how amazing it was. And my Uncle Roger saw it, and had similar sentiments. So, for a time, *The Wild Bunch* became this infamous title in our household. A title that represented an outrageous movie. A movie too outrageous for me.

Another thing that gave *The Wild Bunch* mythic stature was I never saw trailers for it at the movies, or spots on television. So it was just that title, *The Wild Bunch*. And the heavy reputation of outrageousness from my uncles. I actually knew so little about the movie, that for years, I didn't even know it was a western. At first, I thought it was a motorcycle gang movie (I think, at first, so did Curt).

Then in 1971 Sam Peckinpah's *Straw Dogs* was released and its distributor, ABC Pictures International, bombarded the commercial airwaves with vivid and dynamic TV spots, where the announcer always made a big deal about Sam Peckinpah's name, *"From director SAM PECKINPAH, the man that brought you The Wild Bunch."* I didn't see *Straw Dogs* back then either, but a female child psychologist I had sessions with in school did. She knew I loved movies, so when we had sessions we mainly talked about the different movies we saw. And she had just seen it that weekend, so she pretty much (minus the rape) described the whole film to me, including every step of Dustin Hoffman's violent retribution (what a cool lady!).

Warner Bros. kept *The Wild Bunch* in theatres for years and years as the lower half of Warner double features (it's not like they could sell it to television anytime soon). Which was how I eventually saw it that night in 1973 with my mom and a really classy gentleman named Quincy (who looked a lot like Clifton Davis from *That's My Mama*), at the Tarzana Six Movies (back when a six-screen cinema was a big deal).

Obviously, Peckinpah's masterpiece blew my fucking mind. Especially the shot when they slit Angel's throat and the blood—in Peckinpah slow motion, which is about a hundred and twenty frames a second—squirts practically into the camera lens. As far as

I could tell, they just actually slit Angel's throat. It would be years and many subsequent screenings before I really understood the movie. And many more years before I was able to truly comprehend not just the film's power, but its beauty. Unlike his mentor Don Siegel, whose forte was violent brutality, Peckinpah's violence constituted a turn away from mere brutality. The spurting red blood squibs of *Bloody Sam* were closer to liquid ballet and visual poetry painted in crimson (in the eighties John Woo would do the same thing with orange muzzle flash). The shock of *The Wild Bunch* wasn't just what we saw on screen, but our reaction to what we saw.

It was beautiful and moving.

There was a beauty to these rotten bastards opting to risk everything for a member of their team who none of them particularly liked. Something monumentally masculine and profoundly moving about the Bunch's incomparably glorious walk to their destiny/doom (it's truly a moment that can make grown men weep testosterone-salted tears).

Something beautiful in the way they killed (epitomized by Warren Oates' orgasmic turn at the Gatling gun).

Something gratifying about the lack of consideration in the carnage, whether it's blowing the medals off the pig general, or Pike plugging that back-shooting whore with a "*You bitch!*"

Something beautiful about the way they died—filled with little balls of lead, covered in red, spurting blood, Borgnine going down calling Holden's name ("*Pike . . . Pike . . .*").

But *then*, at the Tarzana Six, it was the pyrotechnics that blew my little ass through the back wall of the theatre.

The film finished spooling through the projector shutter gate and the lights came up for intermission. No doubt, I was all mouth talking about how *boss* that was (I'm sure Quincy couldn't believe he was watching *The fucking Wild Bunch* alongside a little kid).

Nevertheless, it was the second movie of the night that left the biggest impression on me, and the one that dominated the discussion on the car ride home.

John Boorman's *Deliverance,* based on the James Dickey novel of the same name, tells the story of four fellas from Atlanta, three of them upwardly mobile family men—*Ed* (Jon Voight), *Bobby* (Ned Beatty), and *Drew* (Ronny Cox)—who follow their roguish bowhunting enthusiast buddy *Lewis* (Burt Reynolds) for a back-woods canoe trip down the Cahulawassee River. Their excursion is a week before a dam is to be finished that will flood the river under ten miles of water.

The difference between the other three and the bachelor *Lewis* is pronounced. Lewis talks tough, acts tough (he alone is not intimidated by the backwoods characters they come across), and looks every inch a macho man (before the red shirt he wore as *the Bandit,* the weird scuba vest he wore as Lewis was Reynolds' most iconic film outfit). Yet author James Dickey—and the movie—makes it clear Lewis is trying to live up to an idea of himself. He's not full of shit, but he's also not the authority he tries to come across as. The way he bluffs the hillbillies over the price of driving their cars downriver is how he bluffs his buddies about his one-with-nature mountain man shtick.

He's full of consumed facts, rather than experience-derived wisdom. He is quite a good bowhunter—but he's a sportsman, not a survivalist. More balls than brains, more opinion than knowledge.

Yes, he possesses more instinct than his three companions. But even his instinct, like his whole macho projection of self, is a pose.

Not to say the pose is a lie. Lewis isn't a fraud—he believes the pose, and it's a comfortable pose. But it's not who Lewis *is,* it's who he wants to be. The people who Lewis models himself on can't turn it off and on. Lewis can. If Lewis owned a sporting goods store and needed an extension on his business loan, he could drop the pose when he went down to the bank to have a meeting with the loan officer. He would and could dress and act and talk like an Atlanta business owner. And that wouldn't be a lie either. Warren Beatty's hairdresser George Roundy couldn't pull off the meeting with the loan officer, but Lewis could. It would have been easy for writer Dickey to give the husbands a genuine (paid) river expert as their guide. He could have served the exact same plot functions as Lewis, down to the same colorful commentary that Reynolds spouts through the whole first half (the best half) of the movie. But Dickey wants us to know that as good a game as Lewis talks, he has more in common with the three husbands than the river folk that they come in contact with. Lewis has eaten shrimp scampi and fried calamari in a fancy Atlanta seafood restaurant.

His cigars are Cohibas, not Dutch Masters. He knows how to order a Brandy Alexander and a Harvey Wallbanger and how they're supposed to taste.

Lewis has seen Jack Nicholson in *Five Easy Pieces.*

Lewis knows who Roman Polanski is.

This makes sense when you realize that Lewis is a stand-in for the author James Dickey, who in actuality isn't a *Tarzan*, but a poet.

The novel is written in the first-person prose of Voight's character, Ed, but it's Lewis that the writer identifies with. And it's Dickey who Reynolds patterned his characterization on. Among the other three, only Beatty's Bobby is taken in by Lewis' "*Tarzan*" act.

Voight's Ed and Cox's Drew follow Lewis' lead, but they're fully aware of what's behind it. The fact it's an entertaining pose is why they enjoy it. And *we* enjoy it too. The whole first forty-five minutes of the movie is a rollicking gas, and the audience's enjoyment is built around Burt Reynolds' running commentary on his fatalistic, yet entertaining, vision of a dystopian future he foresees ("*Machines are gonna fail*"), that only he alone is equipped to deal with.

And a large component of that enjoyment is that the Burt

Reynolds they had become familiar with from his appearances on *The Johnny Carson Show* is still present in the Lewis persona. The dude that sat on Johnny's couch, dressed in his head-to-toe leather outfits, drenched in self-love, cracking jokes about his bad movies was recognizable as the speechifying, sexy stud in the scuba vest. Only a less self-deprecating, more dangerous version of talk show Burt.

On the first day Drew announces, "*I'm goin' with you, Ed, and not Mr. Lewis Medlock. 'Cause I've seen how he drives these country roads he don't know nothin' about.*" The first day of the trip, it's Ed and Drew in one canoe, and Lewis and Bobby in the other. And Lewis barks orders at Bobby all day long. And not out of expertise, or in good natured fun, but as a bully. He refers to Bobby as "*chubby*," diminishing his masculinity inside the male group dynamic. It marks him as a "*soft man*" in ways more than physical. Of this male wolf pack, he's its effeminate member. Even if Ed or Drew were thirty pounds heavier, they wouldn't tolerate Lewis' lack of respect by calling them "*chubby*." But since Bobby *does* tolerate it, it solidifies his position among the other men. Later that night, Bobby whines to Ed about Lewis' treatment with real anxiety, but it's not the tone of an indignant grown-ass man. It's the tone of a whiny adolescent. Neither does he confront the object of his torment. Instead he tattletales to a reasonable surrogate (Ed), in hopes that he'll intervene.

Likewise, the next morning, Lewis tells Ed, not Bobby, "*You take that chubby boy with you today*," further diminishing Bobby's standing inside the masculine quartet.

This trip down the river isn't a roller coaster. It requires the individual achievement of each man working in tandem with one another. It's not like they're on a fishing trip and Bobby proves the most hapless baiting his hook, or he's the most clumsy on the basketball court. Yet, to my novice eyes, it looks like Bobby does a good job. He lacks the confidence of the other men, but he's not an uncoordinated liability.

Inside the group, Ed is the most trusted and liked. Because he's everybody's point of contact. Bobby doesn't know Lewis, he's invited on the trip by Ed. Drew does know Lewis, but not like Ed does. In Dickey's novel, Ed is a graphic artist who's a partner in a dinky ad agency. And Lewis inherited land from his family and lives off his earnings as a landlord. It makes you wonder how Ed and Lewis became friends. How did they meet? What made Lewis invite Ed on their first bowhunting trip? What made Ed go? In the film, Lewis asks Ed, "*Why do you go on these trips with me, Ed?*"

But Ed replies like a movie character would, "*You know, sometimes I wonder about that.*" That sounds like a movie line. But in the book, Ed tells the reader why he goes on these bowhunting trips with Lewis, and it's not to bring home deer meat for his wife to cook up.

He enjoys Lewis' company and even admires him. He informs us, "*He was the only man I knew determined to get something out of life who had both the means and the will to do it.*"

Lewis is quick to expound on his philosophy to the group. He also makes speeches of same to Ed in private. But the speeches to Ed are *much* more intimate. When the group is his audience, Lewis' braggadocio, his survivalist rhetoric, his reckless driving, his daring to provoke the scary backwoods river rats is a performance designed to entertain the group and solidify his position as their masculine leader. Also, having a captive audience for his Nietzsche-inspired monologues entertains an audience of one, himself.

But when the audience is Ed by his lonesome, it may be written by the same speechwriter, but it's delivered intimately *to* and *for* Ed.

A homoerotic courtship plays itself out between Ed and Lewis in the film's first half. Not dissimilar to the courtship dance between Randolph Scott and Richard Boone in Budd Boetticher's *The Tall T.* Lewis doesn't need or want Drew or Bobby's company. He'd much prefer if Ed went on the trip alone. And not for snickering homosexual subtextual obvious reasons. For reasons Lewis not only doesn't understand, but would never occur to him to examine.

It's Ed that Lewis wants to go downriver with. It's Ed that Lewis wants to face the rapids with. The fact that the two men are too shy to share a canoe together during the riding of rough white water is almost adorable. When they do share a canoe, as Ed lounges and Lewis fishes their dinner out of the river violently with his bow and arrow, Lewis performs his macho pose for Ed and Ed alone (it begs the question, who cooked the fish?).

As Lewis prims and poses and opines for Ed's viewing pleasure, he tells him sarcastically, "*You gotta nice wife. You gotta nice kid.*"

Ed, not offended but amused, replies, "*You make that sound kinda shitty, Lewis.*"

To which Lewis (and especially Burt Reynolds) smiles and asks, "*Then why do you go on these trips with me, Ed?*"

Ed drops his smile, and makes an unaggressive stand for himself. "*I like my life, Lewis.*"

On the second day of the trip, it's Ed and Bobby in one canoe and Lewis and Drew in the other. Ed and Bobby get quite a bit ahead of the others (indicating that maybe Bobby isn't as awkward at this river rafting business as we've been led to believe). They pull off to the side of the river to take a break and wait for the other two to catch up. To this point director John Boorman has demonstrated a suspenseful momentum that pulls the audience forward, like the current of the river pulls the men on screen. We feel the pull of the picture. The story and the characters are heading *somewhere* . . . but unless you're hip to the plot . . . you really don't know where. Nor would you be able to guess. Most audiences who saw the movie in 1972 were completely unprepared for the dramatic turn of events;

it's why they were so effective. Most audiences felt there would be a dramatic turn, but that turn would probably be due to the men riding the treacherous rapids down the river. It's clear *something* is going to happen on this trip. But other than the fun and games with the fellas' wolf pack hierarchy, the filmmaker doesn't foreshadow or indicate in the slightest what that *something* is. That *something* is the most profound and disturbing violent sequence in early seventies cinema not directed by Sam Peckinpah. It also became one of the most iconic.

Shortly after Ed and Bobby pull up to the side of the river, they're confronted by two of the backwoods hillbilly mountain folk that live deep within these woods (Bill McKinney and Cowboy Coward). Boorman has the audience's first glimpse of the hillbillies—shot through the leaves on the trees as they descend the hill grade towards the intruders—match Ed and Bobby's perspective of the men. And suddenly—inexplicably—all of us are filled with dread.

The river riders greet the approaching mountain folk with a wave and an awkward *"How goes it?"*

But the two grubby-looking half-wits, one of them cradling a double-barrel shotgun, are immediately hostile.

At first it appears the two city fellas have unknowingly trespassed on some guarded territory, like maybe the location of a moonshine still operated by the mountain folk. Or maybe our protagonists are being mistaken for some sort of representative of authority by the indigenous natives (the Internal Revenue Service, the federal government, county surveyors). But pretty quickly it becomes clear the two hillbillies aren't defensive because these city folk have trespassed on their homeland. Instead these men are more like the other predatory animals that call these backwoods home. And Ed and Bobby are more like a couple of river rats that find themselves suddenly face-to-face with a hungry cottonmouth snake.

Bill McKinney, the more dominant of the two hillbillies, begins immediately manhandling soft Bobby (touching his face, tweaking his nipples). The film begins veering away from standard movie suspense to something we haven't ever felt in *exactly* the same way in a movie before. John Boorman doesn't direct a suspense scene, he stages a *mind fuck*. Because, unlike the manically giggling goofballs that appear in *Death Wish*, the mountain folk that McKinney and Coward portray aren't *movie villains*. They're frighteningly convincing indigenous natives.

Ed and Bobby are forced to move deeper in the woods away from the river—*Get up that hill. Gentlemen, can't we negotiate something? Just negotiate your ass up that hill!*—where Ed is tied to a tree and Bobby is forced to strip naked. Ed is tortured with his own knife, and then McKinney's lead hillbilly fucks the helpless Bobby in the ass.

As the scene plays out before our unbelieving eyes, we seem to be witnessing not just a rape, or a masculine power subjugation—like we might see in a prison movie—but some sort of ancient ritual that might play itself out in a nature documentary.

The way Ned Beatty's soft body is sexualized is genuinely disturbing, but like the extremities of the Romans' beating of Jesus in Mel Gibson's *The Passion of the Christ*, not without its sadomasochistic allure.

It's not "*Oh no, I can't watch this*," it's the opposite, you can't tear your eyes away.

After Bobby's booty is penetrated and hammered from behind, he collapses into the loose dirt and dead leaves, his feminization inside the masculine dynamic now finally complete.

With Bobby busted, broken, and weeping, the mountain folk turn their attention towards Ed, bringing him to his knees as they prepare to make him suck their (likely) dirty dicks.

That's when Ed sees through the trees Lewis and Drew's canoe pull up alongside theirs.

Meaning their victim Voight, McKinney asks Coward what's he want to do with this one?

"*He sure got him a pretty mouth*" is the nitwit's now famous reply.

But as McKinney goes to unbutton the fly of his trousers, bowhunter Lewis lets an arrow fly straight through his chest.

Coward runs away uphill (minus the shotgun), and McKinney—like a game deer slowly performing a kicking dying dance—drops dead.

The rape of Bobby isn't presented like the unfathomable depravity of Andy Robinson's Scorpio in *Dirty Harry*. There's a childishness to McKinney's torment of Beatty. It's why the scene seems so real and doesn't play like a calculated narrative turn. It contains the thoughtless cruelty that only children are capable of. Which is exactly how I reacted to Ned Beatty's torment when I first watched the movie with my mom at the Tarzana Six Movies. The scene scared the shit out of me. Not the *rape* part. Because at that time I didn't know what rape was—even though I had already witnessed a few in movies—even one in *Where's Poppa?* played for laughs. Since I had no idea what sodomy was, I had no idea Bill McKinney was shoving his dick up Ned Beatty's asshole. All *I* knew was Ned Beatty was being bullied and humiliated. And I was right, he was. Pretty early in life that was something any boy who spent some time on a school playground could understand. What really scared me on that first viewing was those two terrifying hillbilly guys themselves. And this happening, isolated in the woods, away from civilization, seemed frighteningly plausible.

The way people were scared to go in the water after *Jaws* was how I felt about the prospect of going camping in the woods after *Deliverance*. Though with Curt out of the picture, and me being looked after by my mom, Jackie, and Lillian, the perils of camping wasn't something I needed to concern myself over. Me perishing like Isadora Duncan was more likely than being taken camping in the woods by my mother.

Dynamic character actor Bill McKinney would essay a plethora of roles all throughout the seventies and eighties, most memorably as a snarling villain (*The Outfit, The Outlaw Josey Wales, Cannonball*). While for two decades he popped up in movies and TV shows constantly, especially after he became part of Clint Eastwood's recurring stock company of players, he never graduated to a villainous character actor that audiences knew by name, the way Neville Brand, Claude Akins, Jack Palance, and William Smith did, but he should have. His performance in *Deliverance* is so authentic most people *still* think he was a real backwoods local (like his sidekick Cowboy Coward and that mongoloid with the banjo) enlisted to appear in the film. But only a *real actor* could control the dynamics of the scene and engage in the performer's dance that he does with his scene partner Ned Beatty. The actor gives his cornholing half-wit a convincing human primitiveness.

John Boorman's movie is about the rape, whether the filmmaker wanted it to be or not. After you've seen it, you can never get over it. Frankly, Bobby seems to get over it quicker than the audience does. But what the story and the theme of Dickey's book is *really* about is what happens *after* the inciting incident of violence.

Boorman's narrative led towards the hillbillies all along like bloodhounds following a scent. But Dickey's narrative propulsion was towards the four angry men's angry debate about what to do next.

The men in *Deliverance* are presented with a social taboo— the rape of a male in their group—that, to one degree or another, will hang over all of them for the rest of their lives. Similar to how Boorman's film presents the same social taboo to the audience, and it hangs over all of our heads for the entirety of the picture (and maybe on the whole car ride home, and when you go to work the next day and tell your coworkers about the wild movie you saw last night).

But the men are presented with an opportunity to bury their

secret, because once the dam is completed the entire area will be flooded under ten miles of water. And as Lewis stresses to the other three, *"Man, that's about as buried as you can get."*

In other words, what happens in the woods, stays in the woods. Then these four men can go back to their ordinary lives, with nobody but themselves the wiser. With the movie provoking the audience with the question, *What would you do?*

Deliverance was Dickey's first novel. He'd only end up writing three. The third one, *To the White Sea*, is practically a one-character book, and the character is basically Lewis if he were an Eskimo. Which means it's Dickey if he were an Eskimo. The first time I was made aware of the book was John Milius telling me how great it was. There was a script in the nineties floating around, written by David Webb Peoples and the Coen brothers, which was terrible. Back then, it was brought up to me once by my agent, and described as a starring vehicle for Brad Pitt. *"Brad Pitt?"* I asked incredulously, *"But the guys a fuckin' Eskimo?"*

Deliverance is a good novel, but strangely incomplete. Most books get reduced when they're adapted into movies. But *Deliverance* benefits from its cinematic transformation. You can imagine Boorman reading the novel and getting excited; *this* adaptation gives him something to do. Boorman makes the story more vivid and compelling. Ed, Lewis, Bobby, and Drew don't pop off the page the way Voight, Beatty, Cox, and especially Reynolds pop off the screen. Neither do the two hillbilly rapists. On the page the hillbillies are stronger than just an idea, they're actual characters, but McKinney and Coward make them flesh. There's an authenticity to their on-screen presence. McKinney, Beatty, and Coward might be acting for the camera, but they're not performing for an audience. We don't *watch* the rape of Bobby, we bear eyewitness.

However, once the debate scene is over, the film peaks. The ambiguity of *exactly* what happened to Ronny Cox's Drew sets the whole third act off on the wrong foot. I'm fully aware it's *supposed* to be ambiguous. But Boorman's staging of that section of the action and his direction of Cox's reaction at first confuses and ultimately irritates. Even *if* Boorman judged it important that the characters be confused over what happened to Drew (I don't think it's necessary), the audience shouldn't be in the dark.

From here on in, the movie, which was as tight as a guitar string, goes slack.

Ed/Voight's rite of masculine passage—climbing the hill, shooting the arrow through Cowboy Coward—is never as exciting or tense as it should be because it's so pro forma its outcome is never in doubt. You worry more for fucking Rambo in *First Blood* then you do Ed climbing that cliff.

And what should be as equally tense as any earlier part of the movie—the survivors facing the authorities downriver and brazing it out—is a damp wick. Because Boorman makes the unfathomably perverse choice of presenting the entire climax—that should be a nail-biter—under-dramatized.

I mean, *what the fuck?*

Is Ed going to climb three-quarters of the way up the cliff, then suddenly fall to his death on the rocks below?

I'm guessing not.

When he comes face-to-face with Cowboy Coward, is the toothless cretin going to blow his face off, then roll credits, close the curtains, bring up the lights?

Doubtful.

But them pulling off their elaborate lie with the suspicious sheriff of the backwoods river community, that could go either way. They all could be as fucked as Bobby.

But Boorman presents it *so* under-dramatized that he could have cut to still pictures as a novelistic narrator filled us in on the eventual outcome. James Dickey himself plays the sheriff, and for the half-assed way Boorman dramatizes the climax he's mildly effective.

But this is the moment when the movie needs another juicy character to come in and bring the story home. With the right actor in the right third act, the sheriff role could have won the game by stealing home from his position on third (think Wilford Brimley in *Absence of Malice*).

But there's an obvious reason why *Deliverance* dribbles to its conclusion. While thematically it's rich, and structurally it's daring to sideline Burt Reynolds' Lewis just before the third act . . . in this movie, cinematically, it's suicidal.

The role that Burt Reynolds had played just prior to Lewis was *Lt. Dan August* on the Quinn Martin cop show of the same name. That role and that show typified his career up to that point. I asked Burt, since he always invested so much personality in his characters, why he had played Dan August so dry?

"Because that's what Quinn Martin wanted," he snapped back. *"Quinn didn't want any horsing around from his series leads. You had to play it just like Efrem Zimbalist fucking Jr."*

Nowadays, since Burt became known as a personality actor, his dry staccato line readings as Dan August prove an entertaining change of pace. It's impressive that, denied his bag of tricks, Burt is still able to deliver. On *Dan August*, his job was to be John Gavin. But Burt didn't want to be John Gavin, and despite an entire machine forcing him in that direction, he successfully resisted. But he wasn't Burt yet either. Only Carson's couch offered him that opportunity. I asked him, if *Dan August* had been renewed for a second season would he still have been able to be in *Deliverance*?

"No way," he said. Adding, *"I woulda been rich but miserable."*

As enjoyable for the audience as show-off Lewis had been in the film's first half, it's Burt Reynolds' officiating over the make-shift court of four that was the finest work the actor had done up to that time.

Watching Reynolds—the sexy stud in the scuba vest—stalking back and forth, making one good point after another as Ronny

Cox's contrarian crumbles under Reynolds' logic and leadership, it's easy to see how every bad Quinn Martin television script he performed in, and every bad movie he was the lead in (*100 Rifles, Sam Whiskey, Skullduggery*), prepared him for the moment when he was able to act in something of quality.

What makes Reynolds so sensational in the "*What do we do with the dead fucking cracker*" sequence is the actor and the character share a duality. Lewis just isn't as compelling in the book as he is in the movie. Boorman's first choice was one of his favorite actors, Lee Marvin. And in the book, yeah, that could be Lee Marvin. But more than likely he would have drunk his way through the role, letting his white hair and white chin stubble give his performance for him. But the book's Lewis needed Reynolds to bring him to vibrant life.

And Reynolds needed Lewis to prove (in the vernacular of his archnemesis Marlon Brando) that he was a contender.

Once Reynolds landed the role, he seized it, the screen, and the audience's attention, and turned the movie into a hit.

Like Burt had waited and prepared his whole life to be at the center of a scene like this, in a "real movie" like this, with actors like these, for a serious filmmaker like Boorman—to finally distinguish himself—is how Lewis had waited and prepared his whole life for a no-turning-back adventure like this . . . where *he* could finally distinguish himself.

Now the survivalist speechifying is no longer *rhetoric*. Now the moral imperative is no longer an intellectual debate. Now the men are no longer laughing off his philosophy as that of a macho blowhard who's in love with the sound of his own voice.

Now he is their leader.

Now they look to him to tell them what to do.

Every buck Lewis ever shot an arrow through, he contemplated *could* he do the same to a man? Now he has. When the occasion presented itself as *do or die*, he rose to the occasion and was not *found wanting*.

He's the greatest John Milius character that John Milius never wrote, and *this* is his *Big Wednesday*.

Despite the seriousness of the situation and the stakes involved, neither Burt *nor* Lewis can keep the smiles off their faces.

The Getaway

(1972)

The imprint of Steve McQueen, and Sam Peckinpah, and the stuntmen, and the location, and the kind of maleness of it all, was so exciting . . . and it's never been duplicated.

—Ali MacGraw on *The Getaway*

The story of both Jim Thompson's novel and Sam Peckinpah's movie is the same. Master bank robber *Doc McCoy*, who's just served four years in prison, is given parole in exchange for orchestrating a robbery for a local bigwig named *Beynon* (played in the movie by Ben Johnson), who sits on the parole board. The deal is brokered by McCoy's robbery accomplice wife, *Carol* (it's inferred in the movie it was her mistake that put Doc behind bars). Once out, Beynon partners him with two unstable accomplices, including a mad dog killing sadist named *Rudy* (played by Al Lettieri). The robbery turns into a bullet festival but the couple get away with the money. When they arrive at Beynon's place to give him his cut, the power broker reveals to Doc that part of the arrangement to get him released was that his wife fuck him. Carol shoots Beynon after his revelation. Now the couple (with the money) make a mad dash across Texas to the Mexican border, with all of the Texas authorities, Beynon's murdering henchmen, and a wounded revenge-minded Rudy all hot on their ass. But the couple have to contend with not only all the enemies after them, but also with each other, because Doc can't forgive Carol for fucking Beynon.

The Getaway was put into production during a serious time of transition in Steve McQueen's life. He and his wife, friend, and confidant Neile McQueen were finalizing their divorce. Steve had moved out of their Malibu home and taken up residence at the Chateau Marmont. During the making of the phenomenally successful *Bullitt*, Peter Yates had gone overschedule by thirty days. Which, before the movie came out and was a smash, prompted Warner Bros.-Seven Arts to end their association with McQueen's production company, Solar Productions. So McQueen and his producing partner Robert Relyea brought the company to Cinema Center Films, a theatrical motion picture arm of the CBS Television network, and a very troubled relationship followed.

After passing at the last minute on *Butch Cassidy and the Sundance Kid*, McQueen embarked on three offbeat projects that all ended in disappointment for the actor.

His family-friendly William Faulkner adaptation with Mark Rydell, *The Reivers*, got good notices, but it was his costar Rupert Crosse who stole the show, the reviews, and received the Oscar nomination (never mind the fact both he and Crosse were way too old for the roles). Also comedy was never the actor's strong suit, and the film required him to mug and overact shamelessly.

Le Mans, the second film on the Cinema Center deal, is today considered one of the key iconic pillars in the actor's filmography and the McQueen mystique. And many (me included) think it's the best racing movie ever made. But at the time it was a terrible disappointment for McQueen. And the town not only considered it a failure, but an ego-driven fiasco, with the financiers, Cinema

Center Films, taking over the production and at one point even shutting it down.

And his last film of the three, Sam Peckinpah's rodeo reverie, *Junior Bonner* (this time made for the ABC Television Network's theatrical picture division, ABC Pictures International), was an outright box office bomb.

So a movie about a husband and wife bank robbing couple on the run was designed by McQueen and Bob Relyea as a way to manufacture a hit.

The project began life when producer David Foster (of the producing team of Truman/Foster) and Mitch Brown optioned Thompson's novel.

McQueen was approached and he said yes.

Then the picture was set up with Robert Evans at Paramount.

The first director on board was Peter Bogdanovich.

He had just done *The Last Picture Show*, which hadn't even been released yet. Nevertheless, in the town he was considered a big-time comer. So big in fact, he was able to line up his next film with Barbra Streisand, and his next film after that with McQueen.

So Bogdanovich hired screenwriter Walter Hill to adapt Thompson's book.

Walter said the director, the producer, and McQueen hadn't any notes, they just wanted a script as soon as possible. Meanwhile Bogdanovich was in San Francisco shooting *What's Up, Doc?*, so *The Getaway* screenwriter was brought out there to work on the script and confer with Peter on set from time to time.

Walter Hill was a fan of Jim Thompson and had read many of his books. Peter wasn't.

When I asked Peter what he thought of Thompson's novel, he described it as "*a good book with a lousy ending.*"

Walter liked Peter, but right off the bat he started having questions about whether or not Peter was the man to direct this material. "*Peter kept saying he wanted to turn it into a Hitchcockian type of adventure. Which, frankly, I never understood. To me it was obviously a movie that should be done more in the style of Raoul Walsh. High Sierra being a perfect example."*

But there was no denying Bogdanovich's ability at handling a big production. Hill would be on the set of *What's Up, Doc?*—usually in the morning—when he and Peter could confer about the script the easiest. And firsthand he watched Peter handle—at the absolute zenith of her superstardom—Barbra Streisand.

"Watching Peter's handling of Streisand," Walter told me, *"was masterful. There really is no other word for it.*

"She'd come on the set buzzing like a hornet about something or other. Then Peter would console her.

"Tell her how beautiful she was.

"'Don't worry, Barbra, you're America's sweetheart, none of this is important.

"'You're amazing in the picture.

"'The critics are going to love you. The fans are going to love you.

"'I watched the rushes last night and practically fell out of my chair laughing.'

"And pretty soon Barbra was purring like a kitten. Now it sounds like I'm just saying he was kissing her ass. Or he was insincere. But that's not it. She was good in the picture. And she was funny in the picture. Quentin, you know as a director, there is a certain amount of that type of handling required. Especially with huge stars of a temperamental nature. And I'd just never seen anybody handle it with the absolute skill Bogdanovich employed."*

However, by this time, McQueen was getting seriously irritated that he had to wait for the ending of *What's Up, Doc?* before he could make *The Getaway.* Of course he was aware that Peter was

---

* Solving the problems, both large and small, of your actors—lead actors especially— *is* the job of a film director.

supposed to do the Streisand picture first, but as time went on, Hill said, "*It made him feel like he was in second position to Streisand.*"

So to make everybody feel like *The Getaway* wasn't stagnating, a meeting between the producers, McQueen, Bogdanovich, and Hill—who was still writing the screenplay—was set up in San Francisco on Peter's day off.

"*By this time,*" Hill said, "*maybe Peter had read twenty or so pages of the script so far. Also, to be fair, Peter was tired from shooting and was probably just happy to have a day off. So it's possible he wasn't taking into account how important this meeting was to McQueen and the producers.*"

So first question to Peter by the producers was, "*How's the script coming?*"

Peter then turned to Walter and said, "*So, Walter, how's the script coming?*"

And Walter said, "*It's coming along.*"

Then McQueen asked Peter a direct question. "*What kind of guns would I use in this?*"

Peter laughed and said, "*Oh, don't worry about that now, Steve. We've got plenty of time to figure that out,*" basically shining on McQueen the way he had gotten used to doing with Streisand.

But McQueen wasn't Streisand.

And to Steve, who knew a lot about firearms and was expert at handling them, armaments were an important thing.

Especially on a movie like this and with a character like Doc.

Hill remembered, "*You could just see from the reaction on Steve's face to Peter's answer that the actor was asking himself 'was this the guy who should be making a tough guy movie?'*

"*And a few days later, Steve decided to cut the cord on Bogdanovich.*"

Hill said he hasn't had any problem with Peter over the years, but at the time there was a feeling on Peter's part that since he'd been fired Walter should have quit.

Walter understood that moral sentiment.

But he didn't necessarily think it applied in *this* situation.

Not only that, he received a memo from Peter Bart at Paramount that told him he should *absolutely* keep writing or he'd be sued. So now there was a big decision, who was going to direct the picture? After the experience with Bogdanovich it was decided that only a filmmaker adept at making tough guy movies would be applicable.

And in that regard there were only two choices, Sam Peckinpah or Don Siegel (either of which would have "*thrilled*" Walter Hill).

After *Dirty Harry* Siegel couldn't have been hotter. But McQueen worked with Siegel in the sixties on *Hell Is for Heroes* and, as mentioned, at different points the two men almost came to blows.

Yet, McQueen had just finished working for Peckinpah on *Junior Bonner* and had a good experience and was very happy with his performance. But that film also ended up being not just unsuccessful, but a *notorious* bomb. The type a popular movie star like McQueen was unaccustomed to. Despite that, it was decided to send Hill's finished script to Sam Peckinpah, with an offer to direct McQueen in the lead.

Sam read it on a flight and according to Walter said, "*Absolutely. It's perfect material for him. And Steve would be sensational in it.*"

The first draft of Hill's script was quite different from the movie that Sam eventually made. Following the book, the first draft was set in 1949. Hill mentioned, "*It read very well, and everybody was pleased with it. But when the Paramount budget people did the numbers, the costs grew to an astronomical amount. So in an effort to bring down the budget, Sam suggested making it a contemporary film.*

"*But even by removing the period element, Paramount still considered the budget too high. Sam pushed back on the figures they were claiming. But both Steve and Sam had reputations for films that went over budget.*"

Leading studio head Robert Evans to say, "*Look, I pay my bud-*

get people to tell me what things are going to cost. If they say it's going to cost too much I oughta listen to them."

So Evans put the film into turnaround.

Evans was sure the other studios would run the numbers and come to the same conclusion, that the whole damn thing was just too expensive, then McQueen and company would be forced back to Paramount, and the studio could dictate better terms at a more reasonable price. But much to Evans' chagrin, the minute it came on the market National General Pictures snapped it up as is.* So now armed with an exciting McQueen action vehicle, a critically acclaimed action director, a script everybody was thrilled about, a budget they could all agree upon, and a home at an enthusiastic studio, there only remained one giant unknown . . .

Who would play the female colead, *Carol McCoy*?

Well, from the moment Robert Evans became involved, he had been aggressively pushing the idea of a teaming between his wife, superstar actress Ali MacGraw, and Steve McQueen.

In retrospect, this is ironic, because it would be while she was making *The Getaway* she would leave the mogul and marry her co-star Steve McQueen. Naturally the producers were excited by the commercial prospects of a McQueen/MacGraw team up, and for good reasons. Ali MacGraw was one of the biggest female movie stars in the world, and *Love Story* was the single biggest hit of 1970. But the actress had yet to do another picture. So *The Getaway* would be MacGraw's follow up to *Love Story*.

---

*NGP was the primary investor in First Artists, the company that was founded in 1970 by Sidney Poitier, Paul Newman, and Barbra Streisand, and in 1971, McQueen joined the team. This arrangement was attractive to McQueen because on all the films he made for First Artists, he would receive meaningful points. Another reason that commercial considerations were at the forefront of everybody's mind.

During the time he was involved, Bogdanovich told me how aggressive Evans was in pushing him to cast MacGraw.

Naturally, Peter wanted to cast his own girlfriend Cybill Shepherd.

"I didn't insist on it. It wasn't like it's Cybill or it's nobody. But I thought Cybill was good casting and MacGraw was bad casting. And I told Evans that. I told him the movie will hurt Ali in the long run. Because since she's miscast, the critics will kill her. Which is exactly what ended up happening. But the character is a barefoot, broad-shouldered Texas girl. That's Cybill!"

He's not entirely wrong. The character in both Thompson's book and Hill's script (which aren't exactly the same) *is* a little closer to Shepherd than it is to MacGraw. But back then the number one person against the MacGraw idea (again, ironically) was Steve McQueen.

His attitude was, *No fucking studio head's going to tell me who's going to be in my movie!*

But even after the movie had switched hands to Warner Bros., Evans was still in there pitching for MacGraw, *"I know it's not a Paramount picture anymore. But don't hold that against Ali. That's not her fault. Her and McQueen would be dynamite together!"*

Sam's choice for Carol was his leading lady from *The Ballad of Cable Hogue*, Stella Stevens. For the character that existed on the page, Stevens was *perfect*. For somebody who could go head-to-head with McQueen, Stevens was *perfect*. But Steve McQueen didn't want somebody who was *perfect*.

McQueen didn't want Carol going head-to-head with him.

Stevens said she had a drink with McQueen when Sam suggested her, and Steve told her, *"I consider you competition."*

And on a McQueen picture, Steve didn't want competition.

That's what had happened with Rupert Crosse on *The Reivers*.

He'll be damned if he does *The Getaway* and watches Stella Stevens get nominated for an Oscar. So Stella Stevens didn't work opposite McQueen in *The Getaway*. But in that same year she did star opposite another *king of cool* movie star—in a big iconic action film hit—when she costarred with Jim Brown in *Slaughter*. And in *Slaughter*, Jim Brown had a chemistry with Stevens that he never had or would ever have again with any of his other leading ladies.

Like McQueen and MacGraw, you can believe Brown and Stevens fell in love on the picture.

I asked Walter Hill who he thought would make a good *Carol*.

He said he liked the Stella Stevens idea, but he thought the obvious choice was Angie Dickinson. "*I don't mean this in a bad way, but I always thought Angie had a trashy quality to her. You could buy her as one half of a bank robbery team.*"

Walter said the actress that got the most consideration was Lauren Hutton. And Neile McQueen told me at one time Geneviève Bujold was in the mix. But that idea ended up blowing up when Steve waited in a bar to meet Bujold to discuss the film, and she came walking in with Maximilian Schell.

You see, after being cheated on time and time again by Steve during their marriage, Neile had decided to retaliate by having an affair with Max Schell. So when Geneviève Bujold walked through the barroom doorway with the man who fucked his wife, Steve got distracted from the purpose of the casting meeting. Instead, after excusing himself from the French-Canadian actress, he asked the German thespian if he could speak with him outside. At which point, according to Neile, Steve proceeded to *beat the living shit outta Maximilian Schell.*

I related that story to Walter Hill, who told me, if that happened, he was pretty sure it would indeed have been a one-sided fight. So after that violent episode, that was it for Geneviève Bujold as Carol.

Hill told me there was a concentrated effort from everybody involved to make *The Getaway* a commercial hit.

After Steve's last three movies, he *needed* a hit.

Sam had never *had* a hit, and he knew this was going to be his best shot at finding out what having a successful picture felt like.

It was the main reason so many of the darker aspects of the novel, including its surreal ending, were jettisoned in the adaptation.

But to the end of being commercial, an obvious choice for the part of Carol would have been Faye Dunaway. Of all the genuine female movie stars of the time, it's Dunaway who's the most like Carol McCoy. And since commercial considerations were at the forefront of everybody's mind, the stars of *The Thomas Crown Affair* reuniting would seem a logical choice.

Walter Hill told me, "*Well, yes, now that seems logical. But at the time, they felt they had to contend with the specter of Bonnie and Clyde, which they were afraid hung over the whole picture. It's why, frustratingly for all, they were never able to even consider Faye Dunaway.*"★

Not only that, Hill told me once Sam came aboard he had a completely different idea for the ending that he really wanted to do. He wanted to end the film in a Sam Peckinpah bloodbath.

He wanted Doc and Carol to cross the border into Mexico with the law waiting for them "*and then shoot 'em dead!*"

Walter said he told Sam, "*That's fine with me, because I know how you're going to shoot it. You see, Sam really didn't like Arthur Penn. And Sam's critics implied Sam borrowed his whole slow motion violence technique from Arthur Penn's ending to Bonnie and Clyde.*" And nothing bugged the hard-drinking director more than being accused of swiping his signature style from, of all people, Arthur Penn.

★And Ronald L. Bowers in the February 1977 edition of *Films in Review* wrote, "*This flashily photographed cops-and-robbers yarn is a second-rate Bonnie and Clyde with only a few good moments of excitement revolving around bank-robber Steve McQueen.*"

Hill told me, "*If you shoot 'em down, I know how you're going to do it. You're going to do it in slow motion.*"

It would have been Peckinpah's chance to outdo Penn with his own ending. But everybody else wanted to stay as far away from *Bonnie and Clyde* as they could. So the Slim Pickens "*happy ending*" was decided as the way to go.

But despite Steve not being into it, the idea of Ali MacGraw never went away. So Sam met with the actress and liked her. "*Then suddenly,*" remembered Hill, "*Sam was pushing for MacGraw. And that really threw Steve for a loop. Personally, I think Sam did like her. Not so much for the part, but he liked her. And you must remember, Sam had never had a hit. And he wanted one. And since everybody thought Ali's involvement would make The Getaway a great hit, he was prepared to go along with it. So once Sam said he liked the idea of MacGraw, that's when Steve gave in.*"

Walter theorized, "*He [Steve] probably figured there were other people who could play this part better, but if everybody else is so hot on her, and it's going to make it that much more of a hit, why not?*"

And let the record state, "*everybody*" was right. *The Getaway* was a massive hit and MacGraw's participation was a major factor to its success.

I first saw *The Getaway* in 1972 when it came out at the *Paradise Theatre* in Westchester, a Los Angeles town by LAX (the Paradise and the Loyola were the two theatres near where we lived in El Segundo that I saw a lot of movies at from 1971 to 1974). My mom would drive me to the cinema on a Saturday or Sunday afternoon, then drop me off and come back and pick me up four or five hours later. And that's how I first saw the PG-rated *The Getaway* when it opened opposite *The Life and Times of Judge Roy Bean*. I liked both films enough to see them again the next weekend. Then the next year, when I was living in Tennessee with my grandmother, I saw *The Getaway* a third time on the lower bill of a drive-in double feature with *Walking Tall*. Then back in Los Angeles one year after that, at a United Artists theatre in Marina del Rey on the lower half of a double bill with *The Outfit*. And all that was before I was fifteen. I later watched *The Getaway* at revival house screenings, not to mention on home video, and countless times since (I have my own IB Technicolor 35mm print).

But while I've always loved it, and I do love it more than some of the other more exalted Sam Peckinpah films (*Ride the High Country*, *The Ballad of Cable Hogue*, *Cross of Iron*), I've always harbored misgivings too.

My main misgiving was that it wasn't the book. It didn't matter that I liked what Sam and Walter did, I held it in contempt for what it wasn't. The changes from page to screen don't affect the story, which stays basically the same. But the biggest difference between the story Thompson told and the story Peckinpah tells is the tone. The Peckinpah movie is tough. But the Thompson novel is far far far more vicious. The characters, the events it describes, and their eventual outcome. And on top of that viciousness (which is what most of us like about Thompson) is a thick layer of pessimism and cynicism, and on top of that is a light coating of surrealism.

The Doc McCoy of the novel is a stone-cold killer.

As Walter Hill said when I brought up the change in Doc from page to screen, "*Compared to the Doc in the book, [Richard Stark's] Parker is a moral paragon.*"

The movie, on the other hand, even more than Hill's script, seems to bend over backwards to portray McQueen's Doc as *not* a killer. This change still bugs the shit out of me.

But the book Doc is different in other ways.

McQueen doesn't say much as Doc.

It's a very internal performance.

And I think it's very real and very deeply felt.

But one of the most defining traits of the Doc in the book is his ability to disarm people with his folksy-sounding charm.

In the book, Doc could talk the birds out of the trees, then break their wings, and stomp on them with his boot.

The most puzzling omission from the book is the sequence when his treacherous accomplice Rudy gets the drop on Doc after the robbery. Rudy's going to plug him, but Doc convinces the killer to take him to Carol because she's got the money. Now convincing Rudy isn't easy, because he doesn't trust anybody, he's a mad dog and he's scared of Doc's reputation. But Doc's folksy-sounding bullshit is so convincing, so sincere, and makes such common sense Rudy, though never taking his gun off Doc, drives to where Carol is.

What's really great about the scene is the drive to Carol's.

What convinces both Rudy and the reader that Doc is on the up and up is during the whole drive Doc never stops talking. Doc just keeps shooting the shit with Rudy about anything and everything. He just keeps pouring on the jokes, the folksy stories, witty observations, and laughs, till the grumpy-jumpy Rudy is forced to (somewhat) join in. The car ride to Carol lasts about an hour. When they get there Doc gets out of the car, casually takes his hat off his head, removes a gun sitting inside of it, and plugs Rudy with it.

As anybody familiar with my work can guess, this is my favorite scene in the book and my favorite scene in any Thompson novel. And it's made to order for a movie.

And yet *two* movies have been made from the book and neither one saw fit to use this scene. When I brought that scene up to Hill to find out why he didn't include it, he had a good answer.

The screenwriter said, "*I liked that scene too. But I was writing a movie for Steve McQueen. That scene is very good in the book, but it's not McQueen. When you're writing for an actor like Steve—or, for that matter, any actor—you gain a lot by being able to fashion the material to their strengths. But you lose some when it comes to characterization, because you're going to avoid things that don't show off that actor in the best light.*"

Another difference is in the presentation of Doc's double crossing nemesis Rudy. On both the page and screen Rudy is presented as a grotesque sadistic brute. But Thompson makes the character physically grotesque. In the book he's known as *Rudy the Pie Head* because when he was born, his head was so large it got stuck in his mother's birth canal. So he had to be yanked out with metal forceps. And those forceps smooshed the two sides of his head together, till the top of his head came to what looked like a point.

Like a piece of pie. Hence, *Rudy the Pie Head.*

Now I can see producers, studios, and movie stars rejecting this aspect of the story as ridiculous. But you would think the man that went rooting around like a truffle pig in the garbage dump that was *Bring Me the Head of Alfredo Garcia* might be inspired by Thompson's Dali-like paint stroke.*

Again, I asked Walter why he didn't include it.

He said he felt that weird "*Rudy the Pie Head*" thing was of a piece with the novel's infamous *El Rey* epilogue. You either go the weird route with it all the way, or you don't.

"*We didn't.*"

Speaking of the Rudy storyline—I'm not a fan. I really don't like Lettieri in the role. It's not that he's a bad actor or gives a bad performance. It's more I find his performance physically repellent.

Now for a character like Rudy, that should be a good thing, no?

No. It's still a movie. I still should *want* to watch the movie and enjoy it. Certain actors can play grotesque bad guys, yet they still have a connection to the audience. We still enjoy them as perform

---

*You can imagine if Sam Fuller did the Thompson novel that aspect alone could have convinced him to come aboard. It's practically a Fulleresque touch.

ers. They do cruel deeds, they're monsters, but we enjoy their monsters because when they're on screen we know something exciting will happen.

For instance, the year after *The Getaway* came out, Neville Brand played a degenerate, murdering serial rapist in the film *The Mad Bomber*. His character is one sick son of a bitch. But he also gives the most enjoyable performance in the film. Every time the film cuts to Brand—as opposed to either Vince Edwards' one-note *Dirty Harry* clone, or Chuck Connors' rock-terrible performance of the title character—you're not only relieved, you're thrilled.

Al Lettieri didn't have that relationship or connection with the audience. I've watched *The Getaway* many times with theatre audiences, and whenever the film cuts to the Rudy/Fran section—you can feel the audience lean back in their seats.

The whole section is ugly, and both Lettieri and Sally Struthers as his hostage turned *sub* Fran, make you physically repel from the screen.

Again, wasn't that the idea?

I doubt it.

There's a sense of sadistic black comedy at play in the Rudy and Fran *dom/sub* theme in Thompson's novel that's absent in Peckinpah's film. If William Smith, or Robert Blake, or Jack Palance had played Rudy, the subplot could have been just as cruel, but it probably would've come off as the sick joke Thompson intended.

Lettieri seems to be trying to give the type of performance that Richard Boone specialized in during the latter part of his career.

But Boone was a gregarious, ferocious bear with tremendous audience empathy. They once asked Elmore Leonard did any actor ever say his great dialogue the way it was in his head. And he said, "*Yes. Richard Boone. And he did it twice.*" (In *The Tall T* and *Hombre*.)

Plus Boone had that great powerful folksy voice (it's a slightly younger Boone who could have pulled off the Doc of Thompson's novel). Al Lettieri's Rudy is intimidating, he's a force, but he's also a bummer.

Every time Sam cuts back to Rudy, you're like, "*Oh, this fuckin' guy!*"

I revealed my misgivings about Lettieri to Walter Hill, curious what his response would be. And was a little surprised he agreed with me.

"*I will address Lettieri's performance. I never really cared for it either. But you see originally it was going to be Jack Palance. Whenever we talked about it, it was always the Jack Palance role. Then they offered it to Palance and he said yes. But then they got into a big fight about price. And once that happened, they just didn't want to refuse Palance—they wanted to punish him. So they pulled the offer. They got into a big fight about it. And Palance sued them and collected!*

"*So they ended up paying him anyway, but they didn't get his Rudy.*

"*And I think the problem was, we thought about it as the Jack Palance role for so long, nobody could ever move off of that idea. At least I couldn't. At one point Jack Nicholson was brought up. And at that time we could have still probably got 'em—you hafta remember he wasn't quite Jack yet. But Sam didn't like 'em. I think he watched Five Easy Pieces and he said—I'll never forget it—'He's a poor man's Henry Fonda.' Yeah, Lettieri was—I hate to say it, but he was kind of repulsive. I mean guys like Lee Marvin and Neville Brand, who I love, played characters like Rudy, and they were always fun to watch.*

"*But having said all that, I feel I must point out, Sam loved him in the role.*"

The other thing that the movie famously loses is the surrealistic postscript chapter in *El Rey*. In the book, El Rey is a getaway no-man's-land that crooks hightail it to on the other side of the Mexican border. El Rey is a pretty unique creation on Thompson's part. A Latin American no-man's-land, where crooks or men on the run end up in, is a staple of both pulp and art. It describes the hellhole that both Yves Montand and Roy Scheider end up in, in *The Wages of Fear* and its vastly superior remake, *Sorcerer.* As well as Tennessee Williams' mythical last stop *Camino Real,* where his ex-boxer hero Kilroy cools his heels with Camille, Casanova, and Lord Byron.

But Thompson's El Rey has different art direction, if not a different outcome. Thompson's El Rey is closer to a luxury resort than the mosquito-infested, mud-and-urine shantytown of *Sorcerer.* But the place really is a Catholic purgatory on earth. It's a destination out of Luis Buñuel or Ken Russell that tips the hard edge crime novel into the territory of science fiction.

Those on the run are offered in El Rey safety and sanctuary.

But at a high price.

Every room, every meal, every drink costs and costs a lot (it sounds like the Cannes Film Festival). And since the people who choose to go to El Rey can never leave . . . eventually . . . the money runs out.

And those people are reduced to beggars and eventually even cannibals. The fate—eventually—of all who enter El Rey.

Including Doc and Carol, who when we take leave of them not only hate each other, but are plotting each other's death in order for their loot to last longer and hold off the inevitability of their hopeless destiny. It seems Thompson, after so much pitilessly presented violence, does have a moral center after all. While we may be bummed out this is how Doc and Carol end up, it's clear the author thinks they and others of their ilk are just getting what they deserve. The cannibal twist demonstrating Thompson's true feelings about the couple.

Now for most readers the last chapter has proven to be the moment of truth. Some people hate it, think it ruins the book.

Some people don't hate it, but they think it spoils the story.

While others love the book, particularly *because* of the ending.

And still others think it's because of the ending that the book reaches masterpiece status.

I used to like the ending more than I do now. Just the whole perverseness of it appealed to me. But now I feel if Thompson was going to pull such a presto chango he needed to write it better.

Frankly, as the book goes on how grim it gets becomes a drag. You may have to force yourself to keep reading. And that's coming from me—someone who equates transgression with art.

Now *maybe* the book's *Doc* and *Carol* deserve this fate, but under no circumstances do you want the movie's couple, McQueen and MacGraw, plotting each other's murder, only for them to eventually end up cannibal beggars. I asked Walter if the El Rey ending was ever considered.

He said, "*Well, I was never told not to include it by the producers. But I was also aware what they were looking for. And that ending wasn't it. Had I included the ending in the book the movie would never get made. And even if Paramount did make the movie, which is extremely doubtful, it would have been a very strange movie. And nobody wanted to make a strange movie. They wanted a good tough guy crime picture starring Steve McQueen, that would do well commercially. But I like Jim Thompson's novel very much. Somebody should do a dark version of The Getaway.*"★

While I love Peckinpah's *The Getaway* there are irritating flaws that are the filmmaker's fault. Dramatic turns of events that clue the authorities on to which direction the fugitive couple are heading are based on plot contrivances (Richard Bright's cowboy con man/locker thief). It seems like through the whole movie the couple can't pass a single Texas extra without them holding a newspaper with their picture in it and that extra doing a double take. Also everybody in the state seems to know not just what Doc looks like, but the make and model of the car he drives. It practically becomes

---

★That somebody should have been Ken Russell. Every fucked up element and grotesque surrealistic touch would have not just been emphasized, but expanded upon.

an unintentional running joke (the TV appearance in the repair shop is convenient, but that one Peckinpah pulls off). Also there really wouldn't have to be a *getaway* at all, if Beynon didn't force Doc to use two unstable half-wits like Rudy and Jackson (Bo Hopkins).

Doc says, "*I pick my own men.*"

But Beynon makes him use those guys.

Why?

We know the minute we see them in that stupid paddle boat they're unreliable.

If Doc is such a "*smart operator*" and a big time pro and Beynon wants to keep his hands clean, why not let Doc pick the men?

As Robert Prosky says in *Thief*, "*If they beef on you, that's your problem. If they beef on us, that's your problem.*"

Because it's a movie, stupid. Or is it because it's a stupid movie?

But, for me, the single biggest problem with the film is the casting of Ben Johnson as Beynon. I don't like Al Lettieri as Rudy, but he still works in the role.

For Sam Peckinpah, Carol fucking Beynon was more important than anything else in the picture. For first time viewers it's easy to assume, to get her man out of Huntsville, she was forced against her will into the sexual bargain. She did what she had to do.

But Peckinpah decidedly does not dramatize it that way.

The film insinuates she was not just willing to do it *for* Doc; she was willing to do it *to* Beynon. It even tries (very unsuccessfully) to insinuate that Carol has to debate her choice of which man to stay with. And in the confrontation scene where Carol shoots Beynon, the movie ridiculously tries to convince us that *maybe* Carol is in league with the Texas power broker *against* her husband.

Later Doc accuses her, "*I think you liked it. I think he got to you.*"

Carol answers Doc back, "*Maybe I got to him.*"

If Beynon wasn't played by Ben Johnson, this whole three-way sexual dynamic *could* have worked. Not putting down Big Ben or doubting his significant masculine charisma. It's not *just* you can't imagine Ben Johnson having sex with Ali MacGraw, you can't imagine Ben Johnson having *sex*. No less Ali MacGraw's Carol *seriously* considering leaving Steve McQueen's Doc (*who she loves*) for Ben Johnson's Beynon.

"*I think you liked it!*"

Yeah, right, Ali MacGraw *liked* fucking Ben Johnson.

"*I think he got to you!*"

I didn't buy Richard Benjamin *getting* to Ali MacGraw in *Goodbye, Columbus*, let alone Ben Johnson.

This whole subplot could have been far more effective if Beynon had been played by somebody a little closer to McQueen in age and dynamic. Joe Don Baker would have been the fantastic natural choice. But I can also see Robert Culp or Stuart Whitman delivering what was required to make the triangle dynamic work.*

Now obviously, more was at stake than just sex appeal.

Beynon represented money, security, stability, and comfort. With Beynon, Carol could have a child and the means to raise it properly. Is she going to have a child with Doc? Probably not. Would Doc be a good father? Probably not. With Doc she'll always be looking over her shoulder for the heat just around the corner.

With Doc, him doing another jail stretch is a possibility, if not a probability.

She waited four years the last time.

Could she wait eight, ten?

Working as his accomplice, she'd probably be sent up the river

---

*Richard Compton directed a fun thriller with Oliver Reed, Jim Mitchum, and Paul Koslo titled in some territories as *Maniac* and others as *Ransom*, and in that film Stuart Whitman as a mean macho Arizona tycoon, dressed in Brian De Palma–like safari suits, gives you a glimpse of how good his Beynon could have been.

too. Beynon's probably not going to jail. And even if he did, she'd have the money and property to handle that.

Still . . . I'd swallow the whole thing a helluva lot easier if it wasn't Ben Johnson.

Walter Hill informed me it was supposed to be William Holden as Beynon. Which would have gone a little way to dealing with my concerns, though I still like my Joe Don, Culp, and Whitman idea much better.

I told Hill my problems with this storyline, and he laughed.

"Boy, Quentin, you're really moving the boulder away from the mouth of the cave to see where all the bodies are buried."

He went on to explain, *"I liked Sam and I enjoyed working with him. And I really appreciated the opportunity to work with him. And it was the success generated from his film that allowed me to be a director. But the whole situation with Carol and Beynon was our only real bone of contention. You see, that was how it was in Thompson's book.*

"She had sex with Beynon, she did it to get Doc out, but maybe her loyalties, for a moment, were divided.

"I didn't think that's the way it should be. I thought it should be clear, it was a condition to the deal of getting Doc out of jail. And that's why she did it, no other reason. I thought it made her side of the argument stronger.

"Carol could have told him, 'Look, that was the deal. So to get you out of Huntsville, I did what I had to do. I did it for you. So grow up and get over it.'

"But Sam said, 'No, it's got to be like it was in the book.' I didn't agree, but it was his movie so I did it the way he wanted it."

The *old-school* genre movie directors dealt within a movie industry I can read about in books, but I really can't imagine. They'd get assigned a producer from the studio that they couldn't stand. They'd get assigned actors they didn't think were right for the part. They'd work with 1st AD's, costume people, directors of photography, production designers who weren't working for them. They were working for the studio.

And it worked the other way around too. Producers and actors would get stuck with hack directors with no feel for the material they were directing, that were just shooting a schedule. Charles Bronson once claimed that was three out of five directors he worked with. Back in those days people would work together and they'd finish their projects despising each other.

Especially Sam Peckinpah.

Peckinpah once said, "*A director has to deal with a whole world absolutely teeming with mediocrities, jackals, hangers-on, and just plain killers.*"

That's not been my experience in the industry.

Directors like Sam Peckinpah and Don Siegel were genre film masters.

But they didn't make genre films the way Jean-Pierre Melville *did*. The way I *do*. The way Walter Hill *does*, the way John Woo *does*, the way Eli Roth *does*. As students of genre cinema, *we* make genre films because we *love* genre films. They made genre films because they were good at it and that's what the studios would hire them to do.

Sam Peckinpah made *The Wild Bunch*, but he would have rather made *Rashomon*. Sam was happy to adapt Jim Thompson's novel. He knew it would make a good picture. It would be terrific for McQueen. And it would possibly deliver him his first hit. But he would have rather adapted Joan Didion's *Play It as It Lays*.

So since this generation of genre directors were forced to make what at the end of the day they considered silly stories about cowboys and cops and robbers, in order to make those silly stories mean something to them, they based them in metaphors that pertained to their own lives.

Sam also came of age in an industry when men cheated on their wives and wives cheated on their husbands and there were violent repercussions, but the show kept going on. A world where producer Walter Wanger would shoot agent Jennings Lang in the balls for sleeping with his wife Joan Bennett. Wanger would go to prison for a few years. Later Jennings Lang would become the head of Universal Studios and Walter Wanger would produce *Riot in Cell Block 11* and *Invasion of the Body Snatchers*, both movies Peckinpah would work on as a young man.

Look at *The Getaway* as a story about Sam Peckinpah from a paranoid Peckinpah's perceived perspective of persecution.

Sam Peckinpah *is* Doc McCoy. A writer-director sitting in movie jail, unable to get work. Beynon, a studio executive he despises, wants Sam to make a movie for him. The executive stands for everything the director has contempt for . . . yet . . . he's the only one who will hire him. The only one to unlock the cell door to movie jail. Doc's wife brokers the deal for the movie. Doc writes the movie. Beynon forces him to work with people the director doesn't want to work with (Rudy and Jackson), but the boss man makes it clear the hired hand has no choice. Due to these incompetent inferiors, the movie ends up being a disaster, and the director is blamed by the executive who placed him in the position to fail from the very beginning.

Then, after the movie is over, the director discovers that his wife, who brokered the deal, as part of the deal, was sleeping with his enemy.

How would Sam Peckinpah react to that situation?

Similar to Doc McCoy in the movie?

Probably.

I think Sam Peckinpah only cared about one thing, his truest expression of artistic self. As Walter Hill told me, *"Sam was a serious guy and he was in it for serious ambitions."*

In Neile McQueen's autobiography, she wrote McQueen was reluctant to do the movie because *"the main thrust of the story dealt with his wife's unfaithfulness.*" She told Steve, "*Look at it this way, honey. You've been through it, you know how it feels.*" Then she laughed as she told me, "*I think he knocked me on my ass after I said that line.*"

"*The Getaway was the last time Steve was in a movie as 'the Steve McQueen' we liked to see,*" Walter Hill stated. "*He did a few other movies and he did good performances, but that special quality that made Steve—'Steve'—was really never on display again.*"

And I agree.

Now a lot of things in the Jim Thompson book I *still* like and some I prefer, especially Doc's cold-blooded propensity, the sequence where he talks Rudy into driving him to Carol then shoots him through his hat, and even Rudy's head shaped like a piece of pie.

But now, while I feel they're good, except for Doc being a cold-blooded killer, they're not necessarily better than the movie that was made. Because watching the movie now, I don't see it as a bank robbery story anymore. I don't even see it as a crime thriller about a pair of on-the-lam robbers, trying to make good their escape, with a massive manhunt coming from both sides hot on their trail.

I now realize what Sam made and what McQueen and McGraw performed was a love story.

The crime story is literal.

The love story is metaphorical.

But it's on the metaphorical level where the filmmakers (and I include the actors in that title) operated most successfully.

Thompson wrote not only a getaway story, he spends the entire book, chapter by chapter, page by page, putting the couple through hell and tearing them apart.

Sam does the complete opposite.

He spends the entire film, reel by reel, scene by scene, putting the couple through hell, then bringing them together.

Nevertheless, when it comes to Peckinpah fans, Jim Thompson fans, Steve McQueen fans, or just fans of seventies crime movies in general, the one thing everybody seems to agree on is that in the role of Carol McCoy . . . Ali MacGraw was *lousy*.

And for the last forty years, I too was one of those Ali Mac-Graw bashers.

That is until recently.

It took me over forty years, but now I see Ali MacGraw's performance differently.

First off, let me start by saying, she's not the Carol McCoy of the book or Walter Hill's screenplay.

If you want *that* Carol, if you *need* that Carol, then nothing is going to replace Sam's first choice of Stella Stevens (except, possibly, star of *Rolling Thunder* Linda Haynes).

No, MacGraw's Carol might not be one-half of the greatest bank robbing couple in crime film literature.

But instead of concentrating on what she's *not* . . .

Let's examine what she *is*.

She *is* one-half of one of the greatest love stories in crime film cinema.

While she doesn't offer the characterization of a professional armed robber, she does offer up the minute by minute, scene by scene, emotional reality of a woman trying to keep a relationship from crumbling into pieces. The couple pass through a physical and emotional gauntlet, and lurch from one catastrophe to another.

While McQueen alternates between keeping his *cool* and losing his *cool*, Carol *feels*, Carol *bleeds*, Carol *hurts*, Carol is *afraid*.

She's heartbreaking and heartbroken when she loses the suitcase full of loot to Richard Bright's cowboy con man thief. She waits there in the train station for Doc, not knowing for sure if he's going to return, in utter despair. *Did I blow it? Did I just ruin everything? How could I be so stupid?*

It's my feeling that Ali MacGraw's moment to moment work in this film is sensational.

In real life she was living through everything that she was hired to portray as Carol.

She's a young woman in over her head—so was MacGraw.

Carol with Doc and this robbery—MacGraw with McQueen at the height of his iconic prowess in a genre film like this.

She's a woman living through a painful betrayal.

Carol with Beynon—MacGraw with her husband Robert Evans.

She's a woman having to deal with a very difficult, mercurial, masculine man amidst a grueling endeavor.

Carol on the lam with Doc—MacGraw making this incredibly difficult movie with McQueen and Peckinpah.

She's a woman in love—so was MacGraw.

When the film came out in the States and England, MacGraw was roasted by the critics.

Torn apart and ridiculed, everywhere.

Everywhere . . . *except* France.

From the very beginning, the French always saw the film as a love story. And in France the critics praised the emotional content of her performance.

The best piece of adaptation that Hill does with Thompson's manuscript is the garbage dump scene. In the book Carol and Doc hide away in one miserable, degrading hovel and hole and cave after another. Hill reduces it down to one moment: while eluding the cops they hide in a garbage dumpster. Then the dumpster gets picked up by a garbage truck, and they're dumped in the back. They spend all night in there and in the morning are dumped out with all the other Texas garbage at the landfill. While they rest in that torn apart Volkswagen bug at the garbage dump, Carol threatens to "*split*."

If Carol loses faith, all is lost.

It's Doc's savvy and survival prowess that keeps them from getting caught. Keeps them getting a little further down the road.

But it's Carol that keeps them together.

It's Carol that saves Doc from his self-destructive impulses.

It's Carol that knows if they don't make it together . . . *they don't make it.*

If she throws in the towel, it was truly all for nothing.

Until Doc can not only forgive her for Beynon, but trust (*completely*) that she did it for the *right* reason, he's still in Huntsville.

Finally, Doc comes to this realization. But Carol demands from her husband, "*No matter what ever else happens, no more about him.*"

And he agrees, "*No matter whatever else happens—no more about him.*" And the two (*fucking finally*) are reunited.

Walking together, one arm draped around her, holding her close. His other arm carrying the pump-action shotgun he stole from the sporting goods store. Backed by a sea of garbage, those terrible trash-eating birds flying around in the sky, and the dump trucks moving mountains of trash . . . yet . . . for the first time in the movie . . . we know they're going to be alright.

"*Whatever else happens.*"

The Outfit

(1973)

Beginning in 1962, the mystery writer Donald Westlake, under the pseudonym Richard Stark, wrote a series of books about a professional armed robber named *Parker*.

I discovered the books sometime in my twenties and went gaga for them.

Parker was a cold, emotionless bastard whose only identity was his armed robber's code of professionalism. He robbed banks, bonds, rare coin collections—you name it, Parker stole it.

The conflict in most of the novels came from the fact that, usually, the other members of whatever crew he was working with weren't as professional as Parker.

And that's when Parker the armed robber could become Parker the unstoppable killer.

Parker may not have been burdened by the normal human emotions most of us have, but that shouldn't suggest he was cynical.

In book after book, he kept expecting his criminal colleagues to be as professional as he was and when they weren't he was appalled.

Some of the books featured Parker helping a former colleague out of a jam, or righting wrongs for a former colleague, or going after a greedy former colleague.

Even though Parker wasn't a professional killer, he dealt in armed robbery and all that implies.

He wasn't trigger-happy (that would be unprofessional), but he wasn't afraid to use his gun if need be.

You always risk certain consequences when you carry a loaded firearm into any endeavor. And Parker was always willing to face those consequences.

In Stark's first Parker book, *The Hunter*, our main character ties up and gags a female secretary in an office he's robbing, and inadvertently ends up suffocating her to death.

Well . . . that's unfortunate . . . especially for her . . . but *them's the risks*. And Parker never shied away from the risks inherent in his chosen profession.

What makes both the character and the books so interesting is their insistence on the code of ethics involved in a criminal activity.

It's as if, by insisting on a professional code of ethics, the characters can convince themselves that being a thief is a trade.

The closest thing to a humanizing trait that Stark allows the character is Parker's genuine fondness, bordering on affection, for his only friend, a fellow thief named *Cody*. Cody appeared in the books every so often and his presence is always welcome.

When I first discovered Parker, what made the character so memorable was he served as an antidote to the horrible homogeneous movies Hollywood was making in the eighties. After growing up in the anything-goes seventies, the eighties marked a play-it-safe decade, like that other horrible decade for Hollywood movies, the fifties. But the eighties were even worse. In the fifties you could claim that it was a repressed society that imposed restrictions on Hollywood, their movies, and their artists. But in the eighties the restrictions Hollywood imposed on their own product were self-imposed. The harshest censorship is self-censorship. And it doesn't always come from the big bad studio either. Many filmmakers watered down their own vision right from the beginning.

The idea that an American studio film of 1986 could have an opening scene like Pedro Almodóvar's Spanish film *Matador*, where a character masturbates to a montage of the goriest scenes in slasher films, was unthinkable.

Elizabeth McNeill's novella *Nine and a Half Weeks* was barely a book. But it did have a certain *something*. It was racy, naughty, and fun. And inside of its slim page count, it suggested an even better movie. You could imagine Radley Metzger making a classic out of it in the early days of seventies erotica. But the movie Adrian Lyne made was scared of even that pipsqueak of a book. And if anybody complained he didn't do justice to the book, he could legitimately say they practically hung me for what I did make! And he's right, they practically did.

De Palma was drawn and quartered for his toothless porn satire *Body Double*. Causing him to retreat to the silly mob comedy *Wise Guys*.

When it came to artists whose film work was of an uncompromising nature in the eighties, you had David Lynch, Paul Verhoeven, Abel Ferrara, Terry Gilliam, Brian De Palma (sometimes), and David Cronenberg.

And that's it.

Yeah, there were one-offs. John Carpenter's *The Thing*. William Friedkin's *Cruising*, Robert Harmon's *The Hitcher*. Kathryn Bigelow's *Near Dark*. Michael Cimino's *Year of the Dragon*. Hal Ashby's *8 Million Ways to Die*. Jim McBride's *Breathless*. Clive Barker's *Hellraiser*. But, *Hellraiser* aside, these directors were usually punished for their perceived transgressions, by the press, the public, and the industry.

I remember when I worked at my Manhattan Beach video store, *Video Archives*, and talked to the other employees about the types of movies I wanted to make, and the things I wanted to do inside of those movies. And I would use the example of the opening of Almodóvar's *Matador*.

And their response would be "Quentin, *they* won't let you do that."

To which I replied back; "Who the fuck are '*they*' to stop me? '*They*' can go fuck themselves."

Now I wasn't a professional filmmaker back then. I was a brash know-it-all film geek. Yet, once I graduated to professional filmmaker, I never did let "*they*" stop me. Viewers can accept my work or reject it. Deem it good, bad, or with indifference. But I've always approached my cinema with a fearlessness of the eventual outcome. A fearlessness that comes to me naturally—I mean, who cares, really? It's only a movie. But at the right age (mid-twenties), and at the right time (the fucking eighties), the fearlessness demonstrated by Pedro Almodóvar led by example. As I watched my heroes, the American film mavericks of the seventies, knuckle under to a new way of doing business just to stay employed, Pedro's fearlessness made a mockery of their calculated compromises. My dreams of movies *always* included a comic reaction to unpleasantness. Similar to the connection that Almodóvar's films made between the unpleasant and the sensual. Sitting in a Beverly Hills art house cinema, watching Pedro's vividly colorful, thrillingly provocative, 35mm images flickering on a giant wall—demonstrating that there *could* be something sexy about violence—I was convinced there was a place for me and my violent reveries in the modern cinematheque.

But the curse of eighties cinema wasn't that they wouldn't let you shoot somebody jerking off to Mario Bava's *Blood and Black Lace*. It was that the complex and complicated lead characters of the seventies were the characters that eighties cinema avoided completely. Complex characters aren't necessarily *sympathetic*. Interesting people aren't always *likable*. But in the Hollywood of the eighties *likability* was everything. A novel could have a low-down son of a bitch at its center, as long as that low-down son of a bitch was an interesting character.

But not a movie. Not in the eighties.

After the seventies, it seemed film went back to the restraints of the fifties. Back to when controversial novels and plays had to be drained of life, changed, or turned into morality plays. As happened with *9½ Weeks, Less Than Zero, Bright Lights, Big City, First Blood, The Color Purple, White Palace, Stick, Miami Blues,* and *The Bonfire of the Vanities.*

Okay, what about Philip Kaufman's *The Unbearable Lightness of Being*? Its open sexuality more or less made it to the screen intact. That meant you can do that kind of thing, didn't it?

Yeah, if you made it dull enough.

The Unbearable Boredom of Watching.

And if you *did* make a movie about a fucking bastard, you could bet that fucking bastard would see the error of their ways and be redeemed in the last twenty minutes.

Like for example, all of Bill Murray's characters.

How does Murray in *Stripes* go from being an iconoclastic pain in the ass, who deserves to get beat up by Drill Sergeant Warren Oates, to rallying the troops (*That's the fact, Jack!*), and masterminding a covert mission on foreign soil?

And *Stripes* was one of the hip movies.

Film critics always preferred Bill Murray to Chevy Chase. Yet, more often than not, Chase remained the same sarcastic aloof asshole at the film's end he was at the beginning. Or at least his conversion wasn't the whole point of the movie as it was in *Scrooged* and *Groundhog Day.*

Admittedly, when you don't give a fuck about other people's feelings, it probably does wonders for your caustic wit. But I've always rejected the idea that Bill Murray's characters needed redemption.

Yeah, maybe he charmed Andie MacDowell, but does anybody think a less sarcastic Bill Murray is a better Bill Murray?

They were no more prepared to do a *real* biography of Jerry Lee Lewis in 1989 than they were a real portrait of Cole Porter in 1949.

In *Wall Street*, it was so obvious that Gordon Gekko was going to have to go to jail at the end that it might as well been preordained by the *Hays Code*.

Naturally, Michael Douglas would end up realizing the error of his ways and drop dime on *The Star Chamber.*

In *Something Wild* and *Into the Night,* was there any chance that Melanie Griffith and Michelle Pfeiffer *wouldn't* inexplicably return to the male hero? Of course not, that would have been a bummer ending.

But it makes no sense why they'd return? Who cares, the movie's over. The people making movies didn't think audiences cared whether or not the happy endings they gave them made sense or not. And while I'd like to say those Hollywood professionals were wrong, I'm not sure they were.

At *Video Archives* I dealt closely with the movie-watching public (usually on a one-on-one basis). Much closer than any Hollywood executives. And, for the most part, they *didn't* care how unrealistic or implausible the jerry-rigged climaxes they were spoon-fed were. They just didn't want the movie to end like a bummer.

Just ask the makers of Demi Moore's version of *The Scarlet Letter*, aka: the triumphant ending version.

Or ask Demi Moore: *"Not many people have read the book."*

When the pursuing posse of local yokels fuck around and flip the On Switch of one-man killing machine John J. Rambo in *First Blood*, instead of slaughtering them like he does in David Morrell's book, he just wounds them.

Does that make the point of the book—that once the government turns a man into a killing machine for the purposes of warfare, keeping that machine turned off back home during peacetime isn't so easy—irrelevant?

Of course, but as Demi Moore would say . . .

As in the fifties, this juvenilization of cinema was a distinctly American problem. Other countries were still making movies for adults. Hong Kong, France, Holland, Japan, and especially England. Alan Clarke's *Made in Britain*, Alen Cox's *Sid and Nancy*, Stephen Frears' London Trilogy (*My Beautiful Laundrette, Prick Up Your Ears* & *Sammy and Rosie Get Laid*).

All of Almodóvar's Spanish films and Verhoeven's Dutch ones.

Every year Nicolas Roeg came out with some crazy movie starring Theresa Russell. Ken Russell still did whatever the fuck he wanted to do, even when he went to America (*Crimes of Passion*).

Still, discovering a heartless, lethal, uncompromising character like *Parker*, during that fucking wasteland of a decade, was a breath of much needed foul air.

The first three Parker books, *The Hunter, The Man with the Getaway Face*, and *The Outfit* are drastically the best ones. Once it became next book, next score, they lost something. But even in the later Parker books I started but never finished, Parker was always true to Parker.

The first three books in the series are connected. The first book, *The Hunter*, was made famous by John Boorman's cinematic adaptation *Point Blank*, with Lee Marvin becoming the first of many movie Parkers (in this one named *Walker*).

The movie doesn't really follow the plot of the book that much, but they both get to the same place. Parker stalking, terrorizing, and murdering a bunch of high-powered mobsters—who aren't used to this type of treatment—over his share of a score they owe him (46,000 dollars). By the end of the book, he's created such bloody havoc throughout the organized crime syndicate (or "*the Outfit*" as they call it in Stark's universe), that even Parker knows he must disappear.

And his attempt to disappear is the plot of the second book, *The Man with the Getaway Face*, which has never been made into a movie.

On the first page, Parker gets a completely new face from a shadowy underground plastic surgeon, who performs such operations for people trying to disappear (a la David Goodis). Unfortunately for Parker, after the operation the plastic surgeon is murdered. The doctor's family believes Parker is responsible. And they intend to alert the Outfit about Parker's new identity and face. Parker insists he had nothing to do with it, and he asks for a week to track down the real killer before the doctor's family does anything drastic.

He spends the rest of the book accomplishing this.

Even, in a stroke of poetic justice, removing the new face the shadowy plastic surgeon gave his killer.

At book's end, he arrives back to the family, explains who the murderer was and why he did it, and presents them with the cut-off face. Only, the doctor's family—sure of Parker's guilt—didn't give him the week he asked for. They've already informed the Outfit of Parker's new identity and new face. Thus rendering everything that happened in the book ironically useless.

The Outfit is the third book in the series. Knowing his powerful enemies are going to come after him—instead of running away from the mob—he runs at them.

Considering what a rough customer Parker is, he's remarkably well represented in movies. There's been as many Parkers as there's been Philip Marlowes. And when you consider Lee Marvin, Jim Brown, Robert Duvall, Mel Gibson, and Anna Karina have all played some variation of the character, quite a wide array.

They haven't always been called *Parker*. Till recently they *never* were. Stark didn't mind selling his books, but he never sold his character.

As the director John Flynn explained to me, *"Westlake didn't want his character to be affected by whatever happened in some dumb movie."*

In my opinion the best movie *Parker* isn't from an adaptation of one of Stark's novels. It's Robert De Niro as armed robber *Neil McCauley* in Michael Mann's *Heat.* While it's not literally based on a Richard Stark novel, it's pretty fucking obvious McCauley is, at least inspired—if not outright based on—Parker.

His professionalism, his creed, his held-in-check emotions, even McCauley's motto, *"Allow nothing in your life that you can't walk out on in thirty seconds flat if you spot the heat around the corner,"* sounds like some shit Parker would say. McCauley is *a little* more expressive than Parker, Mann having him verbalize lines Stark would have expressed in prose. And the end—McCauley missing his window of opportunity of escape and staying in L.A. to get revenge for a respected colleague—is totally a Parker dilemma.

However *if* it had been a Stark book, Parker's professionalism would have led him to flee. Because Parker knows there's nothing more important than *not getting caught.* Sticking to the code is how one maneuvers in this world without getting caught.

Consequently, in twelve books Parker never gets caught and never gets killed. At the end of *Heat,* McCauley gets shot by the law. I never liked the ending of *Heat.* Not just because I wanted to see De Niro get away, not just because I didn't want him to break his code, and not just because I didn't want Al Pacino's detective to win. But from the moment Jon Voight tells him he found the guy who killed Danny Trejo, you know how the movie's going to end. The close-up of De Niro driving, making up his mind . . . incredible. But once he jerks the wheel, you know he's doomed. The by-rote moralistic functionality of the last fifteen minutes, compared to the two hours and thirty-five minutes that preceded it, is a drag.

Of the straight Parker adaptations, most people choose Boorman's *Point Blank* and consider Lee Marvin the living embodiment of Parker.

I've never understood the reputation that baby-boomer critics assigned Boorman's nonentity crime film.

Yes, it has a dazzling (for its time) opening ten minutes. But the truth is, it seemed more dazzling when I was twenty-six than it does now. Even in terms of ruthless Lee Marvin gangster film openings, it can't hold a flickering birthday candle next to Don Siegel's opening for *The Killers.*

What's effective about Boorman's opening is the way it builds and keeps building. The way the forward momentum of Marvin's shoes tap out a rhythm on the floor, brings to mind both the sizzle of a dynamite fuse and the screech before a car collision. And the sequence pays off when Marvin bursts through Angie Dickinson's door, blasting his pistol. But that's by far the best filmmaking in the movie. After the opening ten minutes, except for the violent fight in the discotheque, it never hums again.

After the show-off opening, *Point Blank* settles down into sixties television. It's pretty much indistinguishable from a *Mannix* episode of the same era (actually *Mannix* star Mike Connors wouldn't have been a bad Parker. In fact, when I read *The Hunter*—Parker before plastic surgery—I see somebody like Connors).

I disagree that Lee Marvin is the quintessential Parker. I don't even think it's a good performance. Marvin was one of the most exciting actors of the fifties (*Gorilla at Large, Shack Out at 101, Hangman's Knot, The Man Who Shot Liberty Valance,* and especially *Attack*). And in *The Professionals* and *The Dirty Dozen* he modulated that excitement into stardom. But starting with *Point Blank,* Marvin went from his greatest lead performance in *The Dirty Dozen* to acting like a leafless tree. And for the whole rest of his acting career he swung wildly from these boring iconic death-mask non-performances (*Prime Cut, Hell in the Pacific, Avalanche Express*) to overplayed comedic buffoonery (*Pocket Money, The Great Scout, Cathouse Thursday, Shout at the Devil*, and *Paint Your Wagon*). In the fifties, the way Marvin delivered theatrical dialogue in movies suggested a great theatre actor who knew he was better suited for the camera (his reading of Norman Brooks' dialogue from his play *Fragile Fox* in the movie adaptation *Attack* shows you how it's supposed to sound). But in the seventies, he practically stopped speaking. And then when he did, in Frankenheimer's *The Iceman Cometh* . . . he didn't have it anymore.

But *Point Blank*, when compared to other Stark adaptions, like the abysmal Jim Brown one *The Split* (not Brown's fault), the practically comedic *Point Blank* remake with Mel Gibson, and Godard's non-adaptation *Made in U.S.A.*, which wastes Stark's book, the audience's time, and a lot of *Kodak* film stock, Boorman's movie is at least an honorable effort.

My nomination for best Richard Stark novel adaptation (by far) is John Flynn's *The Outfit*, starring Robert Duvall as *Macklin* (Parker), Karen Black as *Bett* (in the Angie Dickinson role from *Point Blank*), and a perfect Joe Don Baker as Cody.* If you like *Point Blank*, fair enough, then *The Outfit* is its de facto sequel. The events in the book *The Hunter* and Boorman's movie is what leads the syndicate to target both Parker and Cody. And then leads Duvall and Baker to execute a full frontal assault against *The Outfit*. Flynn, forced to start from scratch, has Duvall's Macklin finishing up a prison sentence for getting picked up by the cops in a bar during a vice raid for carrying a hot weapon. He relates that story to someone and they reply, "*Damn, that's some hard time.*"

---

*It was the film author Westlake thought captured Parker the best as well.

As he gets out, his brother is assassinated by two mob triggermen (in a real cool opening that just screams seventies cinema). Then two triggermen (familiar ugly face Tom Reese, who
would've been a great post-plastic surgery Parker), disguised as
quail hunters, show up at the woodsy breakfast diner that Cody
(Joe Don Baker) runs when he's not doing a score. However, they
pick the wrong time, because the local sheriff (who has no idea
about Cody's double life), is in the joint having his morning coffee. But now Cody knows a couple of out-of-town torpedoes are
on his trail.

Macklin/Parker (Duvall) is picked up from prison by his old
lady, Bett (Karen Black), who sets him up for a hit at a local hotel.
She's forced into this betrayal after she endures a torture session
conducted by the Outfit, where they burned a cigarette up and
down her arm (we later find out it was none other than Timothy
Carey who used her arm as an ashtray), but she informs Macklin
in time for him to ambush the gunman (Walter Hill regular Felice
Orlandi), by breaking a bottle across his face (*"I've got glass in my
face"*). Duvall tortures him for information, learning why the Outfit is targeting him.*

Apparently, before he got pinched in the vice raid, Macklin, his
brother, and Cody robbed a bank that unbeknownst to them was
a mob front. Upon his release from jail, the word has come down
from the Outfit's big boss man *Mailer* (snicker-snicker) played by
Robert Ryan to eliminate these small-timers (Ryan was as thin as
a rail, and like Marvin, had a face that looked like it was carved on
a totem pole. But unlike Marvin—in the seventies—Ryan only got

---

*Director Flynn wrote the really tight script with uncredited assistance from
his pal Walter Hill. And the whole opening with Macklin being processed out
of prison, and Bett picking him up, and even the conversation they share in
the car is extremely similar to Doc and Carol's opening in *The Getaway.*

better. It's Ryan, not Marvin, who rises to the challenge of Eugene O'Neill's dialogue in *The Iceman Cometh*).

Macklin and Cody figure the best defense is a strong offense. Instead of running away from the mob, they run at them. With Black operating as their getaway driver, Duvall and Baker start robbing Outfit-fronted operations. Not used to being fucked with, almost every robbery starts with somebody screaming, "*Do you know who runs this place?*" To which Joe Don Baker yells back, "*I don't give a rat's ass if your mother runs it!*" Or Duvall just smashes them in the teeth with his gun. A big part of the movie's enjoyment stems from the mob associates' shock at the brutal treatment they receive at the hands of Duvall and Baker. But there's more to our heroes' plan than just revenge for Duvall's brother and a mad crime spree. Both Macklin and Cody figure if they can cause enough trouble and hurt the syndicate where they're most sensitive, in the pocketbook, since Mailer fancies himself a businessman, maybe they can broker a deal. Well, naturally that doesn't work.

So the movie ends with Duvall and Baker doing an all-out assault on Ryan's home compound. And it's one of the more satisfying sequences of that type I've ever seen, far better than the similar action climax in Michael Mann's *Thief*. While it's not as amazing or as violent as the whorehouse pump-action-shotgun shootout in John Flynn's next film, *Rolling Thunder*, it's still cool and exciting. And the scene between Duvall and Baker on the stairs is the epitome of poignant masculinity. With the picture's final freeze-frame capper displaying a self-mocking tone that ends the whole film on a hearty macho guffaw.

In a 1981 cover story for the magazine *American Film* (done to promote Duvall in *True Confessions*), the writer described him as a "*Hard-boiled Olivier.*" Not a bad description of Duvall's performance in this movie. In the Santa Clarita, California, newspaper *The Signal*, film critic Phillip Lanier wrote about Duvall as

Macklin: "*Earl is one of the most interesting gangster figures to screen in a while. He is intelligent and his brutality is as calculated as it is unsympathetic. To him, robbing and killing is just a nine-to-five job which he has to take home with him too. His [Duvall's] quiet determination brings across a character who appears to be a desperate man by choice. It's a mysterious kind of masculinity that only he seems to possess.*"

Macklin may be Stark's Parker, but both Flynn and Duvall open up the character. Macklin definitely has more of a sense of humor than Parker (in the movie Duvall laughs every once in a while). But it's Macklin's affection for Cody that separates him from the literary Parker. The Parker of the books has affection for Cody as well. But Duvall's masterful performance conveys it stronger without abandoning that turtle shell he uses as a face. And he and Baker make a marvelous team, with Duvall mumbling all the cryptic lines and Baker spitting out all the funny ones. When the two men discuss how they're going to attack Ryan's heavily guarded home compound, they even predate Flynn's greatest cinematic moment, the "*I'll just get my gear*" scene between William Devane and Tommy Lee Jones in *Rolling Thunder*.

While I doubt any actor could be the definitive Parker, Joe Don Baker is absolutely the perfect embodiment of Cody. Joe Don has always been one of my favorite screen actors, but for me, it's his performance in this film that's my personal favorite. The movie even gives Baker the film's terrific curtain line. According to fat hack James Bacon in a profile he wrote on Baker, when director Flynn, producer Carter DeHaven, and MGM studio head James Aubrey went to a screening of *Walking Tall* together, halfway through the picture they shouted in unison, "*He's our man!*"

As I pointed out earlier, *Point Blank* has that canned quality of sixties television. Marvin aside, it even has a television cast.

The whole supporting cast could have been the guest star lineup of an episode of *Cannon* (Angie Dickinson and Keenan Wynn, terrific as they were, did a lot of television).

John Vernon, in the sixties and early seventies, was constantly playing the heavy on episodic TV. And while I like Vernon, it was after *The Outlaw Josey Wales* and *Animal House* that I started liking him a lot more. But back in 1967, Vernon's part in *Point Blank* was too big for him. He couldn't hold his own with even a low wattage Lee Marvin (Keenan Wynn would have been better in Vernon's role).

Carroll O'Connor, before he settled into his role as TV icon Archie Bunker, was all forced comedic bluster. A phony powerhouse, he played everything comedic, because he wasn't a strong enough actor to play it dramatic. But, like Ed Asner with the character of Lou Grant, his ownership of the Archie Bunker role led him to do much deeper work later on (he's terrific in Ivan Passer's *Law and Disorder*. It's Ernest Borgnine who's a braying donkey). But in *Point Blank*, even giving a non-performance, Marvin thoroughly dominates windbag O'Connor.

And then there's fish-faced Lloyd Bochner. The type of tight-lipped stiff who regularly appeared on Quinn Martin–produced TV shows.

Any movie that casts Lloyd—fucking—Bochner has serious casting issues.

But by contrast the supporting cast of *The Outfit* is filled with one terrific actor's face after another (Timothy Carey, Richard Jaeckel, Sheree North, Marie Windsor, Jane Greer, Henry Jones, Bill McKinney).

Director Flynn told me he cast the film with his buddy Walter Hill by going through a book of great B-movie character actors.

When it came to casting, Flynn told me he was happy with the lead cast of the movie. He liked Baker and Black, and thought Duvall was a fine actor and an interesting rising star. But they wouldn't have been his first choice. If he could have, he would have rather gone less modern-day seventies casting, and more film noir. His dream cast would have been Burt Lancaster as Macklin,

Kirk Douglas as Cody, and Angie Dickinson as Macklin's wife. I considered doing an adaptation of the book in the late nineties, with Robert De Niro as Parker, Harvey Keitel as Cody, and Pam Grier as Bett. And just writing that now makes me wish I would have done it.

The Outfit was one of the last films made under the tenure of MGM studio head James Aubrey (aka *the smiling cobra*). And the studio head honcho instituted a new release pattern for his remaining pictures.

Aubrey was pissed off at the way the New York and Los Angeles critics had treated his slate of MGM films. So he began opening new MGM movies regionally first. It took *The Outfit* an entire year to make the rounds through the United States. Starting off in October 1973 in Chicago and Baltimore, and not opening in California (its last stop) till a year later in October 1974. The first press clippings (aside from casting announcements) to appear about Flynn's film were almost all from fat hack James Bacon, who wrote in his syndicated column on Oct 23, 1973, "*Saw The Outfit the other night at a cast and crew preview and it's The Godfather of 1973.*" Wow, pretty impressive, huh? But then ask yourself what was James Bacon doing at a cast and crew preview? Because Bacon had a small cameo in the movie, and that was sort of the deal back then. If you stuck James Bacon's fat ass somewhere in your movie, you could guarantee a few positive notices in his column. But the less-biased critics across the country were in a three-way split between declaring the film a routine crime picture, a slightly above routine crime picture, or a drastically below routine crime picture.

Vincent Canby of the *New York Times* wrote, "*The Outfit is not really a bad movie. It doesn't fail in an attempt to do something beyond its means. It doesn't attempt to do anything except pass the time, which simply isn't good enough when most of us have access to television.*"

Greg Swem of the *Courier-Journal* (out of Louisville, Kentucky) obviously enjoyed the movie, but ultimately concluded, "*It's well written and well directed by John Flynn, but the script and direction are fragmented. The film as a whole doesn't have any great attraction."*

But Gary Arnold of the *Washington Post* declared it *"a lugubrious, derivative thriller."* After he described the plot he concluded, *"This sounds like the outline for a fairly tense little crime exercise, but Flynn has a flat, dawdling way of spinning a yarn, so the essential grubbiness and brutality of the conception aren't leavened with much flair or excitement."*

Jeanne Miller of the *San Francisco Examiner* referred to Flynn's work as *"dismal direction"* and the film itself as *"disastrous."*

Bernard Drew of the *Journal News,* out of White Plains, New York, disparaged Flynn further, *"Writer-director John Flynn, who once unwittingly made one of the funniest pictures of the sixties, The Sergeant, and later succeeded in making a bore out of the holy land in The Jerusalem File, now rises to new heights of ineptitude in The Outfit."*

But Roger Ebert, in his *Chicago Sun-Times* review in October of 1973, gave the film three and a half stars out of four, and wrote; *"The Outfit is a class action picture, very well directed and acted, about a gangster's revenge on the mob death of his brother. An outline of the plot would make it sound pretty routine, but what makes the picture superior is its richness of detail."* Then Ebert went on to clarify, *"We don't care much about what happens, the same things are always happening in action movies, and when you've seen one car burst into flames you've seen them all. But the people in this movie are uncommonly interesting."*

Then a full year later in October 1974, in the *Los Angeles Times,* Charles Champlin concluded his positive review with the summation, *"There is always a particular pleasure in watching a movie which is in command of itself all the way, an exercise in professionalism, and The Outfit offers that kind of satisfaction as the bonus beyond the surprises, the suspense, and the vivid portrayals."*

But it was only John Fox, writing for the *Oakland Tribune,* who offered any serious insight that went beyond a plot summary and a *good, bad,* or *indifferent* verdict. *"The film is perceptive in its understanding of the attitudes men have towards each other. And although the violence may prevent some viewers from seeing the message, there is a fine statement about an individual's ability to overcome a threatening force if only he can find the means and the nerve."*

I first saw *The Outfit* when it played in Tennessee in March of 1974, under the title *The Good Guys Always Win* (actually, if you've seen the movie, not a bad title). Due to Joe Don Baker's incredible popularity in that state because of *Walking Tall*, it was Baker and the Buford Pusser connection that was emphasized.*

And eight months later, when it finally opened in Los Angeles under its original title of *The Outfit*, I saw it again at the *United Artists Cinema* in Marina del Rey on a double feature with Sam Peckinpah's *The Getaway* (talk about an action-packed PG-rated double feature!).

I actually thought I was buying a ticket to the sequel of *The Good Guys Always Win*. No worries. It was even better the second time. And the hearty audience of macho guys scattered around the little cinema made it even more fun. They laughed at everything Joe Don Baker said. Including his terrific curtain line that brought the little house down.

---

*In the state of Tennessee, after *Walking Tall*, Joe Don Baker was only a little less popular than Elvis Presley.

Second-String Samurai

An Appreciation of Kevin Thomas

L ike they did with *Angels Hard as They Come* and *The Hot Box*, Jonathan Demme and Evelyn Purcell killed themselves making the women-in-prison drama *Caged Heat* for Roger Corman. Only this time it's Jonathan as the director and Evelyn as the producer (and second-unit director). And now the day had finally come when their little WIP potboiler would finally be released to theatres and drive-ins around Los Angeles (where it played city-wide alongside Melvin Van Peebles' *Sweet Sweetback's Baadasssss Song* as its supporting feature).

But after all the hard work, there was a little fatalism among the married filmmaking team. According to longtime Demme associate Gary Goetzman, yeah, they knew they made a good little picture for Roger. But ultimately, so what? Who's going to see a sleazy little New World Pictures film called *Caged Heat*, other than the drive-in crowd it was made for? Even when Jonathan and Evelyn met people around town and mentioned they just made a movie, people would ask what was it called.

When they said *Caged Heat* they'd see the contemptible expression on their faces, *what, is it a porno?*

The couple were still happy and excited, but they understood the reality of making exploitation movies in Hollywood.

When it came to *Caged Heat* opening in Los Angeles, Hollywood wouldn't care, the industry wouldn't care, the press wouldn't care, and the public (save for a few teenage drive-in patrons) wouldn't care.

In fact, the only person who *would* care would be Roger Corman.

And to get Corman to offer them another flick is about all they could hope for.

So imagine Demme and Purcell's surprise, when the day after the film opened they paged through the *Los Angeles Times* and read a rave review by Kevin Thomas of their punky little prison picture.

After making clear his contempt for the *women-in-prison* sub-genre (especially the Jack Hill–Eddie Romero Filipino variety), Thomas wrote about Demme's first film as a director:

"With wit, style and unflagging verve, writer-director Jonathan Demme, a youthful and talented exploitation veteran, sends up the genre while still giving the mindless action fan his money's worth. Demme, best known for 'Angels, Hard as They Come,' manages not only to have it both ways but also, in pointing up the absurdity of the genre, points up the absurdity of the often cruel and inhuman conditions of real-life prisons."

Then he ended his review the way all New World Pictures directors *wished* the *Los Angeles Times* would end the reviews of their pictures: *"In every aspect Caged Heat attests to Demme's virtuosity— and to [cinematographer Tak] Fujimoto and [composer John] Cale's as well—and thereby demonstrates that all three of them are ready for major projects."*

If you're going to speak about the early career of Jonathan Demme, you need to speak about his biggest champion, second-string critic for the *Los Angeles Times*, Kevin Thomas. Later (post-

Citizens Band), Demme had a whole host of critics acting as a cheering section. But before Vincent Canby, before Richard Corliss, before Kenny Turan, before Pauline Kael and her *"Paulettes"* fell in line behind Demme, the critic most responsible for the young filmmaker's career progression was Kevin Thomas.

One of the things that I had forgotten, but reading those reviews of *The Outfit* was quickly reminded of, was what Elvis Mitchell called the "Institutional Indifference" to even studio-backed genre product by the newspaper-based critics of the day.

It would appear most critics writing for newspapers and magazines set themselves up as superior to the films they were paid to review. Which I could never understand, because judging from their writing, that was *clearly* not the case.

They looked down on films that gave pleasure, and on the filmmakers who had an understanding of the audience that they did not.

And we're talking about *The Outfit*! A solid studio film, based on a good book, with sensational actors. Forget about the beneath-contempt treatment *actual* exploitation flicks received at their hands.

As a kid who loved movies and paid to see pretty much everything, I just thought they were snide assholes. Today as a much older and wiser man, I realize the extent of how unhappy they must have been. They wrote with the demeanor of somebody who hates their life, or at least hates their job.

For twenty years, almost comically, the *Los Angeles Times*—the newspaper of the motion picture industry—hired critical laughing-stocks for their first-string movie critic positions.

The *New York Times* had Vincent Canby, a good voice for that publication. The *Chicago Sun-Times* had Roger Ebert, who, when inspiration struck him, would examine an offbeat aspect of the film under analysis, like the fact that the Frank Perry film *Diary of a Mad Housewife* was told from the perspective of an unreliable narrator by virtue it was a *diary*. And, despite him and his high-minded colleague Gene Siskel's showboating hissy fit against slasher films in the eighties, Roger was a friend to exploitation films, giving good reviews to *The Last House on the Left, Electric Boogaloo is Breakin' Too*, and *Inframan*, as well as writing the screenplay for the all-time classic *Beyond the Valley of the Dolls.*

But in the seventies the *LA Times* had blurb-whore Charles (Chuckie) Champlin, who reviewed movies the way Ralph Williams sold cars.

In Los Angeles he was known as the "Will Rogers of film criticism—Charles Champlin, never met a movie he didn't like." Champlin wrote as if appearing in as many movie ad pull quotes as possible was an editorial imperative. Also for years he hosted an interview show on local L.A. television called *At One With,* where he'd sit across from actors like Gene Hackman and filmmakers like John Frankenheimer. So he wouldn't do himself, or his local L.A. celebrity status, any favors by being rough with the Hollywood citizens in their hometown newspaper.*

Nevertheless, Champlin was preferable to the person who took his spot in the eighties, Sheila Benson. Benson pretty much ruined the Calendar section of the *Los Angeles Times* for a decade. Her movie reviews read closer to book reports written by a housewife for a night school class on modern American lit.

Back then I only cared about critics' opinions and personality, I never judged their actual writing ability, *except* Sheila Benson.

Myself and my first girlfriend, Grace Lovelace (both of us Pauline Kael devotees), used to quote Sheila Benson's reviews to make the other one smirk. During dinners together in the nineties, film

---

*In fact, Charles Champlin wasn't really a film critic, but an essayist. And the cinema essays he'd write were pretty good. But when he was offered the first-string critic position at the *Times*, even though he probably knew he wasn't right for it, he couldn't refuse.

critic colleagues Manohla Dargis and John Powers drew hearty laughs from everyone at the table by mocking Benson's writing style.

But it's not like Benson didn't have her constituency. To give the devil her due—in a strange way—Sheila Benson was rather an appropriate voice for the Hollywood studio films coming out of the miserable eighties. The middle of the road successful films of that era were right up Benson's alley. *The Big Chill, Out of Africa, Ordinary People, Diner, Gandhi, Stand by Me,* those films were Benson's cup of weak tea.

The problem was her first-string critic position. Writing for another venue other than the *Los Angeles fucking Times,* Benson could have been a perfectly acceptable critic. If Benson—with her PTA mentality—had been writing the movie page for *McCall's* magazine (did *Redbook* have a movie page?) the writer and her readers would have found a happy home. Pauline Kael was fired by *McCall's* for her opinions. Benson would have been so beloved by the readership, they probably would have issued a movie coupon with a picture of her face in the middle of it.

They could have been called *Benson Bucks.*

In the nineties Benson went bye-bye and was replaced by Kenny Turan. Now compared to Champlin, who might as well have worked for the advertising department, and Benson, who was simply unfit for her position, Kenny Turan was a *real* critic. But not a real critic you really wanted to read.

Now, it must be noted for the length of my career—at my hometown newspaper—Kenny set himself up to be my nemesis. Turan wasn't the only critic to give *Pulp Fiction* a bad review. But *his* review wasn't just a pan of a movie he didn't care for, it had an agenda.

To counteract Todd McCarthy's and Janet Maslin's once-in-a-lifetime raves in *Variety* and the *New York Times.*

I thought maybe I'd get him with *Jackie Brown,* but no such luck.

Then for the next few years, Kenny made it a point to bring me up as a negative example of what was wrong with current cinema in every think piece he wrote. In one about Peckinpah's *The Wild Bunch*, he didn't just run me over, he drove around the block to run me over. Turan's animosity towards my work has persisted throughout my career. To such a degree, when he finally responded positively to my film *Once Upon a Time . . . in Hollywood*, he felt the need to explain to the readers the degree to which he had dismissed my work in the past (though by that time the only one keeping score was me). When you share an antagonism with one critic for as long as Kenny and me, you end up having a strange personal connection with each other.

The few times we bumped into each other at an event, we've shared a moment of professional mutual rejection that bordered on intimacy.

But through that entire time, through Champlin, through Benson, through Turan, sitting over there at the *Los Angeles Times* in his second-string critic spot was Kevin Thomas.

Kevin's job as second-string critic was to see the studio-wide releases that the first-string critic couldn't get to. Then see all the art house/independent movies. Then all the foreign films to play Los Angeles. Which in the mid- to late seventies, during the time of Lina Wertmuller, Claude Lelouch, Giancarlo Giannini, and Laura Antonelli was a pretty cool beat. The first time many of us Los Angeles residents ever read about Wertmuller, Fassbinder, and Oshima was in Kevin Thomas' writing. But along with making foreign movies more palpable to regular L.A. moviegoers, the other big job Kevin Thomas had was reviewing most of the new exploitation movies coming into town for the *LA Times*.

And in regard to both positions, nobody in the country did it better.

Consequently, the first time I ever read about Russ Meyer, Jess Franco, and Dario Argento was in Kevin Thomas' writing. On most daily newspapers, the reviews of exploitation movies usually weren't written by the first or even the second-string critic, but pawned off on some staff underling, oftentimes the assignment carrying the sting of punishment. And the pieces they wrote about these flicks displayed a vindictiveness towards the film itself (they weren't just mad they had to write a review, they were mad they had to watch the movie in the first place). That was not how Kevin Thomas practiced his profession or how his aesthetic worked. He always approached every new film from American-International Pictures, or New World Pictures, or Crown International Pictures, or Cannon Pictures, or Empire Pictures with an openhearted optimism and a measure of respect.

Roger Corman received a lot of credit (deservedly so) for launching a lot of young filmmakers from his drive-in pictures to the major studios.

Did Corman deserve the credit for finding these directors? Of course he did. But what really facilitated these directors moving up to studio assignments was if they received a positive notice in the *Los Angeles Times* from Kevin Thomas. The *LA Times* was the morning newspaper most agents and studio executives read. And if Kevin Thomas gave a positive notice to one of Jonathan Demme's flicks for Corman, or Joe Rubin's flicks for Crown International, or Sam Firstenberg's flicks for Cannon Pictures, or Stuart Gordon's flicks for Empire, or Joe Dante's *The Howling*, or Lewis Teague's *Alligator*, or Michael Laughlin's *Strange Behavior*, or John McTiernan's *Nomads* the industry took notice.

Say you're a junior agent at William Morris and you're trying to build up your client list, or you're a junior executive at Warner Bros. trying to pull in promising talent that the senior executives weren't hip to yet. When you read the *Los Angeles Times* over coffee in the morning and Kevin Thomas praised some filmmaker or actor in some exploitation movie that just hit town, you paid attention.

So when Thomas said Jonathan Demme's *Caged Heat* was a good movie, you tracked down a print and watched it in the company screening room. If you agreed, you signed him up as a client, or pitched him at your next meeting of the upcoming films on your slate.

And when your bosses asked "*Who the hell is Jonathan Demme?*" you answered, "*His last movie got a great write up in the LA Times.*"

That is how those directors broke through to the studio level. Corman's position as the movie minor leagues to the studio's major leagues stopped once he sold New World Pictures and opened up his new company in the eighties, Concorde-New Horizons. It stopped earlier than most, because Corman read the writing on the wall that theatrical exhibition for the type of movies he made was becoming a thing of the past. The real market for these movies was home video. So as opposed to in the past, when theatrical box office was the primary concern (right next to the eventual television sale), theatrical exhibition simply became a contractual obligation, so the video advertisement could proclaim "*Straight from its theatrical release.*" Oftentimes in Los Angeles that meant a dumped booking at the Egyptian 3 (a shoebox-sized third screen attached to the historic Egyptian Theatre on Hollywood Boulevard) or the Lakewood One & Two.*

---

* The Lakewood One & Two was a cinema owned by the Pussycat Theatre chain that projected adult entertainment of the Triple XXX variety. However, inconveniently for everybody, the dirty movie house was located directly across the street from an elementary school. So efforts were made by the community to shut them the fuck down. The case came before a judge, who was sympathetic to the community's concerns. Nevertheless, the Pussycat Theatre chain (owned by a fellow named Vincent Miranda) was a legitimate Los Angeles based company that wisely made many political contributions in Los Angeles County. In every brochure of the Pussycat Theatre chain it included a picture of Vincent Miranda shaking hands with Los Angeles Mayor

But with the new Corman product bypassing theatrical exhibition and going straight to home video, it also meant it was bypassing a chance to be reviewed by the local press. So with only a few exceptions (Carl Franklin and Louis Llosa), without Kevin Thomas to act as talent scout, Corman's pipeline to the major studios stopped.

Kevin Thomas wrote about exploitation movies the way a devoted sportswriter might write about a good high school team. Looking for that one player who might possibly possess the talent and potential to take themselves to the next level. And then when they moved up to the college level, he followed them, and wrote whether or not they realized that potential. Then when they made the pros, followed them to the minor leagues, till finally, they made it to the majors. With Kevin Thomas, standing on the sidelines, rooting them on the whole way. When Jonathan Demme finally made his first film out from under the wing of Roger Corman, *Citizens Band* for Paramount Studios, Thomas praised the production, writing, "*Most gratifying of all, the film marks the graduation of Demme, one of the most talented young directors in Hollywood from the ranks of exploitation after a substantial apprenticeship*

Tom Bradley. So the judge came up with a compromise that would have made Solomon proud. Since there were two screens, one could keep showing adult entertainment. But the other had to screen non-pornographic material. At first there was an effort on the company's part to make that second screen work. First they tried showing foreign movies (*Wifemistress, Bread and Chocolate, The Divine Nymph, The Immortal Bachelor*), and when that didn't work they tried turning it into a revival house. So right alongside the new porno film starring Jennifer Welles or Seka you could watch either *The Maltese Falcon* or *Citizen Kane*. Then when that didn't work either the company stopped caring what Cinema #2 showed, as long as Cinema #1 was allowed to remain open. And soon it became a dumping ground for distributors to meet their Los Angeles theatrical distribution contractual requirement.

with Roger Corman that yielded that witty exploitation classic, Caged Heat."

If Kevin Thomas were female it would be easy to make a case that his seemingly permanent position as second-string critic at the *LA Times* was a form of misogyny. But in Thomas' case, I think his editors knew no one in the business could cover his beat half as well as he did.

There were a few areas where Kevin and I parted company. Thomas had a real distaste for mean-spirited violence. He didn't mind graphic violence when woven into a tapestry like George A. Romero's *Dawn of the Dead* or Richard Compton's *Macon County Line*. But one of my favorite movies of the seventies is John Flynn's *Rolling Thunder*. Years later at the Torrance Public Library when I looked up his review, I was shocked at the opening paragraph.

"Well into the press preview of Rolling Thunder someone shouted, 'At least it's not dull.' To give the devil his due, it isn't, but otherwise it's one of the most revolting exploitation pictures to come along in some time."

Damn, Kevin!

But he wasn't through.

"Now the point to be made about Rolling Thunder is that it's not just another cheaply made piece of junk—although junk it most assuredly is. It has been very well directed by John Flynn and superbly photographed by Jordan Cronenweth. . . . Rolling Thunder is some kind of ultimate in cynical calculation. The whole numbing predicament of the returning POW is perceptively, credibly depicted—but only to set up the carnage that follows."

Then he ends the review:

"Of course it could be argued that [William] Devane is only reaping what we sowed in Vietnam, but it will take a much less shallow picture than this to make the connection between American violence abroad and at home."

Obviously, I disagree. But if I *had* read that review, his emphasis on the film's dynamic carnage would have made me pretty gung ho to see it.

Consequently, when his golden boy Jonathan Demme did his own Revengeamatic for Corman, *Fighting Mad* (with Peter Fonda), Thomas took him to task as well. Starting off his review: "*In Fighting Mad, Jonathan Demme, one of the most promising young writer-directors in exploitation pictures, has allowed violence to outweigh ideas to such a degree that the picture becomes a turnoff, little more than a blatantly obvious play to the yahoo mentality.*"

In my opinion the climax of *Fighting Mad* isn't violent *enough*.

Is my taste in cinema more *bloodthirsty* than Kevin Thomas'? Clearly (I'm trying to not take that "*yahoo mentality*" crack personally).

But one man's turnoff . . .

But the review I disagreed with the most (after *Rolling Thunder*) is his critical take on John Carpenter's *Halloween*.

"*Although Carpenter and producer Debra Hill's plot may be full of holes, Carpenter draws upon the resources of the camera to overcome them with ease. Also, his victims are well drawn and well played. With his cinematic flair, Carpenter therefore knows how to generate fear (rather than suspense) and how to make us feel like voyeurs (which makes the film a complete turn-off about halfway through). So what, then, is the point of all this realistically depicted slaughter and terror? With its tree-shaded small-town American setting, Halloween does function metaphorically for the insecure times in which we live. But since it offers nothing more, Halloween becomes yet another in the seemingly endless series of films that simply exacerbate our increasing paranoia—and what is the good of this?*"

It's almost comical in retrospect to read Thomas bemoan "*the seemingly endless series of films that simply exacerbate our increasing paranoia,*" knowing the endless wave of *slasher movies* yet to come that will owe their very existence to *Halloween*. But again, even a

Kevin Thomas negative review reads like a positive review until it gets to the point where Thomas takes psychological umbrage. As with the *Rolling Thunder* review, despite the vehicle, filmmaking craftsmanship always is noted, appreciated, and singled out for praise. And besides, everybody (especially a film critic) is entitled to their opinion, and if he didn't dig *Halloween* and found it a turn-off, so be it. But it would be interesting to see if Thomas' mind would have been changed if he saw *Halloween* not in a practically empty screening room but in a packed cinema of teenagers hooting, hollering, screaming, laughing, and basically having the time of their lives, like most of us experienced when Carpenter's picture first opened.

But then there were the times—and this *never* happened with his colleagues—when I felt Thomas *overpraised* an exploitation picture. This happened when I purchased a ticket, after his enthusiastic review, for the early Sarah Jessica Parker film *Girls Just Want to Have Fun*, which I didn't like at all. Same thing for his positive notice of the bad South African martial arts flick *Kill and Kill Again*. Which was the sequel to the equally bad *Kill or Be Killed*, which I saw and thought was so lousy that I walked out after forty minutes (I'd do that from time to time, but I didn't make a habit of it). After reading Kevin's well-written appreciation of the sequel, I took a chance the film would be different than the godawful original. Nope.

It was just as bad (a friend of mine named Craig Hammon dubbed the films "*designer jeans kung fu*" due to the Sergio Valentes that star James Ryan wore throughout). After twenty minutes, I walked out of this one too. But I never begrudged Kevin Thomas his enthusiasm.

Did I waste money?

Yeah, but I'm not going to pretend I ever gave a shit about that.

I liked Kevin Thomas so much, I was glad *he* at least had a good time. One of Thomas' gifts was pointing out tender moments from some unlikely sources. In his review for the silly and forgettable computer comedy *Electric Dreams*, Thomas notes that the film's two leads, Lenny von Dohlen and Virginia Madsen, were bland when compared to Bud Cort, who voiced the suddenly conscious computer Edgar, and of whom he wrote, *"Bud Cort reminds us of what radio acting at its best was all about."* But then points out the scene where the two young leads finally grabbed him.

"Von Dohlen and Madsen really catch hold of us—and each other—when he comforts her on the loss of her beloved cello, crushed by the elevator doors. By way of comfort, he points out that what's important, and not lost, is what's inside of her—that the cello, after all, is only an instrument."

Usually, when you finally saw the film in question, these moments weren't as affecting as Thomas' description of them. But still, you knew what he meant, and you appreciated his efforts in trying to distinguish something like a piece of fluff calling itself *Electric Dreams*.

One of my favorite Kevin Thomas reviews was for Russ Meyer's *Supervixens*.

Like he was for Demme and Romero, Thomas was a champion of Meyer, even once acting as master of ceremonies at a festival of Russ Meyer's movies in L.A., where he introduced the auteur as *"the only director outside of Alfred Hitchcock whose name above the title means anything."*

"In its first few minutes Supervixens comes on like vintage Russ Meyer, a hilarious, rambunctious combination of fast action and busty babes. But quite abruptly Meyer, the original King of the Nudies, freezes the smile on our faces with a dazzlingly staged, truly terrifying sequence that, in making a direct connection between sex and violence, is truly one of the most impassioned expressions of the battle of the sexes ever filmed. SuperAngel (Shari Eubank), the spoiled incredibly voluptuous, incredibly insatiable wife of a nice-guy gas station attendant (Charlie Pitts),

begins taunting a super-macho crooked sheriff (dynamic, jut-jawed Charles Napier) for his impotence. The more she teases him the more she unleashes in him a sadistic streak—and a masochistic one in herself—so that the tension that builds between them must inevitably be resolved in an orgy of either sex or violence. In the increasing suspense, as either alternative momentarily hangs in the balance before SuperAngel finally pushes the sheriff too far, we are able to see how both are tragically trapped by their sexual stereotypes: As a sexpot SuperAngel is expected to demand nothing less than perfection from her lovers; as a he-man the sheriff must be the ultimate in virility. Anyway, she incites him to such rage that she ends up stomped then electrocuted in her bathtub. Even though this sequence moves as lightning-fast as the famous shower scene in Psycho it is too grisly not to exact its toll. So shocking, so visceral is it in its impact that it's impossible—unless you're pretty unthinking or insensitive—to laugh heartily at the subsequent lusty adventures of Pitts, now on the run since he's the prime suspect in his wife's brutal murder. However, Meyer himself is more serious than ever before. The pioneer and now past master in projecting all-American male sex fantasies on the screen is in Supervixens reflecting the reverberations of women's liberation. Before our very eyes sex goddess dreams turn into nightmares. Indeed, so powerful is SuperAngel that she reincarnates herself as Supervixen, now as good as she was previously evil. With her Pitts finds idyllic bliss—until the sheriff reappears for a final battle with the couple.

A blue-collar surrealist, Meyer used a camera as expressively and rigorously as Hitchcock or Antonioni. In his adept hands a vast desert expanse—virtually the entire setting for Supervixens—becomes a moral landscape. In this film it's as if he had gone and explored, as never before to such an extent, the dark underside of his erotic myths. It's Supervixens, not Day of the Locust, that's genuinely apocalyptic."

After I read that description of the bathtub murder scene, I thought, *I hafta see that!* And sure enough, the scene between Charles Napier and Shari Eubank is one of the great violent sequences in seventies cinema. Right up there with the climax of *Straw Dogs* and the rape in *Deliverance*, as well as the only legitimate rival to Hitchcock's shower scene in *Psycho.*★

Did the power of that scene *"freeze the smile on my face"* like it did Kevin? No. At least not for the same reason that Kevin wrote. In fact, that scene *does* derail the picture, but more because nothing else in the movie can compete with its power. Also, like a lot of Meyer's seventies movies, the final act dissolves into a brand of silliness that I'm not a fan of. But so what? The Napier and Eubank scene is *so fucking* incredible, if you exited the movie theatre once it was over, you'd received *more* than your money's worth for your entertainment dollar. I considered writing about *Supervixens* for this book, but I knew I couldn't match the verve and insight that Thomas brought to bear on the picture.

Also I included that review pretty much in its entirety because it's one of my favorite of Kevin's pieces. But also because it's *classic Kevin. Supervixens* is really, really good, but it ain't *that* good.

That scene is incredible, the rest of the movie—not so much.

Oftentimes the movies Kevin rhapsodized about couldn't live up to his prose. *Caged Heat* is really good, but it's not as good as Kevin Thomas said it was.

I love *Macon County Line*, but it's not as powerful as Kevin suggests it is (and Max Baer Jr.'s performance is no way as good).

Was Kevin Thomas writing about the movies he *wished* they were? Maybe. Hey, I did that all through the terrible eighties or else I wouldn't have liked anything. But sometimes if you read Kevin's review first, the qualities Kevin attributed to the movie, he actually bestowed on the film by virtue of suggestion. There

---

★ Gary Goetzman told me it was Charles Napier's performance in that amazing scene that led Jonathan Demme to cast him in his breakout above-ground role in Demme's *Citizens Band*.

is a depth to *Caged Heat* if you see it after reading Kevin's review that is simply not there if you watch it cold. And even though *Supervixens* is more spectacular and doesn't need Thomas' help quite as much, same goes for it too (excuse me while I rhapsodize about a time when the *Los Angeles Times* applauded "*the king of male sexual fantasies*" for "*exploring the dark underside of his erotic myths*").

Here's a sampling of some of my favorite pieces that Kevin Thomas wrote about some of my favorite exploitation flicks of the seventies.

Death Race 2000

"*A fine little exploitation picture that not only beat the similarly themed Rollerball to theaters but proved to be more coherent and pertinent of the two pictures, although made for far less money in far less time.*"

The Pom Pom Girls

"*No wonder The Pom Pom Girls has been setting records for Crown International in various cities. . . . It's an upbeat, sexy, action-filled tale of contemporary high school life that embodies perfectly what most teen-agers wish their lives were like. . . .*

Talented young writer-producer-director Joseph Ruben, in projecting this postadolescent fantasy, observes the rules. His young people raise hell, but they aren't vicious, cruel or destructive. Even though vehemently anti-intellectual they're a pretty likable bunch, possessing some dimension and, most important, vulnerability. As a result—and because it has an abundant sense of humor—The Pom Pom Girls succeeds as an evocation of the kind of freedom that youth symbolizes but practically no one, today or in the past, ever really gets to enjoy."

The Lords of Flatbush

"*With poignant perception, The Lords of Flatbush suggests that growing up in the '50s was pretty much the same in Brooklyn as it was in San*

Rafael or Modesto (American Graffiti) or even a dying Texas town (The Last Picture Show).

In each instance we're shown high school kids fighting off boredom and struggling with the conflict between their sexual frustrations and an arbitrary, hypocritical moral code. . . .

That The Lords of Flatbush was shot in 16mm (for $380,000) and then blown up to 35 serves only to heighten its sense of reality's harshness. Closer in spirit to Mean Streets—but not as despairing—than to American Graffiti, it is a very New Yorkish film, with its emphasis on characterization and dialogue rather than visual style. . . . Its creators clearly know their people well and care for them deeply, inviting us to share their feelings. A film of acute observation and telling nuances, The Lords of Flatbush is full of devastating vignettes."

Hollywood Boulevard

"At least as far back as Merton of the Movies (1924) Hollywood has been turning its cameras on itself, generally with satirical and often savage intent.

But there's never been anything quite like Hollywood Boulevard, an outrageous, often hilarious spoof of the zany world of low-budget exploitation film-making. And what better company to produce such an effort than Roger Corman's New World Pictures?

To be sure, New World knows its audience too well to attempt anything like an authentic glimpse of the actual hectic, often ruthless and desperate existence of aspiring young talent. Rather, it has played everything very, very broad, making certain there's plenty of fast action and above-the-waist nudity to satisfy the fans of the very films it's making fun of. Yet it is also sufficiently imaginative and knowledgeable to amuse film buffs."

Malibu High

"The title Malibu High suggests a bouncy summer romance featuring sand, surf and bikinis.

Actually, it's anything but that. It tells of an 18-year-old girl (Jill Lansing, an inexperienced but intense young actress) who hates school and is on the verge of flunking out and despises her nagging mother whom she blames for her father's suicide. When her boyfriend (Stuart Taylor) throws her over for a rich girl, that's the last straw. In revenge, she decides to seduce her teachers into giving her A's, turns hooker to get money to buy the luxuries she craves and discovers she gets a kick out of killing people.

All this is as sordid as it sounds, but whether by accident or design director Irv Berwick and writers John Buckley and Tom Singer so identify with their heroine that the film becomes a surprisingly compassionate study in obsession.

They never make fun of the absurdity of her determination to graduate from high school merely as a fierce point of pride nor do they satirize her complete naivete as she becomes a pawn for her underworld pimp (Garth Howard), who gets her to kill for him but treats her with unfailing—and therefore seemingly authentic—tenderness and respect.

This girl brings to mind the frustrated nurse of that B classic The Honeymoon Killers, who would never have turned murderer had she not fallen for a greasy little gigolo, and also Truffaut's equally obsessive Adele H. in her extreme reaction to Taylor's rejection of her.

Produced at the age of 18 by Lawrence D. Foldes, who claims to be Hollywood's youngest producer—and he may well be—Malibu High is often awkward and crude yet is too oddly compelling to be dismissed as the trash it would seem so clearly to be. The girl's story may be utterly improbable but her corruption is persuasive; in this, she's not so unlike Louise Brooks' Lulu in Pandora's Box. Malibu High is a seedy, sleazy little gem best appreciated by cineastes."

When I read his review of *Malibu High* I ran out and saw it that very night. And he was entirely correct. As cruddy as this little tawdry flick was, it had an undeniable power. And the lead actress, Jill Lansing (who never appeared in anything else again), proceeded to get better and better as the film unspooled, till by the final reel, when she's standing naked, towering over the body of one of her victims, she delivers a disreputable tour de force on par with Georgina Spelvin in *The Devil in Miss Jones*.

One review Kevin Thomas wrote in 1980, that I read when I was eighteen years old, was to have a significant impact on my film work seventeen years later. It was a review for the Lewis Teague–directed, John Sayles–scripted *Jaws* rip-off, *Alligator*.

At the time, Sayles had just made his directorial debut with the minuscule-budgeted independent film *The Return of the Secaucus Seven*. Which, as opposed to the films he was paid to write, was not a genre film. In fact, it's the story of a reunion of some sixties former college student radicals, predating Lawrence Kasdan's *The Big Chill*. In his review of the giant alligator movie, which he referred to as *"well made and lots of fun,"* Kevin focused on the two lead performances of Robert Forster and Robin Riker, who, he wrote, *"are delightful and relaxed under Teague's direction."* But then he wrote the line that was to stay in my mind all those years later.

"There's an easy going naturalness to Forster and Riker that makes them seem like one of the couples in Return of the Secaucus Seven."

Now that people barely remember *The Return of the Secaucus Seven*, that might not read as such a big deal, but then *Secaucus Seven* was the critical darling of the year. And to imply the genre characters in a *Jaws* rip-off about a giant alligator contained the same verisimilitude as the independent hit of the season was a bold proclamation.

I saw *Alligator* three times that year (one of those times was on a triple feature with *Rolling Thunder* and a Canadian trucker flick called *High-Ballin'* with Peter Fonda and Jerry Reed), and I agreed wholeheartedly with Kevin Thomas about the charm of Forster and Riker. So much so, when I did my top ten movies at the end of the year, and wrote my little awards (best actress, best actor, best director) it was Robert Forster who was my choice for best male performance of that year (Robert De Niro for *Raging Bull* was number two).

Fifteen years later, I was writing my adaptation of Elmore Leonard's *Rum Punch* (which I retitled *Jackie Brown*), and I had to consider who was to play the novel's likable lead male character, bail bondsman Max Cherry. I had a few choices. Gene Hackman was an obvious choice, as was Paul Newman. I also considered John Saxon. But there was something about Forster in *Alligator* that really stuck with me. I watched the movie again and felt that the character from *Alligator* could *be* Max Cherry, just fifteen years earlier. So I started writing the script as if he was, right down to the discussion with Jackie about his thinning hair. Would I have done that without Kevin Thomas' highlighting Forster so positively in his review?

No.

In the end, what made Kevin Thomas so unique in the world of seventies and eighties film criticism, he seemed like one of the only few practitioners who truly enjoyed their job, and consequently, their life. I loved reading him growing up and practically considered him a friend.

In 1994 I won an award for *Pulp Fiction* from the *Los Angeles Film Critics Association*. When I stepped up to the podium and looked out before the audience of L.A. critics, my first remarks to the room were: "*Gee, thanks, now I finally know what Kevin Thomas looks like.*"

New Hollywood in the Seventies

The Post-Sixties Anti-Establishment Auteurs vs. The Movie Brats

In Peter Biskind's historical examination of New Hollywood in the seventies, *Easy Riders, Raging Bulls*, he relates a story of Dennis Hopper, fresh off his *Easy Rider* success, having dinner with Peter Bogdanovich and his wife Polly Platt and legendary Old Hollywood director George Cukor.

During the dinner, Hopper apparently mocked the old man's generation saying, "*We're gonna bury you.*" With *we* meaning Dennis and his anti-establishment brethren, and *you* meaning Cukor and the rest of the grumpy old farts still making movies at the end of the sixties. Bogdanovich and Platt were shocked and horrified to see this old master, whose work they revered, treated with such an alarming lack of respect. "*I hated Dennis for that,*" Peter told me decades later. And if the story went down how it's been told, Hopper deserved a punch in the nose.

Nevertheless, it does illustrate the attitude that Dennis' *Hippie Hollywood* had about *Old Hollywood* as it gave way to *New Hollywood*.

These new filmmakers had an anti-establishment perspective. To them, John Ford, John Wayne, and Howard Hawks were the establishment. Charlton Heston was the establishment. Julie Andrews, Blake Edwards, and Rock Hudson were the establishment. And since *My Fair Lady* was definitely the establishment, so too was George Cukor.

The Post-Sixties Anti-Establishment Auteurs had just won a revolution. The old studio Broadway musical based extravaganza (*The Sound of Music, My Fair Lady, Hello, Dolly!*) was *finally* at long last dead (many filmmakers today can't wait for the day they can say that about superhero movies). The Hays Code was dead and the rating board was alive.

You could make a movie about any subject (practically) and the material wouldn't have to be compromised. The peekaboo parlor games when it came to sexuality that Hitchcock was forced to play could be a thing of the past. And if you made it—thanks to the rating board—the distributor could release it across the country without some hick sheriff in some jerkwater county claiming you broke their obscenity laws.

These Anti-Establishment Auteurs were as sorry to see the old studio system go bust as the French Revolutionaries were to see Marie Antoinette vacate Versailles.

Now to be clear, the Post-Sixties Anti-Establishment Auteurs were: *Robert Altman, Bob Rafelson, Hal Ashby, Paul Mazursky, Arthur Penn, Sam Peckinpah, Frank Perry, Michael Ritchie, William Friedkin, Richard Rush, John Cassavetes,* and *Jerry Schatzberg.*

Other strong but less prolific members of this group were: *Floyd Mutrux, Alan Arkin, Ossie Davis, Paul Williams* (not the diminutive songwriter), *James Frawley, Francis Ford Coppola* (at the time), *Stuart Hagmann, Melvin Van Peebles, James Bridges, Brian De Palma* (at the time), *Monte Hellman, Harvey Hart,* and of course the *Easy Rider* trio *Dennis Hopper, Peter Fonda,* and *Jack Nicholson.* These were the Hollywood Hills Hippies. The Malibu

Beach Beatniks. And it was the foreign directors of the fifties and sixties (plus *Orson Welles)* that had made them want to be film-makers. But it was the counterculture that had made them want to be artists.

After the devastation of Europe and Asia during World War Two, once countries started making movies again, they found that they were making them for a much more adult audience than existed before the war. And world cinema proceeded to get more and more adult as the fifties turned into the sixties.

However, in America, despite the best efforts of men like Stanley Kramer and Otto Preminger, Hollywood movies still remained stubbornly immature and committed to the idea of *fun for the whole family.* But with the rise of the sixties counterculture, the explosion of a youth culture movement, the new maturity that was introduced to popular music, and the excitement generated by films like *Bonnie and Clyde, The Graduate,* and especially the surprise success of Dennis Hopper's *Easy Rider,* a New Hollywood was ushered in. An adult-oriented Hollywood. A Hollywood with a sixties' sensibility and an anti-establishment agenda.

And by 1970 this New Hollywood *was* Hollywood. And films left over from that other sensibility like Billy Wilder's *The Private Life of Sherlock Holmes,* Blake Edwards' *Darling Lili,* Vincente Minnelli's *On a Clear Day You Can See Forever,* Guy Green's *A Walk in the Spring Rain,* George Stevens' *The Only Game in Town,* William Wyler's *The Liberation of L.B. Jones,* Alfred Hitchcock's *Topaz,* and Howard Hawks' *Rio Lobo* were deemed dead on arrival. And except for Edwards' and Wilder's films, those films *were* dead on arrival (though I can somewhat make a case for Wyler's *L.B. Jones).* But the attitude of both the hip critics and the audience of the day wasn't that much different from Dennis Hopper's at that infamous dinner.

Fuck George Cukor! Fuck George Stevens! Fuck William Wyler! Fuck Howard Hawks!

Like the Movie Brat generation that came after them, these Anti-Establishment Auteurs watched old movies growing up too. But unlike Bogdanovich, Spielberg, Scorsese, and Big John Milius, when *this* era of filmmakers watched old movies on television, they weren't as enamored of what they saw. When *they* watched John Ford westerns they were usually appalled by the jingoistic white supremacy on display. When *they* watched *The Searchers* they didn't see a conflicted man trying to find his place in a society that had outlived his usefulness. They saw a movie about an Indian-hating racist bastard who is ultimately offered absolution by a grateful (white) community. And they saw a director who co-signed that absolution and expected the audience to do the same.

They rejected the morality of the wrap-up at the end of Ford's *Fort Apache*. Where Henry Fonda's genocidal cavalry officer is lionized in death for the greater good of the cavalry, esprit de corps, and for white America as a whole.

The Anti-Establishment Auteurs wanted to remake John Ford movies, but not the way Scorsese and Schrader would do with *Taxi Driver* and *Hardcore*. They wanted to remake *Fort Apache* from the Apaches' perspective. And in the case of Arthur Penn with *Little Big Man*, and Ralph Nelson with *Soldier Blue*, and Robert Aldrich (not post-sixties, hardly a hippie, but absolutely anti-establishment) with *Ulzana's Raid*, they did.

The reason to do historical pictures in this new climate was to *finally* examine and demonstrate America's history of fascism, racism, and hypocrisy. All the elements that Old Hollywood spent fifty years whitewashing in the historical pictures of old.

Jesse James *wasn't* Henry King's dashing Tyrone Power, he *was* Robert Duvall's homicidal religious fanatic in Philip Kaufman's *The Great Northfield Minnesota Raid.*

Billy the Kid *wasn't* Johnny Mack Brown's smiling charmer or even Paul Newman's brooding method acting turn in *The Left*

Handed Gun, he *was* Michael J. Pollard's creepy little punk in Stan Dragoti's *Dirty Little Billy* or Kris Kristofferson's Billy in Sam Peckinpah's *Pat Garrett and Billy the Kid*. A Billy who slays with all the callousness of a modern-day serial killer.

Gen. George Armstrong Custer *wasn't* Errol Flynn's long-haired hard-drinking two-fisted hero, he *was* Richard Mulligan's racial cleansing nincompoop in Arthur Penn's *Little Big Man*.

Wyatt Earp *wasn't* Burt Lancaster's ramrod-straight lawman, he *was* Harris Yulin's fascist cop in Frank Perry's *"Doc."* In Perry (and writer Pete Hamill's) version of events, there wasn't so much a gunfight at the O.K. Corral than Wyatt and his brothers just murdering the Clantons in cold blood. And the reason is made abundantly clear, power and money.

During times of great political turmoil, modern political issues are always conveniently found in America's past. When Arthur Penn, Robert Aldrich, and Ralph Nelson take on the subject of the American Indian wars every parallel with the war in Vietnam is encouraged. To the extent that Penn cast an Asian woman to play Hoffman's American Indian bride who's savagely slaughtered by the cavalry wearing blue coats in *Little Big Man* (*just in case it's not obvious to everyone*).

In Abraham Polonsky's *Tell Them Willie Boy Is Here*, Robert Blake's outlaw Indian on the run for a self-defense murder represents a modern-day Black Panther political fugitive. And Robert Redford's golden-haired posse-leading marshal represents the older white male western archetype. And just in case we don't get it, he's named *Coop*, as in Gary Cooper.

Unlike the Movie Brats who followed them, these filmmakers didn't want to do their version of *Psycho* (*Dressed to Kill*) or *The Searchers* (*Taxi Driver* and *Hardcore*) or *Little Caesar* (*The Godfather*) or *Flash Gordon* (*Star Wars*) or *Bringing Up Baby* (*What's Up, Doc?*).

When these directors would redo films, it's films in the spirit of *Fellini*, and *Truffaut*, and *Renoir* that they aspired to. When Paul

Mazursky was faced with the task of following his surprise smash hit *Bob & Carol & Ted & Alice*, he placed his Fellini influence front and center with his paraphrased take on the Italian's film *8½*, which he titled *Alex in Wonderland*. When faced with his own mortality due to his recent open heart surgery director Bob Fosse looked inward and guess what? He saw *8½* too.

Bonnie and Clyde was originally developed by screenwriters Robert Benton and David Newman as a Hollywood movie for François Truffaut. And when Truffaut turned it down (*he was too scared. Thank god!*), who did they get? Arthur Penn. The only Hollywood director working at a studio level who, in 1965, tried to do a French New Wave–style movie in America, *Mickey One*, starring Warren Beatty.

Almost all of Frank Perry's movies feel like American French films. But he wasn't alone; Coppola's *The Rain People*, Schatzberg's *Puzzle of a Downfall Child*, Altman's *Images* and later *Three Women*, and Kershner's *Loving* and *Up the Sandbox* all play like American versions of European movies.

The first half of the New Hollywood seventies seemed to want to test the limits of both its newfound freedom and the type of edgy material it was allowed to make. And that's why cinema lovers still enjoy discovering those films to this day.

But to the casual moviegoer, who didn't know the difference between New Hollywood and Old Hollywood and lived someplace other than New York City, Los Angeles, San Francisco, or a college campus, all they knew was, if you see a movie, you'd kinda like to understand it.

Did they understand 2001?

How 'bout Catch-22?

How 'bout Brewster McCloud?

How 'bout Little Murders?

Without a critic to tell them what to think did they understand Five Easy Pieces?

Did they misunderstand Joe?

You see a movie you wanna like the hero.

Do you like Jeff Bridges and Sam Waterston in Rancho Deluxe?

Of course not, they're assholes!

You like Donald Sutherland's Hawkeye in MASH.

But do you like Sutherland's Alex in Alex in Wonderland?

Are we even supposed to?

Or work from the expectation that there will be a hero.

Is McCabe a hero?

Is Travis Bickle?

Is Maj. Charles Rane?

Is Elliott Gould's Philip Marlowe?

Are Freebie and the Bean?

Is Warren Beatty's George Roundy in *Shampoo*? I'm not just making fun of people *back then* who didn't *get it*. I'm making fun of people *now*.

I screened *Shampoo* to an Oscar winning screenwriter who had never seen it, and when it was over, her response was; "*So it's just about a guy who's trying to open up a hair salon?*"

And yeah, I'm having a good laugh at Callie Khouri's expense, but she isn't the only person to say that.

The casual moviegoer knew movies had rougher language than before, but that doesn't mean they were ready for *The Last Detail*. They knew movies were more violent now. They liked that *True Grit* was rougher than the usual John Wayne western, they liked the street realism of *The French Connection*, they liked it when Dustin Hoffman's worm turns in *Straw Dogs*, they liked *Dirty Harry* shooting Black Panthers while he chewed on a hot dog, but that doesn't mean they were ready for the throat-slitting scene in *The Wild Bunch*, or the singing-in-the-rain scene in *A Clockwork Orange*, or the male sodomy rape in *Deliverance*, or the climax of *Joe*.

Audiences liked the new risqué elements in movies like *Bob & Carol & Ted & Alice*, *The Owl and the Pussycat*, and *Shampoo*. They liked the funny discussions of sex in *Summer of '42*, they thought it was funny when Hot Lips got exposed in the shower in *MASH*, but that didn't mean they were ready for the *tushy scene* in *Where's Poppa?* when Ruth Gordon bites George Segal on the ass.

Maybe they liked Julie Christie's and Donald Sutherland's making love in Nicolas Roeg's *Don't Look Now*. Maybe (like my mom) they thought Ron O'Neal and Sheila Frazier's bathtub scene in Gordon Parks Jr.'s *Super Fly* was sexy. But were they ready for Oliver Reed and Alan Bates' nude wrestling match in Ken Russell's *Women in Love?* Were they disturbed, aroused, or both by Susan George's rape in Sam Peckinpah's *Straw Dogs?* And *if* they were disturbed, were they disturbed *right away*, or only at the end? And was *that* the disturbing part?

Sequences like these instilled a growing sense of anxiety at what audiences *may* be subjected to inside a darkened theatre with a room full of strangers. I mean, if you bought a ticket to Russ Meyer's *Beyond the Valley of the Dolls* you probably had a good idea what you were getting into. But most audiences who bought a ticket to see *Deliverance* didn't know they paid money to see Ned Beatty get fucked in the ass.

Audiences who didn't live in New York or Los Angeles, or didn't read the *New York Times*, or the *New Yorker*, or the *Village Voice*, began to become afraid of modern movies. After a steady diet of movies like *The Panic in Needle Park*, *Joe*, *Lenny*, *Play It as It Lays*, *The Sporting Club*, *The Hunting Party*, *Last Summer*, and *Dusty and Sweets McGee*, regular moviegoers were becoming weary of modern American movies. The darkness, the drug use, the embrace of sensation—the violence, the sex, and the sexual violence. But even more than that, they became weary of the *anti-everything cynicism*. As Pauline Kael suggested at the beginning of the decade, are the best movies suggesting the only sensible recourse for Americans is to get stoned?

Was everything a bummer?

Was everything a drag?

Was every movie about some guy with problems?

For hip audiences the hero dying futilely at the end of the picture was a *come-on*. It reaffirmed their pose, *you can't win.* When Robert Blake and Stacy Keach died at the end of *Electra Glide in Blue* and *The New Centurions*, and when Fonda and Hopper bought it in *Easy Rider* it was senseless and *tragically ironic*. But that felt good because it reaffirmed the senselessness and tragic irony of American life. The senselessness of their deaths *made* them heroes. In the first half of the seventies you weren't a hero for fighting a war overseas and killing a bunch of enemy soldiers. You were a hero if you fought the war, went back home, and got shot in a liquor store robbery. But that's the Jack Nicholson audience, the Elliott Gould audience, and the Dustin Hoffman audience. Burt Reynolds and Charles Bronson audiences didn't feel that way.

When Burt Reynolds and Robert Aldrich's follow-up to *The Longest Yard* came out, the gloomy cop film *Hustle*, it opened up to dynamite business . . . *until* audiences found out Burt died at the end. And it was a seventies cynical death. Burt's audience wasn't cynical, they liked America just fine. They'd rather watch him crack jokes about his early movies and see what clothes he wore on Johnny Carson for free, than pay to see a bummer.

If you wanted to watch a western-western, it was usually directed by Andrew MacLaglen or his buddy Burt Kennedy and starred old farts like John Wayne, Kirk Douglas, Robert Mitchum, James Stewart, Henry Fonda, or Dean Martin. The youngest guys still doing straight westerns were James Garner and George Peppard. But if it was a true seventies picture, and not a nostalgic throwback for an aging star's aging audience, then it was an *anti-western*. Almost every genre film made for a while was an *Anti-Genre*

Film. With the idea behind the film being to expose the absurdity and unsavory politics that have hidden underneath said genre since the beginning of Hollywood.

And then suddenly a string of movies, *The Last Picture Show, What's Up, Doc?, The Godfather, American Graffiti, Paper Moon, Jaws, Carrie, Star Wars, Close Encounters of the Third Kind,* that were easily understandable, cut for maximum audience enjoyment—not artistic indulgence—and were new takes on old familiar genres. And these movies ended up being the films the public was waiting for.

The Movie Brats, so dubbed because of Michael Pye's book-length critical study of them, were the first film-school educated generation of young white male directors raised on television, who emerged and ended up defining the decade with their snazzy pop flicks. The movement had as its members, *Francis Ford Coppola, Peter Bogdanovich, Brian De Palma, Martin Scorsese, George Lucas, John Milius, Steven Spielberg,* and *Paul Schrader.*

Coppola, the first film school graduate to break into the business, first with Roger Corman and later with Warner Bros., preceded the others from film students to professional filmmakers to auteurs by a decade. And as such he was sort of this group's artistic and spiritual leader (Godfather?). A spot he shared sweetly with John Cassavetes on one end of the scale, and Roger Corman on the other. As John Milius once told me, "*We all wanted to make Hollywood a better place because we were there. But those were Francis' dreams! He was the only one who tried to do anything about it. And in a way you could say all those dreams failed. Hollywood isn't a better place because E.T. made three hundred million dollars. Spielberg's place is a better place.*"

Coppola's championship of Lucas and Milius is well known (Francis produced both of Lucas' first two films, *THX-1138* and *American Graffiti.* And directed Milius' script for *Apocalypse Now,* which started life as a directorial project for Lucas). But his behind-the-scenes support for Scorsese is lesser known. According to Milius, "*Nobody championed the young Scorsese like Francis.*" At one point suggesting Scorsese should direct *The Godfather* sequel, it was Francis who suggested Scorsese to Ellen Burstyn when she wanted a young director to helm *Alice Doesn't Live Here Anymore.* He also suggested Scorsese to Al Pacino and producer Martin Bregman when they went looking for a new director when John Avildsen dropped out of *Serpico.* And according to Scorsese, Coppola even passed on a copy of the *Mean Streets* script to Mr. Pacino.

Coppola and Bogdanovich shared a company together, along with William Friedkin, called *The Directors Company.* It produced one Coppola contribution, *The Conversation* (one of his best), two Bogdanovich films, *Paper Moon* (one of his best) and *Daisy Miller* (one of his most underrated), and absolutely no Friedkin (even though he got a nice slice of those *Paper Moon* profits).

Schrader wrote *Taxi Driver, Raging Bull,* and *The Last Temptation of Christ* for Scorsese, *Obsession* for De Palma, and an aborted first draft of *Close Encounters* for Spielberg. John Milius would produce Schrader's second directorial effort, *Hardcore.*

Milius would dictate over the telephone Quint's speech about the USS *Indianapolis* for his buddy Spielberg and would later write and produce Spielberg's epic comedy *1941.*

Brian De Palma would introduce Robert De Niro to Scorsese, and be the one to hand him Schrader's script for *Taxi Driver.*

And De Palma and Lucas conducted joint casting sessions for *Carrie* and *Star Wars.* Because Lucas was quiet and De Palma did all the talking, the young actors thought George was Brian's assistant.

These filmmakers were and looked young. And they also looked talented and dynamic. Just look at them during this period.

Spielberg naked, except for baseball cap, dirty tennis shoes, and cut off white Levi shorts sitting in Bruce the mechanical shark's mouth on the set of *Jaws*.

Scorsese in his crisp white button-down shirt on the set of *Taxi Driver* scratching his black beard next to Robert De Niro in his weirded-out Travis Bickle mode.

Bogdanovich in a sleek black leather jacket on the set of *Paper Moon* squatting down on his haunches so he's eye level with little eight-year-old Tatum O'Neal in her Addie Loggins overalls.

Lucas almost dashingly handsome in his shearling coat on the set of *Star Wars* sitting in a director's chair alongside Alec Guinness wrapped up in his Obi-Wan Kenobi robe.

Milius in desert headgear to protect him from the Moroccan sun on the set of *The Wind and the Lion* sitting alongside John Huston looking mythic in his ambassador uniform costume.

De Palma, young and slim, viewfinder dangling from his neck, yucking it up with Tom Smothers and Orson Welles on the set of his first studio feature *Get to Know Your Rabbit*.

Coppola in the pages of *Life* magazine dressed in a colorful Hawaiian shirt (trimmer than he's ever looked) traipsing around the massive sets he built in the Philippines for *Apocalypse Now*.

Schrader, built up and beefy like a high school wrestling coach, posing in front of a poster for Joseph H. Lewis' *Gun Crazy* in the pages of *Esquire*.

That *Esquire* article, February 1975, was called the *Ninth Era* and was written by L. M. Kit Carson (*David Holzman* himself). In Kit's piece he's the first to identify this growing group of filmmakers who are taking shape to lead the industry. But Kit's piece prophesied a whole new top of the line. Directors. Producers. Writers. Actors.

Under actors he had *Robert De Niro, Pam Grier*, and *Joe Don Baker*.

Under producers he had *Mike Medavoy, Gerald Ayres, Julia* and *Michael Phillips, Tony Bill*, and *Lawrence Gordon*.

Under writers he had *Schrader, Robert Towne, David Ward, Joan Tewkesbury,* and *Willard Huyck* and *Gloria Katz.*

Under directors he has *Spielberg, Scorsese, Lucas, De Palma, Hal Ashby, Terrence Malick,* and *Ralph Bakshi.*

In his 1979 seminal study of seventies cinema titled *American Film Now,* James Monaco called the group *The Wiz Kids* and included *Bogdanovich, Lucas, De Palma, Spielberg, Scorsese,* and adds *William Friedkin* to the mix. While *Coppola* is given *Pantheon* status alongside *Cassavetes, Altman, Ritchie,* and *Mazursky.*

Diane Jacobs called her 1977 book *Hollywood Renaissance,* and included as *her* Pantheon *John Cassavetes, Robert Altman, Francis Ford Coppola, Martin Scorsese, Paul Mazursky, Michael Ritchie,* and *Hal Ashby.*

And Michael Pye's study with the name that stuck, *The Movie Brats,* kept the film school aspect literal by only including *Coppola, Lucas, De Palma, Milius, Scorsese,* and the wunderkind *Spielberg.*

What set *the Movie Brats* apart from the earlier generation of directors that had come before them, even more then their youth and film school education, was the fact that (*mostly*) they were film geeks.

It's almost amusing to think of a time when filmmakers took an attitude of almost indifference when talking about cinema as an art form. But before Scorsese and Bogdanovich and Spielberg that was the case. Even the generation just before them, the *Anti-Establishment Auteurs* didn't talk about movies the way they did. Bogdanovich talks about the golden age of Hollywood with more authority than any director since François Truffaut. No doubt (*at that time*) Peter had seen more movies in one year then Altman had seen in his life (does anybody really think Altman watched *other people's* movies?). Most filmmakers of earlier eras wouldn't be able to read Paul Schrader's *Transcendental Style in Film,* no less write it.

They were the first generation of filmmakers who grew up

watching movies not just in cinemas, but on television. Which meant they saw a lot more movies. They were also the first generation of filmmakers to grow up watching television on television. The directors before them (*Peckinpah, Altman, Ritchie, Mark Rydell, Sydney Pollack, John Frankenheimer, Ralph Nelson, George Roy Hill, Don Siegel*) were too busy *making* television to watch it.

When *the Movie Brats* were young they grooved on movies the Anti-Establishment Auteurs wouldn't be caught dead watching, god forbid being forced to make. Henry Levin's *Journey to the Center of the Earth*, Richard Fleischer's *20,000 Leagues Under the Sea*, George Pal's *The Time Machine*, Ken Annakin's *Swiss Family Robinson*, J. Lee Thompson's *The Guns of Navarone* (Spielberg can quote the entire James Robertson Justice prologue narration).

Roger Corman, to the generation of filmmakers that preceded the Movie Brats, was a low rent colleague. When Warren Beatty considered working with Corman on a Robert Towne script titled *The Long Ride Home* (made as *A Time for Killing* without Towne's name), Corman screened for Beatty his latest film *The Tomb of Ligeia*, also scripted by Towne. Beatty's response to Towne about *Tomb*: "*When I get married I don't expect my bride to be a virgin. But I'd rather she not be the biggest whore in town.*"

But Scorsese loves *Ligeia* so much he shows a clip of it in *Mean Streets*. To *the Movie Brats*, Roger Corman—even before he became a mentor—was a hero. They loved movies, dreamed movies, even received degrees in movies back when that was a dubious major. When the Anti-Establishment Auteurs did genre films they engaged in genre deconstruction. The Movie Brats embraced genre films for their own ends. They didn't want (*for the most part*) to make art film meditations on genre films, they wanted to make the best genre films ever made. When *Jaws* came out in 1975 it might not have been the best *film* ever made. But it was easily the best *movie* ever made. Nothing ever made before it even came close.

Because for the first time the man at the helm wasn't a Richard Fleischer or a Jack Smight or a Michael Anderson executing a studio assignment. But a natural born filmmaker genius who grooved on exactly this kind of movie and would kill himself to deliver the exact vision that was in his head.

Spielberg's command of *Jaws* showed how clumsy and badly timed most studio genre films were (*Logan's Run, Airport 1975, Towering Inferno,* the '70s James Bond movies).

This new generation didn't aspire, like the generation before them, to adapt the great literature of their day. *Catch-22, Slaughterhouse-Five, The Day of the Locust,* or *Little Big Man.* The books they were drawn to were more popular reads that they thought would make good movies. *Jaws, Carrie, The Godfather, The Last Picture Show, Addie Pray (Paper Moon).*

Also (for the most part) the Movie Brats entered the industry via exploitation cinema.

The Anti-Establishment Auteurs (for the most part) took themselves far, far too seriously to do exploitation films (television yes, drive-in fodder, no).

As far as they were concerned the American-International Pictures logo wasn't a studio presentation credit, it was a stigma. It was the home of horror flicks and biker flicks, over the hill stars (Ray Milland & Boris Karloff), slumming stars (Bette Davis), dubious stars (Vincent Price & Fabian), and the place where failed international productions starring Elizabeth Taylor and Peter O'Toole went to die.

But the Movie Brats were young enough to be the audiences that American-International Pictures were aiming for. They were young enough to see the films in actual drive-ins. They were the first generation of leading Hollywood filmmakers who watched Gordon Douglas' science fiction classic *Them! because* it was about giant ants.

In a way that was the reason that the Movie Brats wrestled the zeitgeist away from the Post-Sixties Anti-Establishment Auteurs that had started the New Hollywood era that the youngsters were thriving in; the hippy directors couldn't understand, or didn't want to understand, that some people watch movies about giant ants and take *Them!* seriously.

Sisters

(1973)

Unlike most of the other *Movie Brats* (Scorsese, Bogdanovich, Spielberg) and their later-day additions (Joe Dante, Allan Arkush, and John Landis), young Brian De Palma didn't grow up devotedly watching old movies on television. Nor did he keep scrapbooks, make notes, and keep files on index cards of all the movies he saw growing up (like Peter Bogdanovich and I did). You see, young Brian wasn't a *film geek*, he was a *science geek*. Keith Gordon's adolescent *Peter Miller* in *Dressed to Kill*, and in adult form, John Travolta's troubled cinema technician *Jack Terry* in *Blow Out* represent the young Mr. De Palma.

In *Blow Out* Travolta's Jack Terry might as well be describing De Palma himself when he was young to both Nancy Allen's Betty Boop–voiced *Sally* and the audience: "*It all started in school. I was the kind of kid who fixed radios, made my own stereo, won all the science fairs, you know the type.*"

The young Brian didn't really get into cinema until college, and even then it was under the guidance of New York theatre legend Wilford Leach. Brian De Palma doesn't become interested in cinema till after he's thoroughly explored theatre (apparently there existed one or two Brian De Palma–penned plays from that period).

But unlike Scorsese, Bogdanovich, and Spielberg, De Palma didn't pray at the altar of movies.

To Brian film was an artistic means to an end.

Similarly, his attraction to Hitchcock shouldn't be read as De Palma being overly invested in the mystery, suspense, horror genre. Even though Brian De Palma would be labeled "*the Modern Master of the Macabre*" (as the text reads over three-quarters of the *Dressed to Kill* one-sheet), it's pretty clear he's not an enthusiastic aficionado of the genre.

But while young Brian may not have been a student of the horror film genre, he was nevertheless drawn to it, because of its capacity for audience manipulation.

When young Brian discovered Hitchcock in school and started seriously examining him, it wasn't Hitchcock's themes that attracted him at first (save for *voyeurism*). It was Hitchcock's cinematic technique, and his practical application of that technique inside of his scenarios, that turned on the young De Palma.

Hitchcock went in for big suspense set pieces, which he usually accomplished through cinematic virtuosity or daring surprises in the narrative. And Hitchcock either pulled them off . . . (the merry-go-round sequence in *Strangers on a Train*, Marion Crane's murder in *Psycho*, the difficult murder of the KGB agent by Paul Newman and the farmer's wife in *Torn Curtain*, *The Birds* in the playground) . . . or he didn't . . . (the Mount Rushmore climax of *North by Northwest*, the rushed rooftop climax at the end of *To Catch a Thief*, the degrading handling of Anna Massey's dead corpse in the "potato sack scene" in *Frenzy*).

For Brian—a kid who tore apart his transistor radio just to see how it worked—to take Hitchcock's suspense set pieces and break them down to their individual components was, no doubt, attractive. But another aspect of Hitchcock's technique, which was not the norm for most of the Old Hollywood picture makers, that probably appealed to the younger De Palma was Hitchcock's *Cin-*

ema First–Camera First shooting style. The *normal* classic Hollywood movie sought for the audience to ignore the camera. Better for you to commit to this exercise of wide awake dreaming, if you *forget* you're watching a movie. So to emphasize or highlight the camera or camera movement was to call attention to the fact that the audience was watching a movie.

Why on earth would somebody want to do that?

Nevertheless, inspired by Murnau, Hitchcock, along with Max Ophuls, sought to give the huge 35mm cameras wings.

For all the huge movie stars that Alfred Hitchcock worked with, the 35mm film camera was always the real star of the show. Well, this approach to cinematic grammar suited the young student filmmaker. Brian De Palma didn't want to become a filmmaker to shoot footage of people talking to each other. I'm sure Brian watched *Rio Bravo* in college too. But unlike Bogdanovich, Scorsese, and me, he probably didn't dig it. He might have thought some of the lines were funny, but for the most part, I'm sure De Palma thought it was just a lot of Howard Hawks shooting footage of John Wayne talking to different people on that damn jail set.★

Same thing with *The Searchers*. I'm positive Brian thinks a

★ When I was attending my very first film festival—the 1992 edition of the Sundance Film Festival—with my first movie, *Reservoir Dogs*, I was introduced by Larry Estes (the man that greenlit *Sex, Lies, and Videotape*) to Gale Anne Hurd, who, due to *Terminator 2*, was the biggest movie producer in the world at that time, as well as being Mrs. Brian De Palma. Once we were introduced, I told her "*Your husband is my hero, but he won't like my movie.*"

"*Why don't you think he'll like it?*" she asked.

"*Because it's just people talking to each other,*" I told her. "*And he doesn't like movies of people talking to each other.*"

Then her face showed surprise, and she said, "*Wow, you really do know him! You're right, he doesn't like movies where people just talk to each other. He was talking about that just the other day.*"

whole lot of *The Searchers* is John Ford shooting John Wayne on a horse talking to Jeffrey Hunter.

And if he did think that, he'd be right.

But "*Hitch*" was different.

He was always *Cinema First–Camera First*.

Not the cinema of capturing actors reciting text.

Not the cinema of pretty pictures.

But an aggressive cinema that manipulated audiences with both its fluid visual grammar and its (at times) savage wit. De Palma's attraction to Hitchcock was always far less personal than Bog-danovich's appreciation for either Ford or Hawks, or John Carpen-ter's attraction to Hawks, or Paul Mazursky's attraction to Fellini, or John Woo's attraction to Jean-Pierre Melville, or Scorsese's attraction to Michael Powell, or my attraction to Sergio Leone, or Australia's Richard Franklin's (the second best to do Hitchcock-like thrillers in the eighties) genuine admiration for "Hitch" (like Bogdanovich, Franklin sought out the elder filmmaker when he was a young man).

Hitchcock's *cinematic fluency* was what young De Palma was enthralled with and wanted to appropriate as his own, less the man. Also, because of Hitchcock's commercial success, Brian realized filmgoing audiences accepted Cinema First–Camera First se-quences more easily when they were done inside thrillers or horror films. A pure cinema approach is always an option for a thriller or a horror film the way it isn't for other genres.

Along with Martin Scorsese (*Who's That Knocking at My Door*), Jim McBride (*David Holzman's Diary*), Shirley Clarke (*The Cool World*), Paul (not the diminutive singer-songwriter) Williams (*Out of It*), and Paul Morrissey (*Trash*), De Palma was one of the leading lights of *the New York New Wave*. Young Brian had directed three shoestring budgeted New York feature films by the time he experienced his first legitimate commercial success, the underground counterculture hippie comedy *Greetings*.

Greetings tells the sixties tale of three young men in Greenwich Village, *Jon* (Robert De Niro), *Lloyd* (Gerrit Graham), and *Paul* (Jonathan Warden), who are trying to dodge the draft (the film is called *Greetings* because that's the first word that appears on the telegram the army sends you on your draft notice). Then the film breaks down into three different storylines following the three lead protagonists. De Niro's budding pornography career trying to capture his Peeping Tom fetish on film, which he calls *"Peep Art."*★ Graham's Kennedy assassination obsession. And Warden going on a series of computer dates.

De Palma made it in partnership with his cowriter and producer Charles Hirsch. The way Richard Linklater's *Slacker* authentically captured *Austin Weird* before the phrase was put on T-shirts and sold at the Austin airport, *Greetings* was a sixties film that played like hippie notes from the underground. As many of the critics at the time remarked, it achieved an authenticity of a film made not just *for* a subculture but *by* it. In many ways, what Ragni and Rado did for Broadway by making *Hair*, De Palma and Hirsch did for film with *Greetings*. If a film version of *Hair* would have been attempted at that time, Brian De Palma would have been a leading contender to direct it. That's how strong his hippie bona fides were (in fact, his split-screen filming of the Performance Group's *Dionysus in '69* could have been his preparation for *Hair*).

While Martin Scorsese's *Who's That Knocking at My Door* barely received any theatrical release, *Greetings*, for an underground

---

★Recently I asked Mr. De Niro, was Jon's whole Peep Art jazz a real artistic expression, or was it just an excuse to shoot women taking off their clothes? He chuckled and said, "*I think it was just an excuse to film women getting undressed.*"

independent film, was just short of a phenomenon, especially in New York. It was the first film to star Robert De Niro, and it established both Gerrit Graham and Allen Garfield as two powerhouses in De Palma's stock company. It generated a sequel, *Hi, Mom!*, that brought back De Niro, Graham, and Garfield, and added Jennifer Salt to the mix.★ But one of the things that turned on its late sixties film-savvy audience is the cheeky way young De Palma took Godard's experimentation of film grammar (with a tiny sprinkle of Richard Lester) and played it for laughs. De Palma even engages in a full-scale spoof of cultural icon *Blow-Up* in the service of lampooning the Kennedy assassination conspiracy.

One of the things that separated *the New York New Wave* from their French counterparts was the New York guerilla filmmakers were usually segregated into their own neighborhoods. The characters in the French New Wave movies all walked or drove down the streets of the same Paris. At any point *Charlie* (Charles Aznavour) of *Shoot the Piano Player* could have bumped into *Arthur* or *Franz* (Claude Brasseur and Sami Frey) from *Band of Outsiders* in a café off the Boulevard St. Germain.

The hippie Greenwich Village draft dodgers of *Greetings*, the Canal Street sharkskin-wearing Italian-American tough talkers of *Who's That Knocking at My Door*, the black Harlem gang members of *The Cool World*, the Alphabet City strung-out junkies of *The Connection*, the Factory freaks of *Flesh*, *Heat*, and *Trash*, the Long Island high school kids of *Out of It*, and lonely apartment dwelling David Holzman might as well inhabit different New Yorks. I

★Actress Jennifer Salt was the forerunner to Nancy Allen in De Palma's work. Appearing in his first film, *The Wedding Party*, and stealing the show in *Murder à la Mod*, then the colead of *Hi, Mom!* and *Sisters*. Apparently she and De Palma lived together for a while during their Greenwich Village years and she was the centerpiece of his dynamic short film *Jennifer*.

mentioned that once to Scorsese and he agreed, "*They were from different countries.*"

Despite having said that, the hippies in *Greetings* break out of their neighborhoods in a way unthinkable for the characters in Scorsese or Morrissey's movies. Way before Ken Shapiro would shoot himself, guerilla-style, singing and dancing his way down Madison Avenue in *The Groove Tube* as amused passersby gape at him on camera, De Palma would stage big run-and-gun scenes in front of larger public places without a permit. The famous four-minute-long one-take of De Niro and Allen Garfield in front of the Whitney Museum (the most hysterical sequence in the film; when it comes to great acting partners for De Niro, before Harvey Keitel, there was Allen Garfield). Gerrit Graham's long-lens assassination in front of the Met. With De Palma's early films you get a real sense of the New York acting scene back then. The performers are almost all young, class-attending, small theatrical production–performing actors of the West Village scene. De Niro, Garfield, Graham, Finley, Salt, Jill Clayburgh, Charles Durning, Jared Martin, Margo Norton, Rutanya Alda, Peter Maloney, Roz Kelly, and many others that didn't do too many movies, concentrating more on the theatre. And that includes the black Living Theatre actors who scared the living shit out of the white crew on *Hi, Mom!* for the *Be Black Baby* sequence ("*Those guys were scary,*" De Palma confirmed to *Cinefantastique* magazine).

Taken as a collective, they all fill the frame with a late sixties zeitgeist authenticity.

After the success of *Greetings*, De Palma and Charles Hirsch wrote a sequel, *Hi, Mom!* (at one point called *Son of Greetings*) that followed the adventures of De Niro's character Jon (once he returns from Vietnam). First he tries to turn his *Peep Art* into a commercial enterprise, getting the backing of smut film producer Joe Banner (returning Allen Garfield). And later he joins a black radical theatre group called *The Living Theatre* in their off-off-Broadway production of *Be Black Baby*. And eventually he drifts into urban terrorism.

While *Greetings* was a zeitgeist explosion of its time captured on film, *Hi, Mom!* is one of the top five movies in De Palma's canon (the others being *Carrie, Dressed to Kill, Blow Out,* and *Scarface*). It appears, at the beginning De Palma planned on designing it like the first film with three (sorta) competing storylines. Jon's attempt to turn his *Peep Art* into a real movie, Gerrit Graham's (a different character than Lloyd) involvement with the black radicals, and housewife Laura Parker's 8mm *Housewife Diary* film, which plays almost like a spoof of *David Holzman's Diary*. But after losing much of the Parker storyline in editing, it became a movie clearly and singularly about De Niro's character.

To me, every single thing in the movie works.

It was as if the first film was a smorgasbord of every effect De Palma and Hirsch could come up with and accomplish. But after its success, De Palma went through the first film, analyzed the most successful elements, and expanded on them. The first film had three protagonists. *Hi, Mom!* focuses on De Niro, the most compelling of the three, keeps Graham (the funniest), and loses the least interesting, Jonathan Warden. Realizing the Allen Garfield scene made the audience laugh the most, he brings back Garfield (seemingly playing a more successful version of the same character), and builds the film's whole first half around him. I also think there's a realization on De Palma's part of what a truly gifted improvisational actor Garfield was, and he utilizes him for the benefit of the second picture. In both *Greetings* and *Hi, Mom!*, it's Garfield who *writes* the text of the scenes through his hilarious improv gifts.

Like a rodeo rider on a bucking bronco, it's De Niro's job during these scenes to hang on for dear life.

But it's the *Be Black Baby* set piece that makes the movie un-forgettable. Suffice to say, no scene in a movie will come anywhere near it till thirty years later during the third act of Takashi Miiki's *Audition.*

So how did a hippie counterculture satirist turn into *"the Modern Master of the Macabre"*?

I'd speculate it was commercial necessity that was the mother of Hitchcockian invention.

Greetings was such a success that Warner Bros. brought De Palma out to Hollywood to make their *"tune in-drop out"* satire *Get to Know Your Rabbit,* starring Tom Smothers (one of the real zeit-geist comedy stars of the era). But after finishing *Rabbit,* (which is really funny), the studio put it on the shelf for three years. After the bad studio experience of *Rabbit,* De Palma realized, by 1970, the sixties hippie aesthetic was dead on arrival. But De Palma's entire identity was tied to that aesthetic. What was required was both a reinvention of self and a commercial genre of cinema he could survive and hopefully thrive in.

But what genre would that be?

For a filmmaker with such an iconoclast reputation, De Palma was acutely aware of the commercial concerns of the marketplace. Some could say to a fault. By this time De Palma had been making movies for almost a decade. He'd already shot five movies. Francis Ford Coppola might have been a mentor to Lucas, Scorsese, and Milius, but to Brian De Palma he was a peer. De Palma had seen directors come and go. He knew in this industry nothing was more important than to keep being allowed to make movies. Also, despite his troubled relationship with Warner Bros., he didn't want to go back to the shoestring, run-and-gun world of independent filmmaking. He *liked* having permits. He *liked* shutting down the street with police control. He *liked* being able to afford a crane.

And the only way to keep in business—unlike Jim McBride, unlike Shirley Clarke—was to make commercial movies people wanted to see.

As he warned me, after he saw and was (surprisingly) impressed with *Reservoir Dogs*, "*Quentin, don't get too esoteric with your subject matter. If you want to be allowed to keep making movies, you've got to give them a Carrie every once in a while.*"

Consequently, he claims that's why he didn't ultimately make Schrader's script for *Taxi Driver* when he had the chance. He didn't feel it was commercial enough. Later he changed that: He felt Marty would do a better job with the material. But I think he told the truth the first time.

So if De Palma's going to move into more commercially viable, less esoteric pictures, what direction does he move?

Action movies?

Well, that's ultimately where he did move in the eighties and nineties. But back in the seventies, making action movies meant making movies with Charles Bronson, Clint Eastwood, Steve McQueen, or Burt Reynolds.

I can't really picture De Palma being fulfilled doing that. Also, it's doubtful those old salty dogs would have the patience to sit around on the set waiting for Brian to execute his rococo camera moves. But I can see a world where Brian De Palma directs *The Groundstar Conspiracy*, or *Freebie and the Bean*, or *Crazy Joe*, or Schrader's original script for *Rolling Thunder*, or *Three Days of the Condor*. I can see De Palma making a great version of *Death Wish*, but probably with someone like Peter Falk or George C. Scott as its star (what a fucking dynamite picture that would have been!).

But Brian De Palma found a commercial niche/genre he could make his own, that wasn't action films, and was related to horror films, but not exactly the same thing.

De Palma's study of the techniques of suspense that Hitchcock employed is as well known as his ultimate dissatisfaction and outright disdain for all of Hitch's movies after *Psycho* (even *The Birds*).

I believe it was the emergence of Roman Polanski with his film *Repulsion* when De Palma began to be intrigued by the idea of doing a new modern type of thriller.

The Polanski movie *worked*.

But where a Hitchcock movie *worked* to entertain, Polanski's movie worked to *disturb*. Hitchcock could disturb too. But ultimately, only up to a point. With Polanski, disturbance *was* the point.

So in this new cinematic landscape, Polanski's Hitchcockian thriller—by way of Buñuel—struck a chord with audiences, critics, and no doubt young Brian.

And then when Polanski followed it up with *Rosemary's Baby*, De Palma must have thought, "*Well, that's that then. Hitchcock is dead and the world has a new master of terror and suspense, and his name is Roman Polanski.*"

At the time Polanski, Peckinpah, and Ken Russell represented a cinematic trifecta of provocation, with Roman proving the most popular and the most commercially successful (by far).

But then, right at the very height of his success, a horrible thing happened to the Polish auteur's wife and unborn child: *The Manson Family*. Then suddenly, for the next few years, Roman would be sidelined out of the picture due to the tragedy.

Polanski's absence left a hole. A hole another classy horror film practitioner could possibly fill.

I also think the American release, reaction, and relative commercial success of Dario Argento's Italian *giallo The Bird with the Crystal Plumage* proved an inspiration for De Palma. Like *Repulsion*, it too used the "*Not since Psycho*" tag on its one-sheet and newspaper ads. Not that I think the snobby De Palma overly admired the Argento thriller. But I do think it's possible that the film did illustrate a modern seventies way to do a horror film that utilized Hitchcockian suspense techniques. Even the fact that Argento committed to staging Hitchcockian set pieces, I think, intrigued De Palma. And the way the ad campaign implied a connection to *Psycho*, but with rougher, more violent implications, must have seemed like a good commercial idea to the young director. Now, while I'm certain De Palma didn't hold Argento in the same regard he did Polanski, there still was something impressive about *Bird with the Crystal Plumage* that could not be ignored. I can also imagine part of De Palma's inspiration to forge a career executing Hitchcockian set pieces was his frustration at how inept he felt the highly praised Hitchcock homages from the French New Wave were. Particularly messieurs Truffaut and Chabrol. I can't imagine De Palma appreciating even a relatively decent one like Chabrol's *Le Boucher* (probably chalking it up to a thrill-less thriller). But I can absolutely see De Palma being appalled at Truffaut's amateur, clumsy fumbling of *The Bride Wore Black*. As well as being dismayed by the affectionate praise heaped on it by the New York film critics (probably the only thing De Palma and Bogdanovich ever agreed upon). It's doubtful a master filmmaker like De Palma was ever charmed by Truffaut's Ed Wood–like amateur bumbling even under more appropriate conditions. But in the service of a Hitchcock-like thriller, backed by Bernard Herrmann music? It must have left young De Palma puking in the aisle. I can hear him ranting to Jennifer Salt, *"How do you do a Hitchcock film without any cool shots? How do you do a Hitchcock film where the camera is unimportant?"*

So with Polanski abdicating his throne, Argento pointing the way, and Truffaut and Chabrol demonstrating there was both a market and an audience for Hitchcock homages, young Brian started his career as a genre horror filmmaker. With the intention of eventually being labeled *the New Modern Master of Macabre*, which he eventually accomplished. But as opposed to other genre masters, while De Palma *liked* Hitchcock thrillers and possessed undeniable talents in that area, I don't believe he made them out of love. I believe he made them to corner a market on a commercial niche he could call his own. If he could be known as the heir to Hitchcock, then—like Hitchcock—he could make film after film.

Leone and Corbucci made westerns because they *loved* them.

Hitchcock and Bava and Argento made thrillers because they *loved* them. While De Palma liked *making* thrillers (for a little while, at least), I doubt he loved watching them.

Hitchcockian thrillers were for him a means to an end. That's why when he was forced to return to the genre in the mid-eighties, they were so lackluster. Ultimately he resented having to make them and was bored with the form.

Hitchcock's *Frenzy* might be a piece of crap, but I doubt Alfred was bored making it.

But back in the early seventies when De Palma was shedding his hippie love beads, he saw not only a genre in cinema that would attract audiences and in which his cinematic talents could thrive and expand. He also saw a hole smack dab in the middle of a genre the young filmmaker felt he alone was equipped to fill.

Armed with a good commercial script (cowritten with Louisa Rose) that accomplished all his Hitchcockian-thriller goals, it was now time to figure out where he was going to set *Sisters* up. After the bad experience of *Get to Know Your Rabbit*, De Palma was weary of dealing with another major studio. This film couldn't suffer any clueless studio interference. If *Sisters* was going to work, it had to be unequivocally *a Brian De Palma movie*.

He first approached Martin Ransohoff, who was running Filmways and making television shows like *The Beverly Hillbillies* and *Green Acres* ("*This has been a Filmways presentation, darling.*"), and films like *The Americanization of Emily* and *The Fearless Vampire Killers*. Why would De Palma, with his leeriness of studio interference, go to Ransohoff, the man who fired Peckinpah off of *The Cincinnati Kid* and took *The Fearless Vampire Killers* away from Polanski and monkeyed around with it?

Well, a few years earlier (1967), Ransohoff began dipping his big toe into counterculture cinema by purchasing the boutique distributor Sigma 111 Corporation. Sigma 111 mostly released foreign films like *Closely Watched Trains* and *Cul-de-sac*. But Ransohoff also released three of De Palma's New York films, *Greetings*, *Dionysus in '69*, and *Hi, Mom!* And the way Sigma 111 turned *Greetings* into a New York box office hit was the reason De Palma had a legitimate film directing career. So based on that friendly relationship and patronage, De Palma initially sold his screenplays to both *Sisters* and *Phantom of the Paradise* to Ransohoff.

The original plan was for Filmways to go independent by having their own distribution company, Sigma 111, theatrically release both films. But that plan never transpired. Instead, Ransohoff ended up pretty much shutting down Sigma 111 and concentrating on producing movies for the major studios (*Catch-22*, *Fuzz*, *See No Evil*).

Then De Palma's worst fears of studio interference came to pass when somehow his scripts were moved from Ransohoff to his rival at Filmways, Ray Stark (Ransohoff and Ray Stark fucking hated each other's guts). Stark was one of the biggest producers in town—he was also one of the town's biggest bullies, and he was responsible for mangling more films than an El Paso drive-in movie projector. Immediately Stark got to work putting his grubby mitts on *Sisters*, insisting that Raquel Welch play the Margot Kidder role of *Danielle and Dominique* (though maybe Stark could have delivered De Palma's original casting choice for the Janet Leigh–like movie-star victim role that surprisingly exits the picture after the first act: Sydney Poitier.)

Around this time, when De Palma was dating Margot Kidder and living with Jennifer Salt(!), the *Out of It* director Paul Williams (not the diminutive songwriter), started hanging around their house. Williams had started a company with his producing partner Ed Pressman called Pressman-Williams Enterprises, and had just made a movie that ended up on Roger Ebert's top ten of the year list, *The Revolutionary*, starring Jon Voight, who, after *Midnight Cowboy*, was a bona fide movie star. So, through Paul, Brian became friendly with Ed Pressman and convinced Ed to buy his scripts back from the clutches of Ray Stark, with Brian even putting up his own money from *Get to Know Your Rabbit* to facilitate the process, and with Pressman ultimately financing *Sisters* completely, then selling it to American-International Pictures as an independent pickup (it's Ed Pressman who owns *Sisters* today).

Sisters was De Palma's first stab (snicker-snicker) at both Hitchcock homage and meta-*Psycho* reworking. The critical pull quotes on the poster and in the newspaper ads strategically evoked *Psycho*. But everything else sought to lure the same audience that was drawn to *The Bird with the Crystal Plumage*. And *Sisters* ended up doing exactly what it set out to do. It accomplished De Palma's entry into commercial Hollywood filmmaking and it did well enough to justify future films from the auteur. But it also garnered good notices that emphasized the director's cinematic bona fides, marking young De Palma as a rising talent to watch.

Pretty much everything a calling card movie is supposed to do, it did. And while, especially compared to his better thrillers (*Carrie*, *Dressed to Kill*, and *Blow Out*), *Sisters* hasn't aged that well (both *Repulsion* and *The Bird with the Crystal Plumage* satisfy decades later in a way that *Sisters* does not), in 1973 it was damned impressive. Compared to the other low-budget horror films to come out that year, *Sisters* played like a really classy picture.

In the film, a man and a woman, *Phillip* (Lisle Wilson) and *Danielle* (Margot Kidder), who meet on a TV game show, go out to dinner afterwards. They hit it off and go back to her apartment where they make love. The next morning she reveals that she lives with her twin sister (*Dominique,* who we overhear—but don't see—arguing with Danielle behind a door) and that today is their birthday. The idea is that the couple (Phillip and Danielle) are going to spend the day together. She sends him on an errand to the pharmacy to fill a prescription. While he's out Phillip stops off at a bakery and buys a birthday cake and has it inscribed "*Happy Birthday Danielle and Dominque.*"

All this has been a *Psycho*-like setup to set the stage for a big showstopping murder sequence, where Dominique kills poor Phillip (despite *Psycho*'s classic status, does anyone really miss Marion Crane once she exits the picture? By comparison, Phillip's death is heartbreaking).

Then the narrative switches to a reporter, *Grace Collier* (Jennifer Salt), who lives in an apartment across the street from the two sisters and witnesses the murder from her living room a la *Rear Window.* The film has a bunch of different elements. Long-standing De Palma stock company regular William Finley playing another creepy red herring. Charles Durning officially becoming a member of De Palma's stock company when he gives the film's best performance as a detective Grace hires to help investigate the murder. Gruff Dolph Sweet plays the first of De Palma's sarcastic police detectives who is more suspicious of our protagonist than of the killer. Like *Hi, Mom!,* there's media-inside-media moments (game shows, news documentaries), as well as Siamese twins, insane asylums, a lot of great Bernard Herrmann music, split-screen sequences, and the first of De Palma's split personality killers. The weakest part of the film, aside from one of the two female leads, is the script, which is more structure than story.

Sisters established the method of Hitchcock homage that the director would later become known for. Which was to take the story points or structural elements from Hitchcock's most famous thrillers and—even more than Polanski or Argento—commit to full blown cinematic set pieces that invoked the master—*except* these suspense set pieces usually led to more violent and gorier outcomes than they did in the Hitchcock fifties.*

In *Sisters*, De Palma takes the structure of *Psycho*: victim *Phillip* and killer *Danielle* are both presented in the film's first act as sympathetic protagonists, all building up to the big murder scene, where the film's two audience-identifying characters are revealed to be murderer and murder victim. In the early sixties audiences were generally fooled into thinking Norman's mother—not Norman—was the killer.

But in 1973, after a slew of movies had made the *Psycho* rip-off a genre unto itself, audiences were more likely ahead of De Palma when it came to his big reveal that *Dominique* was really *Danielle*. But in De Palma's subversive sixties way, the murderer is a white female and the victim is a black male. Upon revealing this switch to the audience, the film continues to follow *Psycho*'s structure of having a new protagonist enter the picture (a witness to the killing) who then begins investigating the murder. However, the way this new character—Staten Island newspaper reporter *Grace Collier*—witnesses the murder is taken from both Hitch's *Rear Window* and the director's own *Hi, Mom!*

Something else introduced in *Sisters* that De Palma would hold on to in some of his other thrillers is the split-personality methodology of the killer. Margot Kidder is *Danielle*, and she's also her dead sister *Dominique*. But, like *Norman Bates*, she herself is unaware of the personality split. And like Norman Bates with his mother, she can engage in conversation between the two personalities without ever being the wiser.

With as little regard as he held for Truffaut's *The Bride Wore*

---

*It must be remembered some of these Hitchcock classics, *Rear Window*, *Vertigo*, and *Rope,* had been out of circulation on the repertory circuit and unavailable on television for many years.

Black, he still tore a page out of François' book by getting Bernard Herrmann, the composer most identified with Hitch, to compose the score to *Sisters*. And it's easily Herrmann's best score of the seventies (only the score for Roy Boulting's *Twisted Nerve* comes close), including a stabbing string section meant to evoke *Psycho* during Phillip's bloody death. But it was De Palma's masterly demonstration of camera pyrotechnics, and his clever use of split-screen and cinema-within-cinema (or TV-within-cinema) that blew away the cinematic techniques employed in the other *Psycho*-like thrillers of that year. Of which there were a lot, mostly coming out of England from Hammer Studios.

But as much as De Palma was adopting the cinematic grammar of Alfred Hitchcock and the story points from some of the master of suspense's scripts (split personality murderer, murder witnessed through apartment window), he still carried over some of the trappings from the counterculture satires of *Greetings* and *Hi, Mom!* With Brian's earlier movies he had established his own vision of New York City (usually centered around Greenwich Village and Manhattan). *Sisters* takes place in a New York recognizable as De Palma's New York from the earlier pictures.

Also in *Sisters*, like *Greetings* and *Hi, Mom!*, De Palma engages in media satires like the crazy game show *Peeping Toms* that starts the film. Like most of De Palma's media satires, as *New York Times* critic Vincent Canby pointed out, what's so funny about them is how authentic they seem. The racial satire of *Hi, Mom!* is dragged into his Hitchcockian thriller (which all by itself places it apart from Hitchcock's work).

The casting of a black male (Lisle Wilson) as the victim of the big set piece murder sequence isn't satire, but actually a progressive stroke. The satire comes in when the film's amateur detective Grace Collier speculates that the cops refuse to investigate the killing because the victim is black. *"Those racist pigs won't do anything about it."* But the film clearly shows that's not the case, and Salt's character, a muckraking intrepid reporter for a local Staten Island newspaper, who writes opinion essays with headlines like "*Why We Call Them Pigs,*" is a blithering idiot.

But the film's funniest racial joke is when the *Peeping Tom* contestants Wilson and killer Kidder are given two free dinners at Manhattan's *African Room*. Where black males in tuxedo tops and grass skirts serve as waiters, which when it comes to ridiculous theme restaurants in movies, ranks right up there with Joe Dante's Canadian-themed restaurant in *Gremlins 2* (a Mountie-costumed waiter asks Zach Galligan, "*Can I get you another Molson's?*").★

But *Sisters'* real claim to fame, aside from establishing the template for the other Hitchcockian/De Palma thrillers to come, is the film's buildup to Wilson' set piece birthday-cake butcher-knife murder, still one of the most accomplished sequences of De Palma's filmography. The problem with *Sisters* as a thriller, however, is once the big murder moment and the successful cover-up section is through . . . so are the thrills. De Palma (and cowriter Louisa Rose) only wrote half a movie, the Wilson/Kidder section. The Jennifer Salt section is simply De Palma trying to wrap the movie up as quickly as possible without spoiling the goodwill generated by the film's dynamic first half. The best moment in the film's second half is a faux media moment. Reporter Grace Collier watches a TV documentary on the Blanchion Siamese twins (Danielle and Dominique) that could have been made for *Hi, Mom!'s ITTV documentary series.*

The problem with the film's second half is twofold. De Palma doesn't create any other real suspense sequences. And the other

---

★Along with Duane Jones in both *Night of the Living Dead* and *Ganja & Hess*, William Marshall's dignified portrayal of *Blacula*, pint-sized Carol Speed's comic vulgarity in *Abby*, and Ken Foree's dynamic S.W.A.T. team leader in *Dawn of the Dead*, Lisle Wilson is one of the only significant black characters in seventies horror.

problem is Jennifer Salt's performance as Grace Collier. De Palma tries to present his women's-lib reporter protagonist as a pigheaded, self-righteous ass. And he tried to have fun with that aspect of the character. In her first scene with Charles Durning's detective, you can tell she's supposed to be exasperatingly foolish. And if you pay attention you might even notice that a couple of her lines are written to be funny. But Salt's delivery just bulldozes over any comedic intent. So instead of being comically foolish, Salt's Grace Collier just comes across as idiotic. Before Pauline Kael would begin to champion De Palma's thrillers, she panned *Sisters*, primarily due to Salt's performance. And for the record, I'm a big fan of Jennifer Salt's earlier performances in De Palma's movies.

However in 1973 when I saw *Sisters* in Tennessee at the South Clinton Drive-In, on a double feature with another bizarre American-International film, *Little Cigars* (a film about a gang of dwarf bank robbers led by curvy blond bombshell Angel Tompkins), I thought it was sensational and the filmmaking thrilling. I had never seen a split-screen sequence before. For years, as I thought about different movies I'd like to make, they always included elaborate split-screen set pieces inspired by De Palma's later use of that device. But I'd eventually do only two: A pretty decent one in *Jackie Brown*, but it turned on a narrative reveal rather than cinematic razzle dazzle. But when Daryl Hannah walks down the hall of the hospital in *Kill Bill vol. 1*, whistling Bernard Herrmann, then it slides into a split-screen, it's almost as if Brian De Palma has seized control of the movie for a moment.

After the success of *Sisters*, De Palma and Pressman would make *Phantom of the Paradise* together, starring Brian's college roommate William Finley as *The Phantom* and Paul Williams (yes, the diminutive songwriter) as the evil Phil Spector–like record producer *Swan*. The duo were initially set to do the movie with American-International Pictures, who were very happy with the

De Palma-Pressman team after *Sisters*. But when the studio balked at the budget that De Palma was asking for, the director and producer again went it alone, both men using their *Sisters* money to grubstake the film's preproduction. Eventually they snagged a real estate developer named Gustave Berne, who had invested in three horror films around that time (*Theatre of Blood*, *Asylum*, *And Now the Screaming Starts!*), and he put up the $750,000 they needed to make the movie (apparently they needed more, because early on the crew's checks bounced every week, and the production was always on the verge of being shut down).

But the funny part about the De Palma-Pressman association is that both *Sisters* and *Phantom of the Paradise* were *Pressman-Williams Enterprises* presentations. Which means *both* Paul Williamses were involved with the making of *Phantom of the Paradise*.★

───────────

★The filmmaker Paul Williams was a real exciting talent during this era of independent filmmaking. His Long Island set high school film, *Out of It*, starring Barry Gordon and a pre–*Midnight Cowboy* Jon Voight, is a charming trifle that surprisingly springs a powerhouse ending on its unsuspecting audience. Voight, post–*Midnight Cowboy*, joined him again when he starred in his interesting *The Revolutionary* (which also included Jennifer Salt). At one point, during the early stages of *Mean Streets* (which Ed Pressman *almost* produced), Martin Scorsese tried to get Voight to star in the picture, playing the role that Harvey Keitel ended up essaying. In his attempt to court Voight, Scorsese even cast David Proval and Richard Romanus, two actors he met in Voight's Los Angeles acting class.

I asked Martin why, ultimately, didn't Voight do it?

He told me, "*Jon Voight was a really wonderful actor and so we talked about it for quite awhile. And he was really starting to think about it. After Midnight Cowboy [Voight] was a major star and to be in a film that, at that point, [Jonathan] Taplin [the producer] had gotten about $650,000 to make, it just didn't seem like the milieu was right. Besides, at that time he was working with a guy named Paul Williams. He was Paul's guy. If he was going to do a low-budget independent feature, it would have been with Paul.*"

Daisy Miller

(1974)

A lot of the American *Post-Sixties Anti-Establishment Auteurs* tried their hand at adapting great authors of literature and theatre. Mike Nichols with Edward Albee, Joseph Heller, and Jules Feiffer. Frank Perry adapted Joan Didion's *Play It as It Lays*. Arthur Penn did Thomas Berger's *Little Big Man*. Paul Mazursky did a modern adaptation of Shakespeare's *The Tempest* and Isaac Bashevis Singer's *Enemies, a Love Story*. Hal Ashby did Jerzy Kosinski's *Being There*. Richard Rush's magnum opus was Paul Brodeur's darkly comic novel of paranoia *The Stunt Man*. And Richard Lester's magnum opus would be his brilliant slapstick comedy reinvention of Alexandre Dumas' *The Three Musketeers* (which I believe is one of the greatest epic film productions ever made).

And their European counterparts would go even further. John Schlesinger would adapt Thomas Hardy and Nathanael West. Roman Polanski would adapt Shakespeare and Thomas Hardy. Franco Zeffirelli would build his career adapting Shakespeare. Milos Forman would adapt Ken Kesey, E. L. Doctorow, and a truly awful version of Ragni and Rado's *Hair*. Ken Russell would do his Ken Russell number on D. H. Lawrence and Aldous Huxley (not to mention all those pseudo-biopics of great composers).

However, when *the Movie Brats* adapted novels, they leaned

more towards popular fiction (*The Godfather, Jaws, The Last Picture Show, Carrie, Paper Moon, The Fury*). This would change in the eighties and nineties, when all the Movie Brats took a turn for the highbrow. Scorsese would adapt Edith Wharton, Spielberg would adapt J. G. Ballard and Alice Walker, Coppola would tackle Bram Stoker's most famous creation, Paul Schrader would adapt Mishima and direct Harold Pinter, and De Palma would fall on his face and never really get back up again after fucking up Tom Wolfe.★

But, back in the seventies, the only one of them to—straight up—tackle classic literature was Peter Bogdanovich's adaptation of Henry James' *Daisy Miller* (yes, I'm aware that Michael Pye doesn't count Bogdanovich as a Movie Brat. But I do).

What sets Bogdanovich's adaptation apart from *Far from the Madding Crowd* or *Tess* or *The Europeans* or *The Age of Innocence* or the whole *Masterpiece Theatre* vibe of most classic literary film adaptations is the director's approach. He tries to turn the first half of the film into a comedy. Bogdanovich's *Daisy Miller* goes for and achieves a rapid-fire pace of overlapping Hawksian comedic rhythm to the dialogue. Does that just mean he has the characters talking fast?

Yes.

But Peter had a facility with overlapping (non-improvised) co-

---

★ During his New York New Wave years, De Palma would film entirely in split-screen, a strange happening of its time, the Living Theatre's production of Euripides' *The Bacchae*, titled *Dionysus in '69*, which no doubt influenced one his greatest achievements, *the Be Black Baby* sequence in *Hi, Mom!*. And technically, *Apocalypse Now* is an adaptation of Joseph Conrad's novel *Heart of Darkness*. But screenwriter John Milius was appalled when the film was put into the Best Screenplay Adaptation category in the 1980 Academy Awards, angrily arguing that the screenplay was an original work.

medic dialogue like none of his peers (it wouldn't be till Bob Clark, in his *Porky's* movies, showed such a similar talent). But admittedly, the film starts off a little bizarre. The tone of the opening scene between Barry Brown's *Winterbourne* and Daisy's nine-year-old brother *Randolph* (James McMurtry) is a little off-putting. You see what Peter is trying to accomplish, but you're not sure it's going to work.

But the film gains power as it progresses and builds to a gut-punch ending. Bogdanovich's film *is* very funny, yet it leaves a viewer profoundly sad as you watch the final credits fade up.

Peter made a film like the breezy and entertaining literary classic adaptations that came out of Hollywood in the thirties and forties. Garbo's *Anna Karenina* and *Camille*, Charles Laughton's *The Hunchback of Norte Dame*, Ronald Colman's *A Tale of Two Cities*, Laurence Olivier's *Wuthering Heights*. Peter tackled the material similarly to the way he imagines his hero Howard Hawks might tackle the assignment in the forties (though there is a level of photographic beauty that would have completely eluded Hawks). Peter even made it for the same reason Hawks would have probably made it. Not because he's overly reverential to Henry James' source material, but because Henry James' source material offered a great star vehicle for Cybill Shepherd (you can imagine Hawks doing it with Frances Farmer).

It's true that Bogdanovich did overestimate Cybill Shepherd's talents. But one of the talents she *did* possess was a facility with rapid-paced comedic Hawksian dialogue. Shown off to good effect in both *Daisy Miller* and the non-singing scenes in *At Long Last Love*. As well as her scenes with Albert Brooks in *Taxi Driver* and Ivan Passer's *Silver Bears*, leading to her spectacular eighties comeback on the smash hit TV show *Moonlighting*.

Shepherd is completely convincing as Daisy Miller. But not convincing like a classic actress playing the role, which is what we're accustomed to seeing when we usually watch classic literature dramatized (Olivia de Havilland in *The Heiress*). By Bogdanovich turning the whole story into one that turns on fast-paced comic repartee, he leans the material into Shepherd's strengths.

But it seems that Bogdanovich also went for a duality of character and actress. Like the cheeky innocent Daisy is in over her head in high society expatriate Rome, Cybill is in over her head in this lavish period production.

But Shepherd, like Miller, rises to the occasion.

Shepherd shares with Miller her delight in slight inappropriateness, her sarcastic sense of humor, and her ability to manipulate men to act out her whims. She also possesses Daisy's American *"fuck you, Jack"* rebellious streak, what used to be called *moxie*. It's that *"fuck you, Jack"* quality that makes Daisy reject *Mrs. Walker*'s (Eileen Brennan) demand to fall in line and get in her society coach. It's a decision that effectively ends Daisy's life in English expatriate Roman high society, and *ultimately* leads to her death.

Shepherd demonstrated that same *"fuck you, Jack"* spirit by taking on Henry James' heroine in a lavish starring vehicle for herself directed by her boyfriend. Both Miller and Shepherd share a consequences-be-damned moxie. But where that moxie in Daisy leads to tragedy, Shepherd, after a settling-in period during the first fifteen minutes, grows into the role (even Pauline Kael had to begrudgingly admit that. Something you could never imagine Kael doing for other of Shepherd's ilk, like Ali MacGraw or Candice Bergen).

In Bogdanovich's telling, Daisy's fate is sudden, and we have an emotional reaction to both its abruptness and callousness.

And that reaction is earned by Cybill Shepherd's affinity with Daisy Miller. The ending leaves you shocked and sad at its conclusion, over the fate of a character you're never really sure you liked.

The conclusion also contains a real-life resonance.

And that's the sad fate of the film's male lead, Barry Brown, playing the American *Frederick Winterbourne*, who chases after Daisy and tells her story to us.

Barry Brown was a young actor who emerged in the late sixties and early seventies, popping up on *The Mod Squad* and *Ironside*, and small parts in movies like Philip Kaufman's *The Great Northfield Minnesota Raid*. He was also, along with Jeff Bridges and Rob Reiner, one of the fraidy cat white kids bussed to the scary black high school in Paul Bogart's *Halls of Anger.*

He was an Andrew Prine–type of leading man.

Skinny, handsome, sensitive, and soft.

A male ingenue.

Brown was also, surprisingly enough, a genre film scholar who wrote regularly for the horror film magazines *Castle of Frankenstein* (the *Fangoria* of the late sixties and early seventies) and *Magick Theatre*. Including, in *Castle of Frankenstein* issue #10, a wonderful piece that chronicles Bela Lugosi's descent into morphine addiction.

But in 1972 *Bonnie and Clyde* screenwriter Robert Benton made his directorial debut with the western *Bad Company*, and he cast Barry Brown opposite Jeff Bridges as the film's two leads.

Brown and Bridges proved a great team. Bridges, all rawboned American farm boy masculinity, and Brown his sensitive and intellectual opposite number.

Then Bogdanovich cast him as Winterbourne in *Daisy Miller*, the film's real lead, and *our* witness to Daisy's comings and goings (it probably didn't hurt that Brown resembled Bogdanovich). Peter had his problems with Brown (mostly due to alcohol), but no matter, it's still one of the finest performances in all of Bogdanovich's filmography.

Cybill Shepherd's biggest hurdle in the film is—in this period piece—fighting against her natural modernness. But in this story, that's not the worst thing, because in the world that Daisy tries to cavort in, she's considered outlandishly modern. But Barry Brown, along with Eileen Brennan, is the most era-appropriate actor in the film. He enters the movie like he stepped out of a Chagall painting to start the story. A painting he will return to once the story is over.

We watch Daisy yank Winterbourne's leash, and we watch him hop.

We watch him try breathlessly to keep up with Daisy, and never quite succeed.

We watch him be enchanted by her liberated spirit . . . till he's not.

And then, we watch him betray her.

And it's only in that final shot that the loss and the cost of that betrayal is felt by us and Winterbourne, all left devastated by it.

What did it all mean?

What was Daisy to him, and what will she be?

Will she just turn into a story he tells?

How will Daisy fare in that story?

Who will Winterbourne be in that story?

Is Winterbourne the only one—save her mother and little brother—to care enough to tell Daisy's story?

The question that Barry Brown's performance asks the audience to contemplate is, will Winterbourne be haunted by his encounter with Daisy Miller, or will her memory become insignificant over time?

After *Daisy Miller* Brown never received another lead in studio movies (but he is the lead of a tremendously entertaining ski thriller, directed by the underrated Robert Butler, titled *The Ultimate Thrill*).

For the most part, Brown returned to television in the late seventies doing guest shots on TV programs like *Police Woman* and *Barnaby Jones*. Though he did have a good part in Joe Dante's seminal *Jaws* rip-off for New World Pictures, *Piranha*.

Then, the year of that film's release, at the age of twenty-seven,

Barry Brown took his own life. Turning all of us who liked Barry Brown, when we watch the end of *Daisy Miller*, into Winterbourne.

Who was Barry Brown?

What did it all mean?

Am I the only one who remembers Barry Brown?

Am I enough?

One of the last pictures ever taken of Bela Lugosi.

BELA LUGOSI
BELOVED FATHER
1882 — 1956

THE

by
Barry Brown

Bela Lugosi's death from a heart attack ten years ago, on August 16, 1956, did not come as an overwhelming surprise, but, rather, as an inevitable eclaircissement of a tragic twenty-year siege of narcotics.

In 1957, a film titled **HATFUL OF RAIN** was released. In its early stages it had been an Actors Studio improvisation project which was developed and expanded by playwright Michael Gazzo. Johnny Pope (Don Murray) is a GI who was treated with morphine to relieve intense pain gained from battle wounds. After discharge, he discovered that, due to his dependence on morphine, he has become an addict. The remainder of the film deals with the struggle to combat this addition and closes with Pope's entrance into a hospital. This dramatization was not unlike the calamitous non-fictionization of Bela Lugosi. Lugosi's struggle lasted a third of his lifetime and climaxed with a moderately triumphant return to prominence.

In 1935, while working at MGM on **MARK OF THE VAMPIRE**, Lugosi began receiving doses of morphine under legal medical attention to relieve what he later described as "shooting pains in my legs." When he was refused additional treatments of the drug, Lugosi established underworld sources for obtaining the narcotic. He developed a strong habit during the following three years. "I knew after a time it was getting out of control," recalled Lugosi during a 1955 interview with a **Los Angeles Times** reporter.

In 1938, Lugosi took a trip to England where he "heard of a drug less harmful than morphine." The new drug Lugosi found was metha-

TRUE FACTS BEHIND LUGOSI'S TRAGIC DRUG ADDICTION

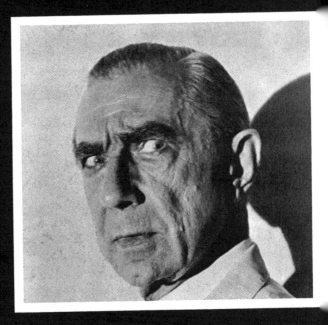

-done (short for methadone hydro-chloride), a white powder stimulant very similar to morphine in its effect. Today, methadone is widely used in withdrawal cures by such treatment clinics as the Lexington Addiction Research Center. Administered in small doses exclusively, it can ease the painful symptoms of withdrawal.

"I smuggled a big box of it back," stated Lugosi. "I guess I brought a pound." From then until the early Fifties, Lugosi's nervous system was made to adapt to methadone and Demerol, a potent morphine-like synthetic which he first used in the late Forties. Demerol (short for meperdine hydrochloride) is a colorless liquid that can be dissolved and taken in a glass of water. Even with the switch to these substitutes, prolonged usage took its toll on Lugosi, who said later, "I didn't eat. I got sicker and sicker."

During this time, his fourth wife, Lillian, did her best to aid her husband in an unpublicized recovery. She persistently reduced his methadone doses to smaller quantities, and this period was undoubtedly an ordeal for her as well. Feeling, perhaps, that she had accomplished a great deal, Lillian Lugosi then left Bela, who had seemingly relinquished his dependence on drugs. Her cure was almost identical to the treatment Lugosi would have received in an addiction center.

But, psychologically, Bela was still unprepared to throw himself back into his career. He later described the experience this way: "She gave me the shots. And she weaned me. Finally, I got only the bare needle. A fake shot, that's all. I was done with it. Then she left me. She took our son. He was my heart was broken."

After his divorce from Lillian in 1953, and the subsequent court decision that awarded Bela Jr. to her, Lugosi lived in an apartment at 5714 Carlton Way. On April 21, 1955, accompanied by writer Manley Hall, who had aided in Lugosi's support since the divorce, Bela entered Los Angeles General Hospital's mental health and hygiene department and requested that he be committed for treatment. At this time, Lugosi's weight was an appalling 125 pounds, a sharp contrast to his former husky and

Fast legal provisions were arranged. Lugosi spent the night at General Hospital and, on the next day, April 22, he attended a 45-minute court hearing in which he pleaded for treatment at a medical center. Superior Judge Wallace Ward granted that Lugosi be committed to Metropolitan State Hospital in Norwalk, California, for a minimum of three months or a maximum of two years.

The news media was comparatively uncompromising in Lugosi's case, plastering front pages with headlines such as "Bela Lugosi Ad-

The former Lillian Lugosi and Brian Donlevy shortly after their wedding last year. Lugosi's wife aided in his recovery.

The Hollywood apartment house where Lugosi died.

since the Thirties. They moved to an apartment at 5620 Harold Way which lies between Hollywood Boulevard and Sunset Boulevard in Hollywood. The 73-year old actor was completely recovered though old age was now seriously hampering him. He was deaf in one ear and suffered from arthritis. Nevertheless, he starred in Banner Productions' low-budget **BRIDE OF THE MONSTER**. Released in February of 1956, it also featured a gorilla and Tor Johnson.

Not much later, Lugosi accepted a supporting role in what was to become his last film—**PLAN 9 FROM OUTER SPACE**. The stars were Tom Keene (1896-1963), Gregory Walcott, Vampira and, of course, Tor Johnson. Lugosi played a scientist in contact with outer space invaders who entered the bodies of deceased Earth citizens. The film was not released until July of 1959.

On a quiet evening on August 16, 1956, Hope Lugosi left the apartment on Harold Way to buy groceries at a store only a few blocks away. Bela was in bed resting. She headed home around seven o'clock, little realizing that an hour or two later she would be saying, "He didn't answer me when I spoke so I went to him. I could feel no pulse! Apparently he must have died a very short time before I arrived. He was just terrified of death. Toward the end he was very weary, but he was still afraid of death. Three nights before he died he was sitting on the edge of the bed. I asked him if he were still afraid to die. He told me that he was. I did my best to comfort him but you might as well save your breath with people like that. They're still going to be afraid of death."

Bela Lugosi, filmdom's disdained but beloved Dracula, had died of a heart attack at approximately 6:45 PM. He was buried two days later at Lot 120 in the Grotto section of Holy Cross Cemetery.

Lugosi's career was filled with ephemeral film plots which all sprang from his one ethereal characterization . . . a cinema milestone . . . **DRACULA**. He died without achieving his greatest wish: to be acknowledged and revered for his dramatic talent. Like the fatalistic suicide of Marilyn Monroe, Lugosi's tragic pilgrimage through the dreary drug world once again proved Hollywood's misuse of true talent.

mits He's Used Narcotics For Twenty Years" and "Bela Commits Himself As Dope Addict." Psychiatrists at General Hospital at first refused to answer any questions about Lugosi's condition or the nature of the drugs, but within a month after the first public word was released, all known details of his unfortunate experience had been exploited.

Lugosi's professionalism and strong will prevailed throughout his tragedy, however, and on August 2, 1955, he passed a staff health examination. On Friday, August 5, 1955, after spending 105 days in the hospital, he was released. In an interview with **Newsweek**, Lugosi stated that his rehabilitation was "the greatest thing that ever happened to me."

Fifteen days later, he began work on United Artists' **BLACK SLEEP** along with Basil Rathbone, Lon Chaney Jr., Akim Tamiroff, John Carradine and Tor Johnson. (Johnson appeared with Lugosi in all the films of his post-narcotics career.) Seven days after beginning **BLACK SLEEP**, on April 24, 1955, Lugosi married his fifth wife —Hope Linninger, a clerk in a film studio editing department who had

Taxi Driver

(1976)

In Martin Scorsese's first feature *Who's That Knocking at My Door*, the film's lead character *J.R.* (Harvey Keitel) starts his relationship with *the Girl* (Zina Bethune) when he spots her on the Staten Island ferry reading a French fashion magazine that he notices has a picture from *The Searchers* in it. Then Harvey proceeds, at great length and detail, to describe the "*Wayne epic*" to Zina.

When the guinea hoods of *Mean Streets* go to the movies after ripping off the Scarsdale kids of their firecracker money, it's *The Searchers* they go see (though in real life I doubt Scorsese would be as tolerant of Tony's buffoonish carrying on in the cinema as Charlie seems to be).

Like the way Kenneth Anger scored *Scorpio Rising* with the rock 'n' roll 45s from his own personal turntable, Scorsese does the same thing in *Who's That Knocking at My Door*, focusing primarily on his fifties rhythm and blues and doo-wop 45s. Defiantly ignoring the music of the day (i.e. the British Invasion), save one group, naturally, *The Searchers*.

Aside from shout-outs to *The Searchers*, other John Ford touchstones in Scorsese's oeuvre include in *Who's That Knocking at My Door* when J.R. holds court with the Girl on Lee Marvin's character *Liberty Valance*.

And in his Roger Corman-produced low-budget epic *Box-car Bertha*, where his whole cinematic conception of the thirties seems derived from Ford's *The Grapes of Wrath*. Also in the way Bogdanovich in *The Last Picture Show*, Spielberg in *The Sugarland Express*, and Milius in *Dillinger* use Ford regular Ben Johnson as the personification of the Ford mythic ideal, is how young Martin uses John Ford regular John Carradine in *Boxcar Bertha*.

Then there's Paul Schrader's two-script reworking of *The Searchers*, Martin Scorsese's *Taxi Driver* and Schrader's own *Hardcore*. *Taxi Driver* isn't a *"paraphrased remake"* of *The Searchers* like Bogdanovich's *What's Up, Doc?* is a paraphrased remake of Hawks' *Bringing Up Baby* or De Palma's *Dressed to Kill* is a paraphrased remake of Hitchcock's *Psycho*. But it's about as close as you can get to a paraphrased remake and not *actually* being one. Robert De Niro's taxi driving protagonist Travis Bickle *is* John Wayne's Ethan Edwards.

In *Scorsese on Scorsese*, the director explained: *"I was think-ing about the John Wayne character in The Searchers. He doesn't say much. . . . He doesn't belong anywhere, since he just fought a war he believed in and lost, but he has a great love within him that's been stamped out. He gets carried away, so that during the long search for the young girl, he kills more buffalo than necessary because it's less food for the Comanche. But throughout, he's determined that they'll find her, as he says, 'As sure as the turning of the earth.'"*

Cybill Shepherd's Betsy *is* Martha (the woman Ethan adores but can't have). Jodie Foster's child prostitute Iris Steensma *is* Natalie Wood's Debbie (the innocent in the hands of savages he can save). And Harvey Keitel's pimp Sport *is* Henry Brandon's Comanche warrior Scar. In *Who's That Knocking at My Door* Harvey talks to Zina at length about Brandon's Scar, *"He was more nasty than Wayne could ever get [that's debatable], but then he was the bad guy. There were a lotta nasty Comanches in that picture."*

In Ford's film it's not just the young girl who must be *saved*, it's her white skin and Anglo Saxon heritage that must be *avenged*, after her life-is-not-worth-living defilement by the dark-skinned savage Scar.

But to get at the heart of the duality between the two pictures, you have to go back to Paul Schrader's script and his original intention.

Taxi Driver tells the story of a lonely man named *Travis Bickle* (played by Robert De Niro). He's one of many faceless people existing by themselves that big American cities are filled with. Solitary men, living solitary lives, without family or friends or loved ones.

His only form of self-expression is a handwritten diary he endlessly pores over which nobody will ever read.

At the film's beginning, you could almost classify Travis as a disaffected innocent. But part of the pull of the picture is watching him slowly *lose* that innocence. And what becomes both scary and thrilling is watching what replaces that lost innocence.

Paul Schrader and Martin Scorsese's sympathetic portrait of this malcontent chronicles his day-to-day, week-to-week, month-to-month existence. And as the film pulls us along through Travis' routine, we see how bloody easy it is for him to drift into violent fantasies, perceived injustices, and a thirst for action that only a bloodletting will quench. We see how easy it is for Travis—all by his lonesome—to become at first a crackpot, then a nutjob, then finally a sociopathic time bomb.

One of the great anxieties of *Taxi Driver* is that it's shot from Travis Bickle's perspective. And that perspective is of a man who's a racist.

Not a loudmouth racist like Peter Boyle's character *Joe*, or the type of troublemaking redneck movie racist that Don Stroud specialized in at the time.

Travis never says anything overtly racist about the black residents of New York he shares the streets with.

He never calls them "*niggers.*"

Characters in *Mean Streets* use that slur. As does Scorsese himself, playing Travis' cuckolded backseat passenger who muses about what a .44 Magnum can do to his wife's pussy.

Peter Boyle's Wizard refers to black folks as "*mau-maus.*"

But the only time Travis refers to black folks it's as "*spooks.*" And he makes a case for his fairness as a taxi driver saying, "*Some won't even take spooks. Don't make no difference to me.*"

Yet the film makes it obvious he sees black males as figures of malevolent criminality. He's repelled by any contact with them. They are to be feared or at the very least avoided. And since we watch the film from Travis' point of view, *we* do as well (that amazing low-angle dolly shot of the black pimp, in the all-night cafeteria, tapping the table with his finger). Part of the anxiety the viewer feels while watching the movie comes from the question the movie forces you to ask yourself.

Is this movie—Taxi Driver—a movie about a racist, or is it a racist movie?

The answer is clearly the former. And what makes the film a gutsy masterpiece is it dares to pose that question to the audience, and then allows them to devise their own answer. In the years since he wrote the screenplay, Paul Schrader has articulated that Travis' racism stems from the fact that the frustrated and powerless poor tend to take out their resentment not on the powerful class above them, but the even more powerless class below them. And while in a larger and more political context that is true, that's not the most important reason that Schrader made Travis a racist. The real reason for Travis' antagonism towards black folks is because it matches Ethan Edwards' hatred of the Comanches in *The Searchers*. Yet as rough as Scorsese's picture is, it's still a watered-down version of Schrader's original nihilistic text. Because in Schrader's original script, all the characters at the end that Travis kills were black. Harvey Keitel's pimp Sport *was* black, as was the guy who managed the fuck hotel that Murray Moston played in Scorsese's film.

According to Schrader, he was asked by the producers and Columbia Pictures to change the character of Sport from black to white because the race riots of a few years earlier still cast a long shadow. And there was a fear if any violence broke out in a cinema, it would cause the film to be yanked from theatres for public safety. As happened, Schrader pointed out, a few years later to Walter Hill's *The Warriors*.

Okay, is it possible Columbia could be timid about a provocative film like *Taxi Driver*?

Hell yeah, over thirty years later Columbia Pictures was timid as hell about the reaction to *Django Unchained*.

But Columbia Pictures was worried about what, exactly?

Violence breaking out among black patrons?

Why, because the film provoked violence, or that black ticket buyers would be so incensed that the film's pimp character was portrayed by a black actor that they would riot in the cinema in outrage?

If that was the case, how come there weren't riots across the country during screenings of *Death Wish*? In that film Charles Bronson pretended to shoot more black actors than white.

The Warriors analogy doesn't really work either. It wasn't that film's on-screen mayhem or Michael Beck that caused violent incidents to break out in a few of the houses screening that picture. It was because since it was a *gang picture, gang members* showed up at some engagements during opening weekend.

Taxi Driver might have provoked a couple of angry think pieces in a few newspapers . . . but actual violence?

Considering, during the seventies, there was no shortage of black male criminality on display on movie theatre screens or TV picture tubes, the studio and the producers' fear of outraged violent black males not only seems far-fetched, it smacks of Travis Bickle's warped reasoning.

So let's get this straight—Columbia Pictures had no problem whatsoever with all those villainous Caribbean brothers plotting, scheming, and murdering in *The Deep*, but *Taxi Driver* was a bridge too far?

Any way you slice it, Scorsese, and producers Michael and Julia Phillips, and Columbia Pictures changing the pimp character of *Sport* from black to white was a *societal compromise*.

And frankly, the only reason it can survive a compromise of that magnitude is the magnetic performance of Harvey Keitel as Sport.

I mean, seriously, *Taxi Driver* without Harvey Keitel?

What would that even be?

You associate Keitel so much with the movie, the movie *without* him seems *as* unthinkable as the movie *without* Robert De Niro.

Yet when the Phillipses first set *Taxi Driver* up at Columbia Pictures—back when Robert Mulligan was the director—it wasn't Robert De Niro who was earmarked for the role of Travis Bickle, but Jeff Bridges, coming off of an Academy Award nomination for *Thunderbolt and Lightfoot* and an acclaimed performance in the critical sleeper *Hearts of the West*.

Now to be fair, seemingly, Scorsese never considered the change of Sport's race from black to white as big a deal as I do.

I'm pretty sure where Mr. Scorsese was coming from—if there was a *chance* of riots leading to the film being pulled from cinema screens that wasn't a chance worth taking. Besides, Marty had wanted the film to have a part for Harvey Keitel and he was frustrated that it didn't (he originally offered Harvey the part of Cybill Shepherd's flirtatious coworker, but the actor turned it down).

So if by making the pimp character white, that opened up a good role for Harvey Keitel, great! Problem solved.

But Keitel forced the fraudulent aspect of the conceit because he wanted to meet a real-life counterpart.

Yes, Harvey Keitel wanted to meet a real-life *white* New York pimp. Not realizing that the "*Great White Pimp*" was a mythological cinematic creation. Nevertheless, Schrader was tasked with hitting the streets of New York looking for a white pimp for Harvey to base his character on. Needless to say, since there weren't any white pimps in New York, Schrader never found one. He said, every once in a while somebody might say, "*Yeah, I think I heard about one who hangs out about six blocks away, but I ain't never seen 'em.*" If there was a white pimp out there, Schrader said, he never found him. So Keitel was forced to do all of his character research with a black gentleman of leisure.

So, granting the idea of *Taxi Driver* without either Robert De Niro or Harvey Keitel is unthinkable, let's think the unthinkable.

Let's imagine that famous scene in *Taxi Driver*, where *Travis* and *Sport* meet each other for the first time and the taxi driver approaches the pimp about *Iris* ("*That bitch will suck your cock till it explodes!*").

Let's imagine the same scene, but with Jeff Bridges playing a less urban, more hayseed version of *Travis*, and Max *The Mack* Julien playing a black, silky smooth *Sport*. No doubt when Schrader first imagined *Sport* in his mind's eye, it was an actor like Max Julien he imagined portraying him (Julien is *so* perfect, Schrader could have written *Sport* with him in mind).

A colorfully threaded *Sport*, sporting a miniature purple fuzzy fedora balanced on his short-haired afro, talking about Jodie Foster "*sucking your cock till it explodes!*"

Does the subtextual racism of *Taxi Driver* now become text?

Or does it just make the whole tableau more convincingly authentic?

And *who* couldn't handle that?

Black audiences?

Or is it more likely that the white folks financing the movie were the ones made to feel uncomfortable by the imagery in Schrader's original script? So uncomfortable that a fear of black males causing violence in cinemas was conveniently trotted out as an excuse to change Schrader's *Sport* from black to white?

With all their anxiety, it begs the question, why did Columbia Pictures want to do Schrader's script for *Taxi Driver* in the first place?

Well, one of the big reasons was because Schrader was one of the reddest hot screenwriters in town, due to the gobsmacking price he elicited from Warner Bros. for his script *The Yakuza*.

Also, it didn't hurt that the three producers of the smash hit *The Sting*, Michael and Julia Phillips, and (superstar producer) Tony Bill, brought the material to Columbia. But what really encouraged Columbia Pictures to green-light Schrader's screenplay (originally with Robert Mulligan at the helm), had nothing to do with its literary allusions to Dostoyevsky's *Notes from the Underground*, or its similarity to Arthur Bremer's diary, but its cracked-mirror reflection of the Michael Winner-directed, Charles Bronson-starring, smash hit vigilante action drama *Death Wish* (as well as other revenge-based dramas, very popular at the time).

With seminal classics like *Taxi Driver*, it's easy to just think of a world where they always existed and were always destined to exist.

But that's not how a hot potato screenplay like *Taxi Driver* gets produced by a major Hollywood studio. The truth is *if* you revere Martin Scorsese's *Taxi Driver* (like I do), then you have Michael Winner's *Death Wish* to thank for its existence.★

The Charles Bronson New York vigilante drama *Death Wish* opened in July 1974. The narrator of its trailer bombastically pro-

---

★Same thing with *The Wild Bunch*. I love Peckinpah, and I'm not fond of Richard Brooks. Nevertheless, without the success of Brooks' western *The Professionals*, there wouldn't have been a *Wild Bunch*.

claimed, "*This is a story of a man who decided to clean up the most violent city in the world!*" By 1975, one year after *Death Wish* and one year before *Taxi Driver*, violent revenge dramas would begin to flood the cinemas of the world. William Margold, first-string film critic for the sex rag the *Hollywood Press*, dubbed the genre (amusingly) "*Revengeamatics.*"

Like Bronson would go after New York muggers over the death of his wife and rape of his daughter in *Death Wish*, George Kennedy would go after European Baader-Meinhof inspired terrorists over the death of *his* family in *The "Human" Factor*.

CIA assassin James Caan would seek revenge against his former partner/best friend Robert Duvall in Sam Peckinpah's *The Killer Elite* (not a great Peckinpah movie, but with the last great *slow-motion* Peckinpah action sequences).

Alain Delon's top-of-the-heap hit man would kill all the Mafia dons responsible for blowing up his wife and child (in a car bomb meant for him) in *No Way Out* (which I saw at the Old Town Mall, with my mother, on a double feature with the Peter Fonda and Telly Savalas violent South African diamond heist flick, *Killer Force*).

Grindhouse men-pushed-too-far potboilers like *Johnny Firecloud* and *The No Mercy Man* would lure cars to drive-ins.

Jan-Michael Vincent's Carrol Jo Hummer would dump sexy bad guy L. Q. Jones in a garbage dumpster and drive his truck, "*the Blue Mule,*" through that big glass sign in *White Line Fever*.

Phil Karlson's seminal action classic of 1973, *Walking Tall*, would get two sequels in 1975. The official one from Bing Crosby Productions, the awkwardly titled *Part 2: Walking Tall*, which included a new actor playing real-life sheriff and real-life fascist *Buford Pusser*, the very good Bo Svenson (who would make the role his own), replacing departing star Joe Don Baker. Nowadays *Part 2: Walking Tall* doesn't play so bad, but back in its day, its mild PG-rated pulse, when compared to the original film's hard R impact, pleased few.

Then original Buford Pusser, Joe Don Baker, and original *Walking Tall* maestro, Phil Karlson, reunited for a Paramount-backed follow-up, the damn good and damn brutal *Framed*, which would prove to be Karlson's last film, and one of the best last films made by one of Andrew Sarris' "*expressive esoterica*" genre cool kids. Karlson's two closest colleagues in the seventies still plugging away shooting movies—Robert Aldrich and Don Siegel—*wish* they exited the stage with a movie as strong as *Framed*.

These films came out the year before *Taxi Driver* opened.

Martin Scorsese's film would open in early 1976.

Later that year, Peter Fonda would be driven *Fighting Mad* and Bo Svenson would be brought to his *Breaking Point*.

Kris Kristofferson would lead a *Vigilante Force* and Jan-Michael Vincent would wage a one-man war against that force in the same movie.

Both Timothy Bottoms and Stephen McHattie would fight back against crooked Southern sheriffs in *A Small Town in Texas* and *Moving Violation*.

And Margaux Hemingway would go after her rapist with a high-powered rifle in *Lipstick* (which is how Stephen McHattie would eventually end his conflict in *Moving Violation*).

And if the trailer narrator of *Death Wish* was correct, and Charles Bronson "*cleaned up the most violent city in the world*," then it was left up to Franco Nero to clean up the second most violent city in the world—Rome—in *Street Law*. The narrator of that film would declare, "*Franco Nero wields the killing cannon in Street Law! If you can survive on these streets . . . you can survive anywhere!*"

In February 1976 *Travis Bickle* would be compelled to rescue New York child prostitute *Iris Steensma* from the sexual bondage of her street pimp *Sport* in *Taxi Driver*. Three months later—April 1976—Robert Mitchum's son Jim Mitchum, as *Big Jim Calhoun*, would travel to Los Angeles to rescue his sister (pretty Karen Lamm) from Hollywood prostitution in *Trackdown* (like Schrader's *Jake Van Dorn* would later do in his *Hardcore*). *Trackdown*'s trailer narrator asked audiences, "*What would you do if it was your sister?*"

When *Taxi Driver* was first released the film had a higher art pedigree than any of the above movies. It won *the Palme d'or* at the *Cannes Film Festival,* it eventually received four *Academy Award nominations,* and great reviews from the best critics. Yet Columbia Pictures revealed its real reason for making the picture one year later in 1977. That was when Columbia rereleased *Taxi Driver* as the lower half of a double feature toplined by a "Revengeamatic" independent pickup titled *The Farmer* (tagline: "*The Farmer doesn't get mad . . . He gets even!*"). Columbia Pictures' ad campaign insinuated that *The Farmer* and *(the) Taxi Driver*'s story and quest were

the same. Two stories, about two heroes, who have been pushed too far and decide to do something about it.

This is how I first saw *Taxi Driver*, on the lower half of a double feature with *The Farmer* at my favorite grindhouse *the Carson Twin Cinema*. While I was fascinated by the TV spot for *Taxi Driver* that played over and over the year it initially was released, I still needed an adult to take me to see the R-rated film. And that year, that didn't happen. But by 1977 (I was 15) I looked tall enough to get into a lot of R-rated movies on my own (especially if they played at the Carson Twin Cinema). But it wasn't till this 1977 *The Farmer* rerelease that *Taxi Driver* was finally doing what the producers and the studio were so nervous about, playing on a large number of screens in black neighborhoods, in front of black audiences. The year before, in its original release, the film never really made it to the secondary markets—cinemas in the black neighborhoods, discount houses, grindhouses, or drive-ins.

So in '77, at the Carson Twin Cinema, alongside *The Farmer* with an (except for me) all-black audience, that's how I first saw *Taxi Driver.*

What was our response?

I dug it, *they* dug it, and as an audience, *we* dug it.

But it's safe to say it didn't play like the subversion of the vigilante action drama that Schrader intended when he wrote the script. In *that* theatre, with *that* audience, on a double bill with *that* other movie, *Taxi Driver* played like a *Death Wish* rip-off.

Yeah, the lead guy was more fucked up than the guy in *Death Wish*, but the guy in *Death Wish* was pretty fucked up. And in both movies—when the lead guy goes up against the bad guys armed to the teeth—you're rooting for him.

The first half was way too stretched out for most exploitation audiences. But, while it was slow, it wasn't boring. And the reason it never grew dull was due to the random moments of street milieu that Scorsese captured.

No film ever made captured the chaos of urban street life in New York in the seventies like Scorsese did in *Taxi Driver*, and the audience laughed with recognition. The violence, the despair, the grotesquery, and the absurd comedy had never been depicted with such verve and accuracy in a Hollywood picture before. The movie had a realistic vibe that we plugged into because we recognized its authenticity.

The only other time I felt *that* level of authenticity with the Carson Twin Cinema audience, and the picture that was playing on the screen, was during *The Mack*.

Before the shoot-'em-up climax, *Taxi Driver* had a few sections where the audience had a big reaction.

Right from the beginning the audience thought Travis was a fucking nut. They found him ridiculous, and the more the film went on, the more ridiculous he acted, the funnier we found him. But we didn't think Travis was just a nut, we thought Travis Bickle was a goofball.

His insipid diary entries drew outright guffaws.

When Betsy walks out of the porno movie theatre and leaves Travis alone on the sidewalk talking to himself, the audience busted up laughing—*What the fuck did you think was gonna happen, you stupid motherfucker?*

When he tipped over his television set and it practically exploded—*what an idiot!*

When he goes to the record store and buys Betsy the Kris Kristofferson album—*You gonna buy it for her? She probably already got it.*

And when Travis stormed into Palantine's campaign headquarters and started acting all crazy, we fell out laughing then too. Especially when he did his little hand-to-hand combat move and made Albert Brooks jump a mile.

For the film's first half—to us, the audience in the Carson Twin Cinema—it was a comedy about a stupid idiot who's turning into more and more of a nutter as the story goes on.

I doubt during its *Grand Palais* screening at the *Cannes* film festival *Taxi Driver* induced as many laughs as it did that Saturday afternoon. But in a way, the black audience laughing at Travis Bickle's antics in *Taxi Driver* wasn't that different from that hip Sunset Strip (mostly) white audience at the Tiffany laughing at Peter Boyle's *Joe*.

Then the moment happened that made the whole theatre burst into hysterics. That one guy walking down the street, ranting and raving that he's going to kill his woman (*"I'll kill 'er! I'll kill that bitch!"*). We laughed so hard at that guy, we were a little disconnected from the movie for the next twenty minutes. Because we kept cracking each other up about it. That guy was so funny, we had to make ourselves stop laughing.

What was it about the *I'll kill the bitch* guy that cracked our audience up so much? Simple, everybody in the theatre had seen *that guy* before. I had seen *that guy*. And when we stepped outside the theatre into the Scottsdale shopping center where the Carson Twin Cinema was located, we might see *that guy* again. But what really cracked us up was we had never seen *that guy* in a Hollywood movie.

But the film's biggest laugh was at the Palantine rally. Scorsese shows us Travis is there by cutting to his shoes in the crowd. Then the camera pans up to him, revealing Travis grinning like a maniac, sporting a Mohawk! When we saw Travis shaved his head like that, the whole theatre burst out laughing. I'm talking hysterically laughing. I'm talking rolling in the aisle laughing—*Get a load of this goddamn crazy fool!* It was a nice reminder that even though the movie was turning more serious, we were still watching the portrait of an insane idiot. And we laughed through his whole bumbling assassination attempt. Especially the overhead shot as Travis runs away from the secret service, bumping into bystanders. God only knows how many times I've seen *Taxi Driver*, and every time Travis'

Mohawk is revealed—in my head—I hear *the Carson Twin Cinema* audience's hilarious reaction.

I n the first half of *Taxi Driver*, it was just the story of a goofy guy going crazy, depicted against a very authentic street/nightlife milieu. When *Taxi Driver* stopped being a comedy about a goofy guy was when child prostitute Iris Steensma hopped into the back seat of Travis' cab.

Travis, who says nothing, watches in his rearview mirror as Sport yanks her out of the cab (*"Bitch, be cool!"*), and tosses that crumbled up twenty-dollar bill onto the front seat (*"Cabbie, just forget about this, it's nothing"*).

That crumpled up twenty-dollar bill was such a strong visual image that it sobered up an audience that had grown accustomed to snickering.

From that point on, not only did the audience start taking the film seriously, it also started taking Travis seriously. Which also coincides with Travis taking his weight lifting and gun handling and preparation for God knows what seriously.

That goddamn crumpled up twenty-dollar bill.

From the moment we saw the effect it had on Travis, and we knew what it represented (the money that keeps the girl on the streets, the cheap payoffs that keep her in her place, the one lone fleeting opportunity that Travis *could have* saved her), we knew—eventually—he *would* save her. Then, a movie that defined itself by its random incidents suddenly snapped into focus. Suddenly all the random incidents didn't seem so random. The filmmakers wanted us to know who this guy was before they sent him off on his moral imperative quest for nobility.

Then the movie started playing like a real movie. But frankly, a *more real* movie than we were used to.

Characters weren't the normal movie good guys-bad guys.

Travis was a fucking loon.

But in this instance, he might be the man for the job.

When De Niro has his first scene with Keitel's Sport, it doesn't go quite like we might have thought. For one, as Pauline Kael pointed out, Keitel's pimp is surprisingly personable. When he makes jokes at Travis' expense, we get the jokes, even if Travis doesn't, and we laugh (my audience *loved* Keitel's Sport, and they also loved Steven Prince's gun salesman, "*The Magnum? They use that in Africa for killing elephants!*").

A small thing that makes a big difference is Sport wants Travis to be a satisfied customer ("*Go ahead, man, have a good time*"). Sport isn't a monster in a monster movie like the gargoyles in *They Call Her One-Eye*. He's a businessman.

Even Jodie Foster's Iris isn't the normal exploitation character. For one, she seems much younger during her lunch with Travis than she does in her streetwalker getup. She talks like a real person (*Niki*, the corresponding character in Schrader's *Hardcore*, is entertaining and we like her, but she always sounds like a character in a movie). Despite the life she's living, Foster's Iris comes across as naive to the cost. Iris isn't hopeless, there is still something to be saved.

An interesting change on Schrader's part when it comes to syncing up *Taxi Driver* with *The Searchers* is what sets Travis off on his moral quest to save Iris, as opposed to Ethan's quest to save Debbie.

Debbie never asks for Ethan or Martin (Jeffrey Hunter) to go on this long journey on her behalf. But—for one fleeting moment of clarity—Iris does. Was it *lucky* of all the cabs in New York she hopped into Travis's? Once when Dan Rather was conducting an interview with me, I mentioned early in my career I got lucky. He scoffed at my use of the word "*luck.*" Declaring, "*Some say, what you call 'luck,' is when opportunity meets preparation.*"

Well, I buy that definition (though I also do believe in Sidney Poitier's definition of serendipity, *"when Providence comes down and kisses you on both cheeks"*). Travis *had* been preparing for some apocalyptic showdown. Some cataclysmic event. A moment of reckoning, or as Big John Milius would call it, *Big Wednesday*—a moment where Travis can distinguish himself.

And when Iris jumps in his cab, hoping to escape, Travis' preparation finds opportunity. He's haunted by that encounter, but so was the audience. Even more than Travis, *we* in the audience know that was a fleeting moment. *We* know that when he eventually approaches her, she'll laugh it off (like she does). She probably won't even remember it (she doesn't). She'll insist she's fine and there's nothing to worry about.

But . . . that one moment when she jumped into the back seat of his cab, she was clearly and unmistakably asking someone to save her from these people.

And then it was only a matter of time before Travis would take all his guns and save *"Sweet Iris."*

And that's when *Taxi Driver* started operating like *Death Wish*, like *Trackdown* (which I had already seen), like *The Farmer.*

Paul Schrader is crystal clear that he's subverting the *Death Wish* movie model. In fact, Schrader would have gone far further than Scorsese ultimately did with Travis' standoff with the pimps. If Schrader had directed the film, he would have surrealistically painted the hallway walls of the fuck hotel with crimson red blood, like in a Kenji Misumi samurai film. Schrader always saw Travis' last stand as a *"samurai death with honor,"* that's why he has Travis try to commit suicide (but his gun is empty). That's why he always saw the shootout at the climax as Japanese-style surrealism, the splashing red paint against the walls creating an abstraction of the violence. While Martin understood where Paul was coming from, he didn't comply. When I asked him why not, he humorously snapped back, "*Because I'm not Kon Ichikawa, that's why. I could only stage the scene from a world I knew.*"*

Yet, Scorsese also told David Thompson, "*I was shocked by the way audiences took the violence [in Taxi Driver]. Previously I'd been surprised by audience reaction to The Wild Bunch, which I saw in a Warner Brothers screening room with a friend and loved. But a week later I took some friends to see it in a theatre and it was as if the violence became an extension of the audience and vice versa.*"

"*Shocked*"?

Really?

You were "*shocked*"?

So let's get this straight, a Roger Corman alumnus, Martin "*Boxcar Bertha*" Scorsese, who came within an inch of directing *I Escaped from Devil's Island*, directs one of the most kinetically charged violent climaxes in cinema history . . . and he was "*shocked*" that audiences were turned on by it?†

No, he wasn't.

That's just the kind of horseshit that a director would tell a David Thompson, or a Stephen Farber, or a Charles Champlin, or a Rex Reed, or a Rona Barrett and they'd let them get away with it.

But Scorsese being "*shocked*" by the audience's reaction to the climax of *Taxi Driver* is the kind of horseshit that film directors in-

---

*The effect that Schrader hoped to duplicate was probably something closer to the magnificent outrageousness of the candy apple red blood geysers in Kenji Misumi's *Baby Cart at the River Styx* than to Kon Ichikawa's *Fires on the Plain*.

†Forget about the sacrilege of suggesting Scorsese enjoyed a screening of *The Wild Bunch* more in a Warner Bros. screening room than he did with a wild, enthusiastic audience.

sincerely mumble when they've crafted a tremendously violent and controversial sequence and then find themselves on the hot seat with some interviewer having to answer for it.

They never say cinematic violence is fun.

They never say, I just wanted to end the movie with a bang.

They never say, I wanted to shock the audience out of their movie-trope-fed complacency (Ken Russell *might* say that, but very few directors who have ever lived had the balls that Ken Russell had).

No, like Peckinpah before him, Scorsese had to bend over backward to disingenuously describe those magnificent *exhilarating* violent scenes he crafted as *horrifying*.

I've already described how different *Taxi Driver* was from the other Revengeamatics that screened during that year and the year before that. Its characters, its milieu, its objective, its authorial voice, its literary aspirations.

But where *Taxi Driver* lined up with *Coffy, Fighting Mad, Johnny Firecloud, Trackdown, The "Human" Factor* and the other Revengeamatics that unspooled on the Carson Twin Cinema screens was the way the whole film built to a climactic and orgasmic explosion of violence. A climactic explosion—in Scorsese's hands—that is as brilliant and kinetic as any shootout sequence ever captured on film.

So *exactly* what was the *"shocking"* part of the audience's reaction to *Taxi Driver* when Scorsese first saw it during its initial release?

Scorsese explained to Thompson, "*I saw Taxi Driver once in a theatre, on opening night, and everybody was yelling and screaming at the shootout. When I made it, I didn't intend to have the audience react with that feeling, YES DO IT! LET'S GO OUT AND KILL!*"

Well, maybe they were yelling and screaming because the audience had been led to both that ending and that violent explosion the entire film. And now—*at the film's climax*—they reacted like an American movie audience and yelled, screamed, and cheered.

And on opening night of *Taxi Driver*, a big part of that screaming, yelling, yelping, and even laughing had to do with the audience's jumping-out-of-their-seats reaction to Scorsese's graphic gore effects in the final shootout.

Of course they're rooting for Travis. He's saving a twelve-year-old girl who's been put out on the sidewalks of New York to sell her prepubescent pussy to anybody walking by with twenty-five dollars. Twenty-five dollars she's not even allowed to keep.

Of course we're rooting for Travis to win his one-man stand against the sleazy pimps, even if he did start it.

If we're not meant to (at least sorta) root for Travis' success in his mission, why make Iris a child?

If Iris was nineteen or twenty nothing in the story would be any different. She could *still* be lost and brainwashed. She could have *still* had the same moment of clarity. She could have *still* hopped into Travis' back seat hoping for rescue. The only thing in the scenario that her not being a child would have changed, would be Travis' moral imperative and the audience's perception of that quest.

The structure of most Revengeamatics is the audience is driven mad watching the lead character get fucked in the ass for the first half of the film, and then is brought to climax as the lead character wipes out all the offending fuckers in the film's final reels.

Now Scorsese monkeys with this structure during *Taxi Driver*'s first half, but by the film's last forty minutes—structure-wise—*Taxi Driver* might as well be *Trackdown*.

Scorsese has jerked us off so hard throughout the film, now that we're heading towards the climax, going where the whole movie has always threatened to go, we can't wait to cum. And when Travis blows Murray Moston's brains out the back of his head—and they go *splat* against the wall of Iris's fuck hotel room—we do.

Which brings me to my rhetorical question to maestro Scorsese:

When you direct one of the most kinetic and outrageously violent action scenes ever contained in a studio-produced motion picture . . . *violent catharsis* surely must have been one of the filmmaker's goals, right?

Is Travis Bickle disturbing and troubling?

No doubt.

Yet, as much of a wacko as the movie presents him, neither Schrader, nor Scorsese, nor De Niro go all the way in indicting the character. Steering him far closer to Charles Bronson's *Paul Kersey* in *Death Wish* than Peter Boyle's *Joe Curran* in *Joe*.

As opposed to the climax of *Taxi Driver*—where Travis kills the sex traffickers—during the climax of *Joe*—when Joe blasts hippies at the commune with automatic weapons—it didn't turn audiences on.

It wasn't a great action scene.

It wasn't intended to be kinetic.

And we weren't meant to find it cathartic.

Its intention was to be horrifying and ironically tragic.

And that's how audiences reacted to it.

Also, *Joe* doesn't engage in any societal compromises or audience pandering. On the contrary, it flew in the face of compromise and pandering. *Joe*'s great screenwriter, Norman Wexler, *could have* given Joe some bullshit backstory in an attempt for the audience to get their bearings on this challenging lead character. But Wexler doesn't attempt to try and explain Joe or for Joe to explain himself.

Joe is just who he is.

Even Paul Schrader—in regard to Travis Bickle—slightly invests in this type of character Tom Foolery by suggesting Travis is a Vietnam veteran, and that he did a tour of duty during the war.

Horseshit.

No fucking way was Travis in Vietnam.

The extent of Travis' paranoia of black males is only credible if they are an *other* that he has only had superficial contact with.

How do you do a tour of duty in Vietnam and only have superficial contact with black dudes? The answer is you can't.

Okay, say he did serve with black dudes in Vietnam, does that mean he has to like 'em?

No, not necessarily.

But it's not convincing he would *fear* them the way Travis does.

In the movie, he fears them as an *other*. If you serve in war with six or seven black guys (officers and enlisted men) they wouldn't be an *other* (unless, possibly, if Travis was an MP).

I don't have a problem with Travis' fraudulent claim in the movie.

The only proof the movie offers up of Travis' military service (no Vietnam flashbacks) is his account to Joe Spinell and his jacket.

Fine, Travis spends the entire movie demonstrating to the audience that he's an unreliable narrator, completely delusional, and he constantly presents himself to characters in a fraudulent manner (usually to get something he wants at the moment).

He bought the jacket in an Army Navy Store.

Scorsese further clarified to Thompson his intentions in regard to the audience when he was making *Taxi Driver*: "*The idea was to create a violent catharsis, so they'd find themselves saying, YES KILL, and then afterwards realize, OH MY GOD NO.*"

Okay, that's slightly less horseshit.

But . . . if the goal was "*OH MY GOD NO,*" then show a movie about a man who spends the entire movie speaking about cleaning up the scum of the city, and demonstrate that it's black males he considers the scum of the city. Then at the climax he kills a bunch of black males because of their defilement of a young white girl and is turned into a hero by the very same city (i.e. white society).

That would have been viewed by audiences as *OH MY GOD NO!*

And *that* would have been *The Searchers.*

Cinema Speculation

What If Brian De Palma Directed
Taxi Driver Instead of Martin Scorsese?

Brian De Palma introduced me to Paul Schrader. We made a pilgrimage out to see Manny Farber, the critic, in San Diego. I wanted Paul to do a script of "The Gambler" by Dostoevsky for me. But Brian took Paul out for dinner, and they contrived it so I couldn't find them. By the time I tracked them down, three hours later, they'd cooked up "Obsession." But Brian told me that Paul had this script, "Taxi Driver," that he didn't want to do or couldn't do at that time, and wondered if I'd be interested in reading it. So I read it and my friend [Sandy Weintraub] read it and she said it was fantastic: We agreed that this was the kind of picture we should be making.

—Martin Scorsese in Scorsese On Scorsese

Yes, that's right, Brian De Palma was the actual first of the Movie Brats to read Paul Schrader's screenplay and contemplate directing it.

The story goes Brian De Palma and Paul Schrader became friendly associates when Schrader—a critic at the *Times*—wrote a good review for De Palma's new film, *Sisters*. Leading to critic Schrader interviewing the young filmmaker for his newspaper. During the interview, the two men continued to get on well, with Schrader revealing to De Palma that he plays chess. Since De Palma does too, they proceeded to play chess. Which, for these two career strategists, to start their relationship battling it out over a chess board is so metaphorically perfect as to be suspect as legend-building public relations.

While trying to capture the other man's bishop, Schrader just happens to mention he's written a screenplay. "*Oh no, not another one!*" De Palma groans.

Schrader calms him down; "*I'm just saying, since we're talking, I wrote a script once.*"

The script he was referring to was the first draft of *Taxi Driver*.

And despite De Palma rolling his eyes at the mention of this film critic's screenplay, he eventually did read it. And recognizing the material as a genuine piece of work, was tempted to do it himself.

In later years he shrugged it off as, "*I just thought it was better suited for Marty.*" But sometimes he admits the reason he didn't do it. He didn't think it was commercial enough.

Admittedly, that's a rather depressing reason.

It wasn't commercial enough?

So it *was* commercial enough for Columbia Pictures?

And it *was* commercial enough for the original director, Robert Mulligan?

And it *was* commercial enough for Mulligan's original leading man, Jeff Bridges?

And then after winning Ellen Burstyn the Academy Award for Best Actress, it's commercial enough for Martin Scorsese?

And after winning the Academy Award for Best Supporting Actor, it's commercial enough for Robert De Niro?

But it *wasn't* commercial enough for Brian De Palma?

In all fairness to the young De Palma of that era, a movie that would put asses in seats is what Brian was looking for. His brand-new Twentieth Century Fox rock 'n' roll musical extravaganza *Phantom of the Paradise* was playing in New York to empty auditoriums.

He didn't want that feeling of watching another of his movies being indifferently projected on a screen in a sparsely populated auditorium.

So the next film out of the gate should be a hit.

And while it's clear he considered making *Taxi Driver*, he ultimately decided to enlist Schrader to write with him a *Vertigo* retread titled *Obsession* that would further play into De Palma's "the New Hitchcock" personality. So the choice for De Palma in 1976 isn't between *Taxi Driver* and *Carrie*. It's *Taxi Driver* and *Obsession*. Brian De Palma does *Taxi Driver* in 1976, instead of *Obsession*, and still does *Carrie* later that year! Or he does both *Obsession* and *Carrie* but he holds on to the script of *Taxi Driver*, and does it after *Carrie* in 1977 instead of *The Fury*.

But just because Brian De Palma was commercially motivated doesn't mean he was prescient. It was *Taxi Driver* that ended up connecting with audiences, and it was his slow, lush *Obsession* that audiences ignored.

Now *Obsession* isn't a *bad* movie, just a bit of a dreary one. And Cliff Robertson's lead performance is extremely unappealing, especially for a movie about a doomed love story. Robertson is about as sexy as grandpa's big toe. But in all fairness, Geneviève Bujold's tremendous performance is far more memorable than Cliff Robertson's creepiness. And she's at the center of, up to that time, *Be Black Baby* aside, the finest De Palma cinematic set piece of his filmography.

The sequence where Bujold in a closeup reverts back to a seven-year-old little girl, and remembers what actually happened the night of the kidnapping.

Despite all my misgivings about *Obsession* (Robertson's lead performance, the film's lack of humor), the doomed love story at its center *kinda* works. As does the impact of Vilmos Zsigmond's dreamy-floaty camera and Bernard Herrmann's lushly pounding score. So by the time you reach the climax at the airport—as Herrmann's score seems to hurl the lead characters (Robertson and Bujold) towards each other—you could be legitimately on the edge of your seat.

Also Schrader's melodramatic doomed love story—despite lacking common sense—also *sorta works* in a preposterous *Magnificent Obsession* kind of way.

It's unmistakably *a Brian De Palma movie.*

But due to its complete absence of humor, it's kind of a *bad* Brian De Palma movie.

All in all I wish De Palma had written the film himself. For a filmmaker who didn't start out as a screenwriter, De Palma was a pretty good screenwriter. At least he knew how to write *Brian De Palma movies* better than Paul Schrader.

It's a little funny-peculiar that De Palma found Schrader's script for *Taxi Driver* initially uncommercial. Because the commercial niche that Columbia Pictures later had no trouble exploiting was as a movie in the vein of *Death Wish.* The trailer suggested *Death Wish* with an even more seriously disturbed dude at the center. But the trailer decidedly does not announce itself as, *"This is the story of a dude with a fucked up head."* Instead, it paints a picture of a lone man in the crowd, rising up to be heard, who's had enough.

Like *Billy Jack.*

Like Joe Don Baker.

Like *Mr. Majestyk.*

Since Columbia Pictures did such an effective job selling *Taxi*

Driver as a *Death Wish*–style vigilante film, it's curious that aspect didn't occur to De Palma after his first read. Especially, since I can see De Palma, right after *Sisters*, doing a remarkable job on a film like *Death Wish*.

That's the kind of commercial gig Brian was on the hunt for (and he found when he read *Carrie*).

However once Marty read Schrader's material that was it. Marty once told Paul, "*When Brian De Palma gave me a copy of Taxi Driver and introduced us, I almost felt I wrote it myself. Not that I could write that way, but I felt everything. I was burning inside my fucking skin; I had to make it.*"

But it's still interesting to contemplate how close we came to a Brian De Palma directed *Taxi Driver* and *exactly* how that movie might have been different. I mean it would have been based on the same screenplay, how different could it have been?

I suspect, *mighty* different.

In fact, if the film's original director, Richard "*Summer of '42*" Mulligan, had shot Schrader's screenplay with Jeff Bridges playing Travis, I think *that* version would have been closer to Scorsese's version then De Palma's telling of the same story (in 1978 Richard Mulligan would do *his* version of a Scorsese movie, when he adapted Richard Price's second novel, *Bloodbrothers*).

The main difference I see between a Scorsese-directed version of Schrader's screenplay and a De Palma–directed version would be the matter of point of view.

I think it's entirely doubtful De Palma would have empathized with Travis Bickle the way Schrader does and the way Scorsese and De Niro did. With the film Martin Scorsese made, when you watch *Taxi Driver*, you *become* Travis Bickle. Regardless of whether or not you empathize or sympathize with the rituals of Travis' existence, you observe them. And in observing them, you come to understand them. And when you understand this lonely man, he stops being a monster—if he ever was one to begin with.

Scorsese, Schrader, and De Niro make you witness a man—from that man's perspective.

I'd speculate, when Brian De Palma first read Schrader's manuscript, he didn't see it as the first-person diary dream that Schrader intended. I'd bet De Palma's first reaction would have been along the lines of, "*Oh great, this can be my Repulsion.*"

I do believe that De Palma would have observed Travis the way Polanski observes Catherine Deneuve in *Repulsion*. A De Palma *Taxi Driver* wouldn't be linked with *Death Wish*. De Palma's *Taxi Driver* wouldn't have been a first-person character study disguised as a vigilante thriller. Nobody's going to misinterpret De Palma's Travis as heroic. Brian De Palma's *Taxi Driver* wouldn't have been *just* a thriller, it would have been a political thriller (kind of what *Blow Out* ended up being). De Palma would have focused on the story's political assassination element: Travis Bickle's story would have been how some looney becomes a political assassin. From Travis' place of displacement inside of society, to getting the big idea to whack out Palantine, to every little thing he does along the way, leading to the assassination attempt by Bickle (in full Mohawk glory) at the outdoor rally.

As opposed to the big clumsy fiasco that Scorsese stages, I see Brian shooting it—like the prom sequence in *Carrie*—as one of his grand slow-motion ballets. An action set piece of Bickle's failed attempt, scored by Bernard Herrmann—which would have no doubt been an extremely different score than the minimalist car noise—asshole with a sax—score Herrmann pawned off on Scorsese.★

And since *Taxi Driver* is the movie he would have done before he shot *Carrie*, you need not do anything but watch the whole *Car-*

★ Pauline Kael, who saw an earlier score-less cut of *Taxi Driver*, always claimed she preferred it without Herrmann's score.

rie prom sequence to see how De Palma would have orchestrated the assassination attempt scene in *Taxi Driver*.

What's the bucket of pig blood scene but an assassination scene?

Carrie White and Tommy Ross win an election (king and queen of the prom).

The victorious candidates are brought on stage where they're applauded by their cheering constituency.

However, among all this cheering, there's an individual with an imagined grudge against the female candidate.

Nancy Allen's blond-haired, red-lip-glossed *Chris Hargenson*, whose desire is to assassinate the candidate in front of her constituency at the very moment of her biggest triumph.

That filled-to-the-brim bucket of pig blood, falling with its full weight onto Carrie White's face, is Jackie getting JFK's brains blown in her face.

The assassin Chris enlists a likeminded army of volunteers to help her pull off this conspiracy (especially second-in-command evil girl *Norma*, played by baseball-cap-wearing, pigtail-sporting P. J. Soles). As well as a group of guys (John Travolta's *Billy Nolan* and Norma's boyfriend *Freddy*, played by Michael Talbott) who are duped and manipulated by the assassins into assisting.

Including rigging the entire election, so the assassins can make sure candidates Carrie and Tommy will win.★

Even smiling *Sue Snell* (Amy Irving), Carrie's secret campaign manager, standing with—yet apart from—the cheering crowd seems pleased with her media creation.

★One of the many fucked up things in *Carrie* is because of Chris Hargenson's vote-tampering shenanigans, we never learn who really won king and queen of the prom. Judging from the honest reaction of their classmates, it's entirely believable that Carrie and Tommy could have legitimately won without Chris' vote tampering.

In De Palma's *Taxi Driver*, I can see Cybill Shepherd's *Betsy* (if made after *Carrie*, a great part for either Nancy Allen or Amy Irving) being enlarged to practically colead status. I wouldn't be surprised if Schrader and Scorsese's imperative—to not have any scene in the movie not from Travis' perspective—wasn't monkeyed with by De Palma in order to feature a few scenes from Betsy's perspective. Maybe it's even Betsy who figures out Travis' plan beforehand, and it's because of her that his assassination attempt is thwarted. I'm not suggesting any of these hackneyed ideas involving Betsy would be an improvement on the film Scorsese made. But the same movie done in a more Hitchcockian manner? I can see those changes woven into the scenario.

The other change from a De Palma version and a Scorsese version, would have been the whole *Searchers* angle. When Paul Schrader writes his thematic *Searchers* remake, then lucks out and lands Scorsese as helmer, he doesn't just land an interpreter, but a coconspirator. Jesus Christ, Marty even features a clip from the fucking *Searchers* in *Mean Streets*. As Schrader tells Marty about the duality of Ethan Edwards and Travis Bickle, Scorsese doesn't need subtitles, he tells Paul the Comanche-Buffalo story.

I think it's fairly safe to assume that De Palma was not as enamored with either John Ford or *The Searchers* as Scorsese was. And it's doubtful that Brian would have leaned into the similarities between the films as heavily as Marty did. I can hear him telling Schrader, after he's heard Paul refer to the Ford epic one time too many, *"Look, Paul, maybe the script you wrote was based on The Searchers. But the movie I'm going to make is going to be Repulsion."*

Next big question, *if* Brian De Palma shot *Taxi Driver*, who would have played *Travis Bickle*?

And if you just jump to Robert De Niro because of the two men's past association—not so fast.

Despite Brian and Robert starting their careers off together, they wouldn't work with each other again till *The Untouchables* in the eighties.

I always assumed the two men must have had a falling out.

But recently I asked Mr. De Niro about working with Mr. De Palma in the times of *Greetings* and *Hi, Mom!*, and the actor remembered the director fondly. *"It was always good to work with Brian, he was a great audience and he knew what he wanted."* Then I asked was there any falling out between the two men? And De Niro categorically denied any bad blood between them. *"No,"* he explained, *"When the two of us were in town [during the seventies], we'd get together and share a coffee and catch up."*

I asked how come they didn't work more together, and Mr. De Niro said, *"Well, Brian became a pretty big director then. And he was doing his stuff and I was doing mine."* And it's true, if you think about the movies De Palma did in the seventies, none of them are conspicuous by De Niro's absence. It's not until *Jack Terry* in *Blow Out* that a role right for Robert De Niro presented itself.

But what about *Taxi Driver*?

Well, you have to remember, Robert De Niro wasn't attached to *Taxi Driver*. The film was already set up at Columbia Pictures with Jeff Bridges in the lead role, and the Phillipses and Tony Bill attached as producers. Scorsese wanted De Niro for the role, but the studios didn't think he was a big enough star yet. But he was playing the young *Vito Corleone* in Francis Ford Coppola's upcoming sequel to *The Godfather*. So, according to Schrader, they decided not to shoot it with Jeff Bridges (which meant saying adios to superstar producer Tony Bill), and wait for *The Godfather: Part II* to come out and hopefully make De Niro a bigger name. Well, that worked, Robert De Niro won the Best Supporting Actor Academy Award that year for his role as Vito Corleone. But then Scorsese had another problem, De Niro had signed on to be one of the two leads in Bernardo Bertolucci's Italian epic *1900*. And now Marty had to sit on his hands and wait, seemingly, fucking forever for Bertolucci to finish his magnum opus.

That's how convinced Marty and Paul were that Robert was the right actor to play Travis.

However, I can see Brian De Palma being very happy with a green-lit film at Columbia Pictures, produced by the three producers of *The Sting*, and starring Jeff Bridges. I don't see De Palma waiting a year for Bobby. And even if Bridges dropped out, I can see Jan-Michael Vincent proving an effective Travis Bickle for De Palma.

But now comes the 64,0000 dollar question, how about changing *Sport*'s race from black to white?

I know I'm making a big deal out of this, because to me it's a very big deal. The entire debate between social responsibility, social compromise, and integrity can be boiled down to this one decision.

As I've stated before, I don't think Scorsese considered the changing of the character's race as that big of a deal. And it does appear the producers and the studio properly intimidated the director with their worst-case scenarios of rioting black audiences. And as I also mentioned, Scorsese was looking for a good role for Harvey Keitel anyway.

But Brian De Palma wouldn't be breaking his neck to get Harvey Keitel in the movie.

Would he have faced the same pressures brought to bear on Martin Scorsese?

Undoubtedly.

Yet, with a less sympathetic and more *Repulsion*-like Travis Bickle, events might have played out differently. The guy's a fucking lunatic. A lunatic can kill anybody. Also, it must be said, if the director who brought you *Be Black Baby* felt the script should stay as it was written, I'm pretty positive De Palma would have been more successful.

Rolling Thunder

(1977)

John Flynn's *Rolling Thunder* tells the story of Air Force *Major Charles Rane* (William Devane), who during the Vietnam war was shot down over Hanoi. He was held prisoner in what one character describes as a "Hanoi hellhole" for seven years. The film starts in 1973 when the POW's are finally being released. When Maj. Rane steps off the plane in San Antonio, Texas, alongside his fellow captives, including his buddy *Sgt. Johnny Vohden* (Tommy Lee Jones), he's greeted to a hero's welcome, including cheering fans, dress uniform military brass, and even the local high school marching band (one of the first images in the film). Also, among that cheering crowd is the wife he left behind seven years ago, *Janet* (Lisa Richards), and his nine-year-old son *Mark* (Jordan Gerler).

Charlie Rane enters the picture not dissimilar to Martin Scorsese's description of John Wayne's Ethan Edwards in *The Searchers*. Returning home from a war he fought and lost, which left unhealable wounds to his humanity. As Scorsese described, *"he has a great love within him that's been stamped out."*

The way Ethan Edwards in his mind probably romanticized his brother's wife Martha during his bloody conflicts is no doubt similar to how Charlie Rane romanticized his own wife during his captivity.

It's humorous comparing the two characters, because in *The Searchers* Ethan Edwards is far more self-aware than Charlie. Ethan may covet his brother's wife (when he arrives at the massacre aftermath, it's her name, "*Martha!*" he calls out in frightened panic, not his own brother), but he would never claim her as his own. It's doubtful he would do that to any other man, *especially* his brother (or should I say another white man. It seems Debbie has been married to Scar for several years). But far more important to Ethan's discipline is he knows he's no good for her. He's well aware he's incapable of the love and strength it would require to be a loving husband and father.

When Charlie Rane comes home to pick up where he left off, he's not self-aware enough to know that would be impossible. After seven years of captivity, Charlie is not the same man his wife and two-year-old son said goodbye to on a military airfield.

He's unemotional, unresponsive, and stoic to the point of not being among the living. He can't sleep with his wife in their bedroom, instead moving into a toolshed in the backyard that duplicates his prison camp cell. His son doesn't remember him—and though Charlie tries to make an effort—the boy finds it awkward and rejects the advances.

Once the family arrive home on Charlie's first night back, he and his wife settle down in the front room to share their first time alone together in seven years.

Janet confesses, "*I've been with another man.*"

Charlie's actually nonjudgmental, telling her calmly, "*We* [meaning his fellow POW comrades] *all knew. Couldn't a been any other way.*"

But Janet isn't through with the devastating revelations. She reveals that she's fallen in love with a local Highway Patrolman named *Cliff* (Lawrason Driscoll), who's asked her to marry him and she's accepted.

Charlie turns cold, *"I don't think I'm up for any more of this,"* freezing her to death long before her ultimate fate.

But if Charlie could get past the homecoming daydream he's carried in his head for seven years, he'd see clearly that—like Ethan Edwards—he's physically and emotionally incapable of being the loving husband and father that Cliff would be.

Another comparison between the John Flynn film and the John Ford film is both pictures' sense of community ritual on display. Charlie may be a stranger to his family, but to the townspeople of San Antonio he's a hero. The residents of San Antonio don't seem to be conflicted about the Vietnam War at all. Nor did they forget him while he was away. For seven years a sign sat in the local park that read *"Send a letter to Hanoi Release Maj. Charles Rane."* As a hometown act of symbolic solidarity, a local Texas belle, bar waitress *Linda Forchet* (played by the magnificent Linda Haynes), wore his ID bracelet the entire time he was in captivity. In honor of Charlie's service to his country and community a local car dealership gives Maj. Rane a brand spanking new, big ass, candy apple red Cadillac convertible. And in an act of symbolic reimbursement for his sacrifice, a local department store offers him a gift of two thousand five hundred fifty-five silver dollars, one for every day of his captivity (including one for good luck).

To the locals of San Antonio he's not only a hero, but a local celebrity. Charlie can't walk into a bar without the bartender buying him a drink. Linda Forchet describes herself as a Charlie Rane *"groupie,"* a term she has to explain to Charlie.

The bitter irony is while his community accepts and even reveres him, his own family rejects him. At home he can't elicit a smile from his son, and his wife is so guilty she can't even look at him without bursting into tears.

This opening thirty minutes is a grippingly detailed character study, and by the time it's over the audience doesn't just sympathize with Charlie Rane, we really do understand him. Apparently better than anybody else in the film. It's a much deeper depiction of the casualties of war than the contrite *Coming Home*, with its para-plegic hippie Jesus figure telling it like it is.

Then one late afternoon, Charlie drives his big ass Cadillac into his driveway. And just as soon as he steps across his threshold, the barrel of a gun is jammed against the side of his head, and he's yanked inside.

Enter *the Acuna Boys.*

The Acuna Boys are four Texas scumbags (two white and two Mexican, though only the white ones have any real dialogue) that have broken into Maj. Rane's house to swipe his two thousand five hundred and fifty-six silver dollars. Not being able to find it when the house was empty, they wait for the Major to come home so they can force him to hand them over. The ringleader of the Acuna Boys is a puffy-sweaty-disgusting-no-name cowboy with fancy boots, played to a fare-thee-well by *Rosco Coltrane* himself, James Best.

Best demands the silver dollars and informs Charlie that they're prepared to torture him to get them. What they're not prepared for—after seven years of practice—is Charlie's ability to *withstand* torture.

The Vietnamese knew if they could make Maj. Rane disavow his own country, it would only be a matter of time before the other prisoners followed suit. But despite their best efforts, they never could break Charlie. So after seven years of torture at the hands of his communist captors, when these Texas shitbirds suddenly show up demanding information, Charlie ain't talking.

The only difference, while the communists might have been more skilled at torture than these scumbags, the VC didn't want to kill Charlie Rane, they wanted to break him.

If they killed him, in a way, Charlie won.

If they killed the Americans' commanding officer, none of the other soldiers would break. It was a propaganda victory that was important to the enemy. But the Acuna Boys not only don't care if Charlie dies, it's pretty apparent that killing him once they get their hands on those silver dollars was the plan from the start. So out of frustration to the stoic defiance that Charlie shows their amateur-night violence, they shove his hand down the kitchen sink garbage disposal and grind it off.

Then his wife and son come home, and in an effort to save his father (a meaningful moment for both Charlie and us), Mark tells the bastards where the money is.

Then, in their own sign of symbolic Acuna Boy gratitude, they shoot—execution style—both Janet and Mark dead, then shoot Charlie dead . . . or so they think.

From here on end, what follows is Maj. Charles Rane, now armed with a sharp pointy hook where his ground-off hand used to be, in his big ass red Cadillac convertible, with a boot full of weapons, accompanied by dishwater blond barfly Linda Forchet, driving through Mexico, tracking down the Acuna Boys, in what my character The Bride would call "*a roaring rampage of revenge.*"

When I first saw *Rolling Thunder* with my mother and her boyfriend Marco in 1977 on the film's opening night in Los Angeles, on a double feature with *Enter the Dragon*, it blew my fucking mind!

What was it about the movie I dug so much?

Well, at that age—*Revengeamatic* films—with dynamic blood-all-over-the-walls climaxes—were my idea of a good time at the movies.

I loved *Rolling Thunder* so much that years before it became available on Vestron Home Video—for a period of ten years—I followed it all over Los Angeles, whenever and wherever it played (before home video, cinephiles used to do things like that). Which would be easy enough once I had a car and knew how to drive. But before I knew how to drive or had a car, I'd travel by bus, hours away from my home, to some really sketchy neighborhoods to see *Rolling Thunder* unspool in some very unique movie theatres. A few of the more memorable were the beautiful but dilapidated *Orpheum Theatre* in Downtown Los Angeles, on a 35mm print with Spanish subtitles, on the lower half of a double feature with Burt Reynolds' *Hooper*. And at *the Palace Theatre* in Long Beach (which was hardly a "palace") on a triple feature with Joe Dante's *The Howling* and Chuck Norris' *Good Guys Wear Black*.

Initially, when I chased Charlie Rane and his hook for a hand all over L.A., it was to grindhouses and second-run theatres. But later in the eighties, *Rolling Thunder* started appearing as part of Vietnam programs at many different revival houses. Which led to me taking in screenings of the John Flynn film at *the Nuart* (in West Los Angeles), *the New Beverly* (on Beverly and La Brea), *the Vista* (where Hollywood Boulevard and Sunset meet), and *the Rialto* (in Pasadena), on double bills with films like *Go Tell the Spartans*, *Who'll Stop the Rain*, and even *Apocalypse Now* (a rather long night at the movies).

So was it just the spectacle of the powerfully depicted explicit violence that made me love Flynn's film as much as I did?

Well . . . maybe that initial screening, yeah.

But after I watched it a few times, I began to have a deeper understanding of the film. In fact, a deeper understanding than I had ever had to any film prior.

When I was promoting my first book, the novelization of *Once Upon a Time in Hollywood*, I appeared on a fun podcast called *3 Books with Neil Pasricha*. The idea of the show was for Neil to discuss with an author three books that had a formative influence on them. Not necessarily their three favorite books. But three books that had an influence on them, usually earlier in their life. One of the books I chose was Dan Jenkins' *Semi-Tough* (to this day the funniest book I ever read).

I described to Neil one of the things that really grabbed me (I read it at fifteen or sixteen) was Jenkins wrote the whole book as if his lead character, Billy Clyde Puckett, was speaking into a tape recorder. I had read first-person narratives before. But never something so causal, or immediate, or naturalistic, or funny.

I remember thinking, "*You can write a book this way? If you can write a book this way, maybe I could write a book?*"

Then Neil (bless his heart) said, "*Ahhhh, that's the book that gave you permission to be a writer.*"

And he's right, it was.

Well, *Rolling Thunder* was the movie that gave me permission to be a critic. The first time I analyzed a movie.

John Flynn's film and William Devane's performance was the first time I looked deeper into a film's character than just what was on screen. There was a depth to Charlie Rane and a three-dimensionality that revealed itself to me the more I saw the film. Charlie Rane was the first movie character that I examined after the movie was over.

What I used to claim about *Rolling Thunder* was it was the best combination of character study and action film ever made.

And it still is.

The film also made me a champion of its director, John Flynn. At least the three action films he did in a row in the seventies, *The Outfit*, *Rolling Thunder*, and *Defiance*. It seemed all the cool critics had their special filmmaker to champion and Flynn was mine.

So much so that I sought him out at nineteen to interview him. How did I manage that?

Simple—if not easy—I looked up every *John Flynn* in the phone book, called them up and asked, "*Is this John Flynn?*" If they said yes, then I asked them, "*The John Flynn who directed Rolling Thunder?*"

Till eventually one said, "*Yes it is, who is this?*"

Wow! It's him, it's fucking him!

I had never spoken to a movie director before. No less the

director of one of my favorite movies. So I introduced myself and
told him I was writing a book on film directors, and could we get
together and interview him about his career. And he agreed, and
we set a time, and he invited me to come over to his house and
conduct the interview.

Holy shit, I'm going to see what a movie director's house looks like!

As we sat down in his living room to conduct the interview,
he poured me a glass of red wine, and put on his turntable Mor-
ricone's soundtrack to *The Sicilian Clan*, and I began asking my
questions and testing my theories about *Rolling Thunder.*★

Flynn explained to me the history of the project as such. Paul
Schrader wrote *Rolling Thunder* after writing his first script, *Taxi
Driver*, and before he wrote *The Yakuza*, and the three scripts to-
gether create an interesting trilogy for the young writer.

Besides the fact that they're good movies, they also share complex male Schraderesque protagonists at their center, and all three
scripts end in Peckinpah-like blood-all-over-the-walls violent catharsis (which in all three motion pictures are spectacularly achieved).

The script for *The Yakuza* takes the Daiei Japanese yakuza film
and plays it pretty straight, just fashions it for Western audience
consumption.

But both *Taxi Driver* and *Rolling Thunder* take popular sub-
genres of the day (vigilante movies and Revengeamatics), appear
to be offering up another entry, but instead offer a cracked-mirror
blistering critique of the genre.

★ I was so inexperienced at what I was doing that I brought my tape recorder
with me, but I only brought one cassette. I couldn't imagine him giving me
more than an hour. So once both sides of the tape were done, I didn't want
to look like an idiot, so I just kept flipping it over and re-recording over what
I had just recorded. So all the stuff on his early career and *The Outfit* was lost
forever.

Rolling Thunder was sold to Lawrence Gordon, who was head of production at American-International Pictures, after Schrader's high-profile sale of *The Yakuza* screenplay to Warner Bros.

The writer fashioned the script to be his first film as a director. And you can believe that, because especially in the first half of the screenplay, it's pretty much directed on the page, and directed well, I might add. If I filmed it, I would shoot the first half exactly the way Schrader dictates it in the screenplay. But nobody at AIP was willing to back this high-profile script purchase with Paul behind the camera. John Milius told me Paul wrote it for him to direct. I do believe Paul wrote it for himself, but once that option was off the table, and since Milius had just finished directing his first feature, *Dillinger* for Lawrence Gordon and AIP, I can see Paul thinking Big John was a good candidate to make the hard-hitting script into a powerhouse film.

And he's right, seemingly, Milius would have been perfect.

He at least would have shot Schrader's script, because he loved it, Milius told me. *"Boy it was a good script—with wonderful stuff in it."*

But John didn't want to make it.

I asked *"Why not?"*

Milius said, *"I don't know. I guess at the time I didn't want to do something that dark."*

Then at AIP it almost came to pass in a real interesting incarnation. In an interview, George Romero revealed that around 1974 the film was set up as a package with him as director. Romero explained, *"Schrader was hot in town because of The Yakuza screenplay sale, and Joe Don Baker was hot because of Walking Tall. And I was hot because of Night of the Living Dead. So a package deal with those three principals was set up at AIP. Then The Yakuza came out and bombed. Then Golden Needles [a Joe Don Baker film with Jim Kelly] bombed, and the deal fell apart."*

It hung around as an unmade hot potato at AIP until Lawrence

Gordon left the company to become an independent producer and took the script with him. Because as Flynn said, "*That was Larry's favorite script from his AIP days. He was determined to get it made as one of his first projects as producer.*"

Gordon took the project and set it up over at Twentieth Century Fox.

Having made *Hard Times* with Walter Hill, Gordon offered the film to Hill's buddy and director of *The Outfit*, John Flynn.

Flynn agreed and they started looking for their Major Charles Rane. Reading the original Schrader script, it's pretty fucking obvious that the role of Rane was written for Joe Don Baker. And Baker had of course acted in Flynn's previous film. So it seems like a natural fit.

And Flynn told me they sent the script to Baker to read. "*Baker never slept at night. So we sent it to him and he read it during the night.*" But for some reason nobody can remember, in the morning Baker passed.

Then it was sent to David Carradine, who also passed. Though Carradine later said, "*At the time I knew I should have done it. But I was trying to get another revenge type movie made. And I kinda knew this [Rolling Thunder] was the better script. But I had spent too much time on the other one and I couldn't give it up. Then the way it came to pass, we never did get that other revenge movie made.*"

At a screening at one of my *QT Film Festivals* in Austin, Texas, in 2001, Carradine watched *Rolling Thunder* for the first time with me and he loved it. He told me, "*Boy, I was a dummy and turned down a lot of good stuff in my career. But me turning that down has to rank with the dumbest.*" And because of the timing he obviously read the Schrader original. As we walked away from the Alamo Drafthouse, David remarked, "*The script I read wasn't as good as the movie we just saw.*"

After William Devane gave what many people still consider the best portrayal of John F. Kennedy in the two-part TV event *The*

Missiles of October, his star was on the rise in Hollywood. He was looked at as another potential dynamic actor/could-be star. A so-ugly he's handsome kind of guy with serious chops who could also be a leading man (George C. Scott, Roy Scheider).

Devane followed up his Kennedy portrayal with lead roles in two big-deal TV movies, *Fear on Trial* (with George C. Scott) and *Red Alert*. Then when he moved into movies he entered as a comer. He received a good part with above-title billing in the hit thriller *Marathon Man*. That ended up being the first of three pictures he did with director John Schlesinger (the other two being *Yanks* and the underrated *Honky Tonk Freeway*). Then he was one-quarter of the lead quartet that starred in Alfred Hitchcock's last film, *Family Plot* (he replaced Roy Thinnes after Hitchcock fired him).

And the same year as *Rolling Thunder* he also starred in one of my favorite sequels of all time, *The Bad News Bears in Breaking Training*.

He was offered the Schrader script by Twentieth Century Fox, who according to Flynn, *"were very high on Devane."*

Both Flynn and Devane felt the idea and the structure of Schrader's script was solid, but the material itself was, in the exact words of John Flynn, *"unfilmable."*

Well, I'm here to say, that's horseshit! It's a terrific piece of writing. Truly Paul Schrader at his best. It wasn't that Paul Schrader's script was *"unfilmable,"* you just needed the balls to film it.

Why they felt it was *"unfilmable"* is pretty obvious, but I'll get into that later. So at Devane's suggestion, his screenwriter friend Heywood Gould was brought on to do a rewrite. Gould was sort of famous inside Hollywood for writing the screenplay *Fort Apache the Bronx*, which was a script that got passed around the industry that everybody loved but no one would produce (they eventually produced a really mediocre movie out of it in 1981 starring Paul Newman).

Gould and Flynn and Devane hung out together for weeks

fashioning a shooting script and turning it into the movie *they* wanted to make.

As Gould remembered it, "*I was working as a bartender in Soho, living in a residential hotel and generally having a blast. Bill Devane had read a draft of a script I wrote called Fort Apache the Bronx, plus my novel One Dead Debutante. I don't know what was happening behind the scenes, but I know they were already in prep when they decided they needed a rewrite and Bill suggested me.*

"*So they flew me to L.A. and I met Larry Gordon, the producer, and the director, John Flynn. I read the script that night and as I remember it was a relentless bloodbath, which I guess they didn't want.*

"*At the meeting the next day I said they could keep the structure of the story, but needed more scenes to explain Rane, more emotion in his family life, more realistic bad guys, and they definitely needed a plausible, sympathetic woman* [who doesn't?].

"*I did a little writing out of sequence because they wanted scenes for the auditions. I wrote the scene in the bar where Rane meets Linda Haynes first and then the scene in the garage where he relives the torture for Cliff* [the line "*You learn to love the rope*" became the motto for the shoot when the temperatures went over 110]. *Then the homecoming scene with Rane and his wife and stuff with his son.*

"*I pretty much wrote the picture in L.A. and then went home. Then the next week they called and flew me to San Antonio to do a production rewrite based on the locations they had chosen. I stayed about a month and ended up writing new scenes for Rane and Linda and rewriting the fight scenes and the big brothel shootout at the end.*

"*I wanted to show some unspoken love and communication between the two men* [Devane and Jones] *because I objected to what I considered to be the original's heavy-handed snobbery about working people. A picture changes a lot when the reality of the cast, locations, and schedule sinks in. John wanted scenes punched up and new scenes written. I wrote the target practice scene between Rane and Linda after he looked at the dailies and decided the relationship was playing well and he wanted more.*"

What's fascinating about comparing the Gould and Schrader drafts is they tell the same story; the two scripts share basically the same structure, and many of the same scenes. But inside of that, Gould pretty much does a page one rewrite. The dialogue in the original script is some of Schrader's best. Yet only two nondescript lines make it into the finished film. But Gould writes some pretty terrific dialogue for the characters himself. Paul Schrader has long disowned the film, even recently—when it was brought up in an interview—he said, "*It was a movie ruined in the rewrite.*" While I understand his feelings (that's how I feel about *Natural Born Killers*), I don't agree it was "ruined," but, as with *Taxi Driver*, his thematic conception was jettisoned.

Rolling Thunder is a really rough film. It was a hard R in *1977*! But Schrader's script was even harder, more violent, more cynical, with a jaw-dropping turn of events at the climax that frankly is so fucking brilliant I'd still love to see it done in a movie.

But since practically none of Schrader's script made it on to the screen, if you love the movie like I do, then what you love is Heywood Gould's rewrite, as well as the radical direction that William Devane took the character of Rane.

There's plenty in Schrader's script that's better than Gould's rewrite, but there's also plenty in Gould's screenplay that improves on Schrader's original (all the movie's classic scenes are Gould's).

In Schrader's original script the Acuna Boys are after Rane's back pay. It was Gould who created the symbolic silver dollars. In Schrader's script Linda Forchet is just a Texas tramp who slips her phone number to a married man, in Gould's she wore Charlie's ID bracelet while he was in captivity. In Gould's draft the shotgun that Charlie later does so much damage with during the climax was a homecoming present from his son Mark.

In a nice touch we learn Cliff helped the boy pick it out.

Charlie: "*Well, that was very nice of Cliff.*"

And the *worst* scene in Schrader's script—the dinner at the home of Charlie's fellow prisoner Johnny Vohden with his annoying family—is the *best* scene in Gould's script and Flynn's movie. As well as being the most cathartic scene in the whole Revengeamatic genre. But even that's too puny a description of the scene. Of all the scenes in all the movies I've ever seen with audiences, no other scene gets quite the bloodlust reaction from a roomful of people quite like the scene in *Rolling Thunder* when William Devane gets Tommy Lee Jones alone.

```
                    RANE
        I've found the men who killed my son.

                   JOHNNY
          I'll just get my gear.
```

That scene and those lines never fail to drive audiences wild wherever and whenever it's projected. And trust me, I've seen *Rolling Thunder* with every type of audience imaginable.

Despite the film's sugary theme song,

San Antone it's really good to see you.
It's been awhile but you've been on my mind.
I've been a lotta places, but I think I've always known,
one day I'd come back to San Antone,

when Linda asks Charlie while they're in Mexico if they're going back to San Antone Charlie says, "*I don't care if I ever see that town again.*" One of the biggest differences between Gould's conception of the character and Schrader's is Gould's Rane doesn't even seem to be from Texas, he's just stationed in San Antonio due to the Air Force base. While Schrader's Rane is a Texan through and through, and not even from San Antonio but Corpus Christi. He's also a Mexican-hating, Jane Fonda–cursing, country music–loving redneck.

But the Charlie Rane that Heywood Gould fashioned for his script rewrite is itself drastically different than the Charlie Rane that finally reached the screen.

William Devane's Rane is practically monosyllabic. Where Gould's Rane might be equally damaged, he's actually quite loquacious. And the first half of the movie is built around scenes where Rane speaks eloquently about himself and his mental state.

The only one that survives is the excellent scene in Charlie's garage when Cliff—the man the Major's wife is leaving him for— tries to have a man-to-man talk about their dilemma (*"You learn to love the rope"*).

But Gould also wrote an earlier scene, when Charlie speaks with his wife, on his first night back home, he tries to explain to her why he's sleeping in the small sewing room instead of their bedroom.

Gould has Rane delivering an actual monologue.

                         RANE
        Anyhow about the sewing room. You
        have to think of it like a . . .
        decompression chamber. You know the
        deep-sea divers have to take a lot of
        time coming back up into the real world.
        Down below, they work under incredible
        pressures and it compresses the gasses
        in their system. If they come up too
        fast, the gas turns into little

                       (MORE)

> RANE (CONT'D)
>
> bubbles instead of being reabsorbed. And the bubbles can kill them or cripple them. You see? That's the way it's been with me and the other guys. We were under incredible pressure there. Unbelievable. We were at the bottom of a human sea. Only now we have to come back into the real world. But we have to decompress. The sewing room is my decompression chamber. Does that make sense to you?

If you've seen *Rolling Thunder* as often as I have, to read that is to say out loud, *"Who the fuck is this guy? I mean, Jesus Christ, that's more dialogue than Charlie says in the whole fucking movie!"*

Well, it turned out the final author of the character of Charlie Rane was not either one of the two screenwriters, but the actor playing the role.

John Flynn informed me, *"Twentieth Century Fox was very high on Devane, and the actor had a lot of leeway to shape the character as he saw fit."* And even though Heywood Gould was brought in at the actor's request, Devane *"saw fit"* to slash Rane's dialogue by half, making the character far more interior and far more damaged. He's not quite the walking zombie that Tommy Lee Jones' Johnny Vohden is, but Charlie's not really alive anymore either. He even refers to himself as dead (*"I remember that song from when I was alive."*).

The other characters that Devane's Charlie deals with, his wife, her lover Cliff, Linda Forchet, even the Acuna Boys, are filled with messy emotions and are vibrantly alive when compared to Charlie.

The emotionless Major spends three-quarters of the movie

hiding behind dark aviator sunglasses. Oddly enough, other than his pump-action-shotgun-wielding Acuna Boy–killing sidekick Vohden, the only other character in the film that seems as stoic as Maj. Rane is his nine-year-old son Mark. This is beautifully articulated in a scene that shows Devane's Rane arriving at a little league game his son is playing in. He watches the boy play baseball behind a chain link fence. Desperately trying to make an unspoken connection with Mark. His son watches him watch, and without a word of dialogue spoken, the boy's rejection of the man's attempt is abundantly clear.

Yet the film demonstrates that Mark's relationship with his mother's lover Cliff is one of warmth and affection. Emotions Maj. Rane—through no fault of his own—is incapable of.

This is the Charlie Rane I've grown up with, and *this* Charlie Rane was completely William Devane's conception.

It even extends to the character's revenge. The movie Rane makes it abundantly clear that his revenge is for his son and his son alone. Once his wife tells him she's accepted a marriage proposal from Cliff, the Air Force officer closes the iron door on her. Even her execution-style murder doesn't unthaw his heart. I asked director Flynn about this and he confirmed, *"Devane's thing was he didn't really care about the wife."*

This whole conception of the character is absolutely essential to Devane's characterization and the finished film's subtext.

But it's not part of Schrader's manuscript.

Schrader's Charlie seems to understand his wife's dilemma in a way that would be unfathomable in the Devane characterization. Cliff even has dinner with the family, and yeah, it's awkward, but everybody seems to get along. And even though Janet is leaving her husband, she still makes herself available to Charlie emotionally and physically. Schrader's Janet doesn't spend the movie weeping, wringing her hands, with a guilty look on her puss. She truly cares about Charlie and *tries* to help him. She offers herself to him, and not out of sympathy, but because she loves him. But Charlie can't handle it.

Schrader includes in his original screenplay a scene where Janet tries to have sex with Charlie. He refuses for a myriad of reasons, and leaves the house. He gets into his big red Cadillac and drives to a Texas drive-in that's showing *Deep Throat*. As he watches Linda Lovelace in the pornographic film, he looks to the man in the car next to him, it's *Travis Bickle*! The two Schrader antiheroes share a stare moment.

As the writer puts it, "*two fuses slowly burning down.*"

But if you love *Rolling Thunder* as much as I do, then one of the things you love is William Devane's performance, because it's sensational.

But from talking to Flynn, Devane's power position on the production rubbed the director the wrong way. He didn't badmouth the actor, but there was a decided lack of affection when he spoke about him (always calling him "*Devane*," never "*Bill*"). Even telling me he tried to get Twentieth Century Fox to dump Devane and replace him with Tommy Lee Jones ("*If you want the next Burt Lancaster, it sure as hell ain't Devane, it's Tommy*"). One of the reasons for Flynn's frustration was Devane had just finished directing a play, and he kept trying to stick actors from the play in the cast, "*which was a problem,*" Flynn told me. And in a film just overbrimming with outstanding performances, the two duds are the actors from Devane's play. Lisa Richards as Charlie's wife Janet, who's just a one-note simpering mess. And Lawrason Driscoll as her lover Cliff. Driscoll spends his performance indicating his frustrations rather than feeling them, and in his big scene between Charlie in the garage where Charlie relives the Hanoi Hilton torture with Cliff as the torturer, Devane devours the weak actor. Flynn was especially frustrated about the casting of the wife because at one point Barbara Hershey was interested in the role.

In Rane's search for the Acuna Boys, he (inexplicably) brings along Texas barfly cocktail waitress *Linda*—played to perfection by Linda Haynes—who can also be seen in *Coffy*, *The Nickel Ride*, and *Brubaker*. But it's her performance as Linda in *Rolling Thunder* that has created a small but devoted cult following for the naturalistic actress. And when it comes to *the Linda Haynes Fan Club*, consider me a forty-five year member. Ms. Haynes quit performing in the eighties; both Vincent Gallo and I have tried to persuade her back to acting, but unfortunately to no avail.

It's a superb characterization and one of my favorite female performances in seventies cinema. As Vincent Canby remarked in his *New York Times* review when the film came out:

"[Haynes] manages simultaneously to look beautiful and slightly ravaged (something it took Ava Gardner years to achieve)."

In John Flynn's movie (as opposed to Schrader's script) Linda serves a similar function as Jeffrey Hunter's *Martin Pawley* sidekick does in *The Searchers* and Season Hubley's bleach-blond astrology aficionado sex worker *Niki* in Schrader's self-directed *Hardcore*. Like Hunter's Martin and Hubley's Niki, Haynes' Forchet is obviously a good and sincere person attached to an emotionless (save for revenge) killing machine. But Hunter's character Pawley is part Native American, giving him a shared ancestry with the object of Ethan's bloodlust. While Martin Pawley is an Indian, he's no savage. And while Linda Forchet is no murdering scumbag, her Texas barstool-warming floozy shares a similar white-trash lineage with the object of Charlie's bloodlust.

To love *Rolling Thunder* is to love Linda Haynes' Linda Forchet. She's really remarkable, and her dynamic with Devane is one of the main reasons for the film's success. Just like Charlie can't get over his homecoming daydream of a loving family welcoming him back from hell with open arms, Linda can't get over her daydream of Charlie and her running off to Alaska.

Charlie's not going to fucking Alaska.

He's never going to leave Mexico alive. Charlie knows that. The audience knows that. Hell, even Linda knows that. But she keeps the pipe dream alive as long as she can. I told director John Flynn that one of my favorite closing shots in cinema history was his shot of Devane walking the wounded Tommy Lee out of the blood-drenched brothel, the floor littered with the dead bodies of their enemies, as the closing credits rise up across the screen and the film's soft theme song plays.

He told me they originally had an epilogue to that ending. Linda Forchet sitting on a bench waiting for a bus to take her back to San Antone (the lyrics of the film's theme song). And Charlie parked in his big ass red Cadillac convertible about a half a block away out of her line of sight, silently observing her. Is he contemplating picking her up and taking her with him, or is he just making sure she gets home alright, or is he just taking one last look at the only woman who will ever love him?

That's up for the audience to decide.

Then the bus arrives, she climbs aboard, and the bus heads for El Paso, while he turns the Cadillac around and drives deeper into Mexico . . . alone. I think he thought about picking her up and *wishes* he could. I don't think Charlie loves Linda, because he's not capable of loving anybody anymore—what's that line Scorsese says of Ethan Edwards? "*He's a man capable of a great love that's had it stamped out of him.*"

But while Charlie might wish he *could* love Linda, he respects, admires, and appreciates her sincerity. Yet, he knows taking her with him would be impossible, because Charlie knows he's going to die. At some point the federales will track him down, and after spending seven years in a Vietnamese prisoner of war camp, the last thing he's going to do is spend the rest of his life in a Mexican prison (or any other prison). So the day they catch him, will be the day he dies, because he's going to blast Mexican cops till they blast him back. The only thing Charlie has left to give Linda is keeping her out of the line of fire. The Linda who climbs aboard that bus and goes back to San Antone with her tail between her legs may be a sad Linda, but at least she'll be alive. Flynn liked that ending, but they ran out of time on the schedule and it had to be abandoned.

Over the years I've enjoyed Linda's character so much, Linda's performance so much, and Haynes and Devane's chemistry so much that it *rarely* occurred to me how contrived it was that Charlie takes Linda with him on his bloody trail of vengeance in the first place.

At least in the movie that exists, it doesn't make any sense that Charlie takes a tagalong girl he barely knows on such a perilous journey. *If* he clued her in on what he was up to, and they were conspiring together . . . *maybe.* But just sending in this blond white girl (as she's described in the movie, "*a real piece of ass*") to these cutthroat Mexican bars to ask some sketchy folks a bunch of suspicious questions doesn't make any fucking sense. But as per usual when it comes to Schrader writing genre scripts, he cuts corners, and cliche supporting characters always supply the lead protagonist with the information they need to get to the next script plot point.

As opposed to the movie version of the story—where Charlie and Linda don't really have anything in common—Schrader's Charlie and Linda are both two Mexican-hating, Texas white-trash peas in a pod. The couple have a lot more in common, they get along better, have a helluva lot more to talk about, and Charlie does seem to genuinely need her. And not just to do Schrader's illogical plot-lifting, but for her companionship.

When the movie's Charlie leaves her sleeping in the morning in their motel room, to meet up with Johnny Vohden to kill the Acuna Boys, he sneaks out before she wakes up (in a nice touch he covers her up with the fallen blanket). Instead of saying goodbye, he just leaves a big wad of cash on her bedside table (as John Flynn told me, "*Like you would a whore*"). But we know he's not being insensitive, it's just literally all he has to give her. But Schrader's Charlie Rane isn't the burnt-out shell of a man that William Devane essayed. In Schrader's script, once Charlie's family is massacred and he goes on his search for their killers, his personality blossoms.

He seems relieved to jettison the pressures of fitting into society. And during Charlie and Linda's time on the road he gets along better with her than he does anybody since he returned home. They even have a really wonderful scene where the two talk about their favorite country music singers (Loretta Lynn, Kitty Wells, Connie Smith, Conny Van Dyke, Jeanne Pruett, and Miss Tammy), which would be unthinkable coming from Devane's Rane (in *Taxi Driver* Betsy tries to talk to Travis about Kris Kristofferson, but Bickle can't keep up. *I wonder if Travis has favorite porn stars?*).

The real reason Schrader feels the film was *"ruined"* in the rewrite, was because, like *Taxi Driver*, his thematic conception was jettisoned. Like Travis in *Taxi Driver* is paranoid about black folks, Rane has no use for Mexicans. In Schrader's script, when Linda asks him when they're in a motel room, *"Don't you ever clean up behind yourself?"* he answers, *"That's why god made Mexicans."* (Obviously a line Schrader heard somewhere along the way.) And like in *Taxi Driver*, where Travis is paranoid about black males, then goes on a moral imperative quest that allows him to raise arms against black males, all the Acuna Boys who murder Charlie's family are Mexicans (I believe that's what Flynn meant when he said Schrader's screenplay was *"unfilmable"*). The producers and the studio had Heywood Gould change the killers from all Mexican to half of them Mexican and gave the two white scumbags (James Best and Luke Askew) all the good lines. So once again a societal compromise was forced on another Paul Schrader screenplay. And, like *Taxi Driver*, they get away with it because of the excellent casting. *Rolling Thunder* without Luke Askew's *Automatic Slim*, or

James Best's no-named, slightly humorous Acuna Boy ringleader is as unimaginable as *Taxi Driver* without Harvey Keitel.

As is the movie without Jimmy Best's classic line reading, when Charlie's wife asks Rane why he let them grind off his hand in the kitchen garbage disposal rather then tell him where the silver dollars were. Best delivers the greatest line reading of his long career, "*I'll tell you why, lady. Because he's one macho motherfucker.*" Which brings down the house in every single screening of Flynn's film I've ever seen.

So, like Travis Bickle, Charlie Rane is a racist son of a bitch who has an excuse to go hunting for the objects of his disdain. Nevertheless, in this instance, these Acuna Boys deserve to die. And we root for Charlie and Johnny to track them down and (in true Schrader fashion) paint the walls with their blood.

But it's in Schrader's blood-soaked climax, when Charlie and Johnny track them down to a Mexican whorehouse and go on their killing spree that Schrader flips his genre script.

Because Schrader has Charlie and Johnny wipe out everybody!

Now in Flynn's film, Charlie and Johnny end up killing many more folks than the four that came to his house, most because they take up arms against them. But not all. When Johnny bursts into a room where a bunch of Mexicans are playing poker and says, "*Adios, boys!*" and sprays the table with shotgun shells, it's obvious he's now just on a killing spree, or as Kevin Thomas wrote, "*Charlie is just reaping what America sowed in Vietnam.*" The idea seems to be: if they're Mexican, don't take any chances—shoot.

But that still is (director) Flynn's, (producer) Gordon's, (star) Devane's, (writer) Gould's, and (studio) Twentieth Century Fox's societal compromise.

Because in Schrader's script—just like the napalm they dropped on villages in Vietnam—Charlie and Johnny blow the fuck outta everybody!

Acuna Boys, whores, customers, every single human being they come across. And in an amazing touch—that I can't fucking believe they didn't include in the film—both Charlie and Johnny speak to each other in Vietnamese during the firefight.

By the final page Schrader's point is made clear.

A point nobody at Fox wanted to make (everybody who talks about the freedom of cinema in the seventies should talk to Paul Schrader).

So Schrader's savage critique of fascist Revengeamatic flicks was turned by its makers into a savage fascist Revengeamatic.

Yet . . . the greatest savage, fascist, Revengeamatic flick ever made.

Which frustrates Schrader to this day.

Paradise Alley

(1978)

T he first time movie audiences got a taste of Sylvester Stallone's voice as an artist (writer/actor) wasn't 1976's *Rocky*,
but 1974's *The Lords of Flatbush*. It's a low-budget New York independent film directed by Martin Davidson, who would go on to
have a nice little filmography that would include the like-minded
Eddie and the Cruisers, *Hero at Large* (after *Lords*, my favorite), *Almost Summer* (which enjoys a very very tiny cult following among
devotees who saw it when it came out), and the William Petersen
& Sissy Spacek nineties romantic comedy *Hard Promises* (which,
apparently, I alone like), and codirected by Stephen Verona, who
would go on to direct the ill-fated Gladys Knight–starring feature
film vehicle *Pipe Dreams*, which costarred her sketchy ex-husband.

The *Lords* of the title are a group of four Brooklyn street
toughs—too small to actually call a *gang*—they're more like four
buddies who just had jackets made up and wear them all the time.
Stallone's *Stanley* (hands down the biggest and the meanest), Perry
King's *Chico* (the handsomest), Henry Winkler's *Butchey* (the smart
aleck of the group and the one Jew among the three Italians), and
Paul Mace's *Wimpy* (the little guy and the most authentically New
York member of the crew. You can spot Mace hanging out with the
other junkies in Jerry Schatzberg's *The Panic in Needle Park*). The

film follows their lives and loves (really only Chico and Stanley) in doo-wop era fifties New York. This shoestring-budgeted independent feature was made for nothing and filmed in a bare-bones manner. It was either shot on 16mm and blown up to 35mm, or it just *looks* like a 16mm blow up (the interior lighting captures to a tee the Roger Corman cinematography maxim "*Get an image*"). Yet, miraculously, it was picked up for distribution by a major studio (Columbia Pictures) and paired with the amazing fifties time capsule wonder *Let the Good Times Roll* (one helluva concert film, and apparently in its initial first run engagement Columbia even struck 70mm prints!). The reason Columbia picked up this grubby-looking independent feature and stuck their grand lady with a torch logo on the front of it was . . . well, it's a really good movie.

But also, the success that Universal had with *American Graffiti* precipitated—right smack dab in the seventies—a large wave of romanticized fifties nostalgia, which at one point threatened to engulf the entire decade. A nostalgia that I, as a little boy, was especially susceptible to (back then I loved everything fifties and prided myself on my wealth of fifties trivia knowledge).

During this tsunami-like wave of fifties ephemera came oldies-based radio stations, and fifties hit collections sold on TV (most people my age first learned who Chubby Checker was from these commercials). After a fall from grace during the hippie sixties, James Dean was reintroduced to the pop culture zeitgeist (you could buy his posters in head shops again, right next to Tim Curry's *Frank-N-Furter*), and *The Wild One* replaced both *On the Waterfront* and *A Streetcar Named Desire* as the seminal Brando film (again, those were the pictures and posters sold in head shops). And on TV there was the *American Graffiti* inspired hit situation comedy *Happy Days* (lest we forget Ron Howard starred in both), and then later its feminine opposite number *Laverne & Shirley*. And last, but certainly not least, the ascendancy of Henry Winkler's *Fonzie* to the schoolyard pop culture stratosphere (I just watched *The Goodbye Girl* again recently and was amused to see a poster of Fonzie prominently hanging on the wall of Quinn Cummings' bedroom). Well, some sly shrewd fox over at Columbia noticed that not only was *The Lords of Flatbush* fifties-based like *American Graffiti*, but it also sported Fonzie among its cast. Now except for the smart cookie at Columbia who picked up on that, the rest of the industry hadn't yet realized what a big deal that was. But to us schoolkids that was a very *big deal*! So even though Henry Winkler didn't really have a tremendous amount of screen time,* Columbia Pictures cut together a terrific TV spot that featured Henry Winkler's footage (Fonzie's drawing power among young schoolkids was no joke), and *the best and most catchy* commercial jingle ever written for a movie TV spot, which I can sing perfectly to this day. All this made the movie both a modest success and a very fondly remembered artifact of its era.

And like *American Graffiti* before it, and *Dazed and Confused* after it, *Lords* had a cast of young actors who would distinguish themselves in the future. Obviously, both Stallone & Winkler, but also the lovely and talented Susan Blakely (who was almost unbelievably beautiful), who starred with Nick Nolte and Peter Strauss in the first official miniseries (which they called "*a novel for television*"), *Rich Man, Poor Man*, and in my opinion, the better Frances Farmer movie. In *Lords* she plays *Jane*, the (relatively) rich WASP beauty from the other side of the tracks that Chico falls head over heels for (the song *You and Me* that accompanies their dates together is one of the film's terrific song score's highlights. A song score written by disgraced tunesmith Joe Brooks). And as Chico,

---

*Amusingly, in Italy, *Lords of Flatbush* was titled, *Happy Days: La banda dei fiori di pesco*. And dubbed to turn Winkler's character of Butchey literally into Fonzie, and the whole film into a Fonzie origin story.

Perry King, who for a while had a string of feature film leads in interesting movies like *Mandingo*, *The Possession of Joel Delaney*, *The Choirboys*, *Foster & Laurie*, and *A Different Story*, till by the eighties he was wearing Hawaiian shirts and drinking out of coconuts on TV's *Riptide*.

The story goes King was a replacement for the role of Chico. Originally Chico was played by a young Richard Gere, three years before his breakout roles in *Looking for Mr. Goodbar* and *Days of Heaven*. And, apparently, Stallone and Gere hated each other so much that Stallone kicked his ass and then Gere either quit or was fired. Another humorous element of Stallone's "*Lords Legacy*," after super producers Robert Chartoff and Irwin Winkler read the *Rocky* script and wanted to make it, they were told they had to do it with the author as the lead.

"*Well, what has he done before?*" they incredulously asked.

Stallone's agent said, "*He's the lead of Lords of Flatbush.*"

So naturally they screened the film and were completely beside themselves with excitement about the actor and his potential to play a great *Rocky* . . . because they thought *Perry King* was Sylvester Stallone!

While I've always felt *The Lords of Flatbush* spent too much footage on the Chico-Jane relationship, their breakup scene, set to a *breakup* version of *their* song *You and Me*, has always punched me in the heart. It's after that scene you realize how good this dinky little movie really is.

In retrospect, watching *The Lords of Flatbush* when it came out was an interesting experience for the fourth-grade me. Because it was the first time I was introduced to the New York independent low-budget film aesthetic. Before I saw *Mean Streets*, I saw *Lords*. Before I saw Claudia Weil's *Girlfriends*, I saw *Lords*. Before I saw Jim Jarmusch movies, I saw *Lords*. Before I saw *Smithereens*, I saw *The Lords*. And I liked it and my friends liked it. Though we all felt a little gypped that Fonzie didn't have more to do. But the film's cast was excellent. Along with who I've already mentioned, there was disco's court jester Paul Jabara, the beautifully annoying Renee Paris as *Annie,* Chico's disposable sex partner (even that's too romantic a description for what she is), and best of all the *great* Maria Smith as Stanley's longtime, long suffering, but ultimately triumphant girlfriend, *Frannie.* And to this day, Smith remains Stallone's best female on-screen partner. I wouldn't be surprised at all to find out he originally wrote the role of *Adrian* in *Rocky* for Smith. As good as everybody is, it's Stallone and Smith who dominate the movie. Stallone not only dominates the screen as Stanley, he wrote or rewrote many of the scenes he's in—earning him that long ago banished from the Writers Guild credit, *Additional Dialogue.* And frankly anyone familiar with Stallone's witty street-smart dialogue can tell. Especially in two of the film's best scenes. One, a very Brandoesque monologue delivered by Stallone to King next to his rooftop pigeon coop. And the other, which is not only the film's best scene, but one of the standout scenes in seventies independent cinema, where Stanley's fiancée Frannie lures him into a jewelry store to purchase an engagement ring the poor slob clearly can't afford. The scene that follows is hilariously funny, hilariously real, and even a touch sad. Throughout the entire film Stallone's Stanley is a beast. In any other movie he'd be the bully bad guy of the piece. It's only Stallone's sarcastic witticisms, said out of the corner of his mouth, that keep him vaguely sympathetic (though *sympathetic* is way too strong an adjective). But at the height of the hysteria that Frannie and her best friend Annie create in the jewelry store, you actually realize how over his head the big gorilla is. The scene ends in a tremendous victory for Frannie. But also, despite Stanley's brutish behavior throughout the film, we realize the depth of feeling he has for Frannie. And we never look at him the same way again. It's really a wonderful scene, and Stallone's writing fingerprints are all over it.

After his success with *Rocky* (both as writer and star), Stallone would give interviews and journalists would ask how he started writing.

He famously said he started trying to write screenplays after he saw *Easy Rider.* He remarked, "*I could do at least as good as that.*"

So after *Lords*—and sometime before *Rocky*—Stallone penned his magnum opus, the mini street epic *Hell's Kitchen.* The script is a hodgepodge of every Warner Bros. street film, Clifford Odets play, and Damon Runyon story Stallone had ever seen or heard. But while those are the touchstones that Stallone and the critics cited at the time of release, the script's true inspiration was *the East Side Kids* series of films made by Monogram Studios in the forties (it's why even though the film feels like it *should* take place during the Depression, it actually takes place after World War II). By the time Stallone eventually made the film, post-*Rocky,* and now re-christened *Paradise Alley* with Stallone himself at the helm, those *East Side Kids* movies were enjoying a renewed wave of popularity on local television stations all over America (primarily due to their public domain status). In Los Angeles on KHJ-TV's channel 9, they played every Saturday at ten o'clock, right after the Saturday morning cartoons wrapped up, and two hours before *Soul Train* aired on the same station.

The East Side Kids movies starred Leo Gorcey, Huntz Hall, Bobby Jordan, and (sometimes) Gabriel Dell. Now more often than not, when people refer to *the East Side Kids,* they confuse them with *the Bowery Boys,* as if the two groups and two film series were interchangeable. Which, since Gorcey and Hall starred in both and played similar characters, is understandable. That is— understandable—*if* you've never seen the two different series. If you have, you know the two series are vastly different in both style and quality. Almost every film in *the East Side Kids* series is pretty fucking good, and almost every film in *the Bowery Boys* series is pretty fucking lousy.

For the uninitiated, a little history might be required. Now this gets a little complicated, so keep up. One of the most successful shows on Broadway in the thirties was the Sidney Kingsley play *Dead End*. It was a socially conscious drama about life in the slums of New York. Almost all other stories of its type, whether it's *Blackboard Jungle*, or *Boulevard Nights*, or *Boyz n the Hood* is a descendant of *Dead End*.

The big sensation of the play were the young street kids who played the juvenile delinquents in the show, Billy Halop, Huntz Hall, Leo Gorcey, Bobby Jordan, and Gabe Dell. They were so popular they became known as *the Dead End Kids*. And for a while, the boys were one of the most successful acting ensembles in the history of Hollywood. Jack Warner put them under contract and began putting them in Warner Bros. crime pictures alongside their biggest gangster film stars, James Cagney, Humphrey Bogart, John Garfield, Pat O'Brien (but not Bette Davis or Errol Flynn). They did seven films for Warner Bros. as *the Dead End Kids*. And some of them were the best Warner movies of their era, including the greatest Warner gangster movie of all time, *Angels with Dirty Faces*. As good as the films they did at Warner's were, I always had a bit of a problem with *the Dead End Kids*.

In *Dead End* the kid with the biggest part was Billy Halop. So consequently in the movies at Warner's featuring *the Dead End Kids* they always featured Billy Halop most prominently. But I always found Billy Halop the least interesting and most one-note of the fellas. If they mixed it up a bit, it would have been better, but they never did. It was always practically *Billy Halop and the Dead End Kids*. So eventually their contract ran out at Warner's, which pretty much coincided with the studio pulling back on making gangster films. So now the boys were free agents. So they split up and created two separate groups. *The Little Tough Guys*, led by Billy Halop, who signed with Universal. And *the East Side Kids*, led by Leo Gorcey, who signed with Monogram Pictures. But Huntz Hall, Bobby Jordan, and Gabe Dell appeared in both groups. And considering how many movies they did, I'm not really sure how they accomplished it. Especially considering Universal didn't just put *the Little Tough Guys* in features, but starred them in four serials as well. Now back in their Warner Bros. days they starred in some of the biggest movies on the lot with the studio's biggest stars. This was definitely not the case with Monogram and Universal. The movies they made for them were hour-long B programmers. But this was back when studios knew how to make B programmers. So yeah, they were cheaper, but they were still pretty fucking good. And now the boys didn't have to share the screen. The movies were about *them.* They were made by some of the best B movie directors in town, Wallace Fox, William Nigh, Ray Taylor, and Ford Beebe. And in the case of *the East Side Kids* many entries by the great Joseph H. Lewis. And two *Little Tough Guy* films were made by none other than German emigre Joe May (director of the German classic *Asphalt* and Fritz Lang's mentor). And by the time Halop was starring in *the Little Tough Guy* movies, I liked him much better (especially in Joe May's *You're Not So Tough*, which is a dynamite little picture).

But for me, it's all about Leo Gorcey and *the East Side Kids.* Gorcey was a bulldog-looking, hot-tempered little guy who strangled the English language with "*dees,*" "*dems,*", and "*does.*" Also, despite his size, he could knock anybody's block off. And he was a tremendous *Smart Alec* and *Wise Guy* (both the names of two of his movies). When Robert Blake became a superstar in the seventies due to his cop show *Baretta,* he was sorta the second coming of Leo Gorcey. In the movies Gorcey played *Ethelbert "Muggs" McGinnis,* the ringleader of *the East Side Kids,* which consisted of cute Bobby Jordan as *Danny* (who wore practically the same striped T-shirt in every film and kind of resembled a young Keanu Reeves), Huntz Hall's *Glimpy,* who was the genuinely amusing comic foil to Gorcey's straight man, former *Little Rascal* Sunshine Sammy Morrison as *Scruno,* the one black member of the gang, and usually Gabe Dell as the gang member most susceptible to corruption (if the local gangsters were going to get their hooks in one of the boys, it was always Gabe Dell), and then a couple of other guys who spent the movie hanging around but didn't have names, or lines, except maybe a random, "*You tell 'em, Muggs!*"

As a young man in the late seventies, when all my on-screen role models were tough ethnic New York street guys (Robert De Niro, Sylvester Stallone, John Travolta, Robert Blake, Richard Gere), Leo Gorcey was the forebearer. He had the size and sass of Cagney, he looked a bit like John Garfield if somebody dropped an anvil on Garfield's head from the top of the Empire State Building. And no doubt he could beat the shit out of Bogart. And as film series go, few other series lasted as long, did as many entries, and kept up as consistent a level of quality as Monogram's *East Side Kids* films. The series definitely had some standout entries, but my two favorites were Joseph H. Lewis' *That Gang of Mine*, which features a thoroughbred racing plot, an off-beat story, an out of character turn by Gorcey, and a highly dignified performance by black thespian Clarence Muse.* Muse and Morrison share a scene and a dolly shot that is not only unlike any other scene in the series, it's unlike any other scene in a *white Hollywood* film of its era. It wouldn't be until the sixties that another black actor was the focus of a dolly shot.

My other favorite is also one of my favorite boxing pictures, and my two favorite performances by both Gorcey and Jordan, Wallace Fox's *Bowery Blitzkrieg*. It's also the film that most resembles Stallone's *Paradise Alley*, or at least the type of picture *Paradise Alley* is trying to be. Due to its public domain status, *Bowery Blitzkrieg* has been available for decades on shitty quality video tapes.

---

*This dignified use of black thespian Clarence Muse was a staple of Joseph H. Lewis' work and sensibility. It's a quality that also distinguishes his nifty Bela Lugosi horror quickie *The Invisible Ghost.*

But every video tape I've ever seen of the film (and believe me, I've looked), doesn't include the scene that made me fall in love with the picture when I saw it as a kid on Channel 9. Just before Gorcey's Muggs has to get to the boxing arena and fight the big climactic fight, he gives a pint of blood to save Jordan's Danny, who's lying in a hospital bed fighting for his life. The scene that's always missing is a prayer/monologue to God, where Muggs begs the man upstairs to save his pal. It's corny, it's sentimental, and I'm tearing up just typing this.

And it could have been written by Stallone.

It was only towards the end of the film series run, when hacks like William Beaudine started wielding the megaphone, that the boys stopped being tough and started being goofy (the haunted house entry *Ghosts on the Loose* with Bela Lugosi and a young Ava Gardner is the pits).

Then Leo Gorcey got tired of working for producer Sam Katzman, quit *the East Side Kids*, started his own production company (where he'd own 40%), and started *the Bowery Boys*, originally called *Leo Gorcey and His Bowery Boys*.

And then the movies became terrible, but not right off the bat.

The first one, directed by Phil Karlson, isn't bad. But pretty quickly the boys went from being tough guys to subpar Three Stooges–like buffoons.

The East Side Kids movies played like hour-long versions of the same types of movies that the boys used to make at Warner Bros. Boxing movies (*Muggs becomes a boxer*), racetrack movies (*Muggs becomes a jockey), Muggs and the boys break up a ring of counterfeiters . . . etc., etc. . . . .*

But whatever realistic grit *the East Side Kids* movies had was lost when they started doing the stupid *Bowery Boys* movies. And Billy Halop had it worse. After *the Little Tough Guys* he went over to PRC Releasing company and with Carl "*Alfalfa*" Switzer started *the Gas House Kids*, which were to *the Bowery Boys* what *the Ritz*

Brothers were to *The Three Stooges.* (Pauline Kael inexplicably always sang the praises of Harry Ritz and the Ritz Brothers. Well, whatever film on them that survived that was any good, I've never seen.)

Stallone has never acknowledged *the East Side Kids* as his inspiration for *Paradise Alley.* But when I saw the picture when it opened in 1978, when *the East Side Kids* played every Saturday morning on television, the debt was obvious.

Stallone's film tells the story of *the Carbonis*, three Italian brothers (post-WW2), living in a garishly beautiful, Hollywood backlot depiction of New York's Hell's Kitchen (one-half empty booze bottles—the other half fairy dust). Fast-buck con man *Cosmo* (Stallone, in the Gorcey part); mammoth-muscled ice block deliveryman, the sweet but simple-minded *Vic* (the extremely effective Lee Canalito in the Bobby Jordan role, if Jordan was the size of Steve Reeves); and burnt-out mortician with a war wound in his gimpy leg *Lenny* (Armand Assante in the susceptible to corruption Gabe Dell role).

The first act of the story follows Cosmo's hairbrained schemes to make a buck in the neon lit slum streets of Hell's Kitchen. Cosmo has a million ideas to make a million dollars, but he mistakes a big brain for a big mouth. Then he gets the idea to talk gentle giant Vic into entering the hundred dollar wrestling match that's held at *Paradise Alley*—a local combination bar–wrestling arena.★

Vic ends up winning the match against the Paradise Alley champion *Big Glory* (John Milius regular Frank McRae). Then the fast buck opportunist Cosmo and sensitive older brother Lenny start

---

★Paradise Alley, the combo tavern and wrestling joint, is extremely reminiscent of *Glory Alley*, the combo tavern and boxing joint and hep-cat jazz club, that figures prominently in the Raoul Walsh picture of the same name.

managing Vic's wrestling career. And the sweet Vic, now dubbed *Kid Salami*, turns into the Carboni brothers' meal ticket as he continues to win matches and work his way up the ranks. But as Vic's wrestling career does better and better, a personality change happens between the two managing brothers. Cosmo begins worrying more and more about Vic's safety, and Lenny turns into a cold, callous fight promoter out of *Body and Soul*.

When Stallone first wrote the script—like *Rocky*—it was designed as a way to showcase himself in a real movie. So in his dream scenario it was supposed to star Robert De Niro as Cosmo, Al Pacino as Lenny, and himself as the beefy Vic. A hat trick he couldn't quite pull off. But at one point it was almost made as an ABC TV movie. Stallone, his beautiful wife, Sasha, and that prehistoric beast of a dog he owned, Butkus (the one in *Rocky*), had just arrived in Los Angeles from New York. Their car broke down on Sunset Boulevard and Sly called the only person he knew in L.A., his costar from *The Lords of Flatbush*, Henry Winkler. So Winkler picks them up and drives them to a motel, Winkler remembering Butkus leaving three gallons of drool on his back seat. Winkler was riding high at the time on his TV show *Happy Days*, and his character *Fonzie* was just starting to take off. Henry asks Sly, what are his plans? Stallone shows him the script for what was then *Hell's Kitchen* and says he wants to get it produced. Winkler reads it and really responds to the material. Knowing, due to the growing popularity of *Fonzie*, that he had a little pull over at ABC, Winkler asked Stallone permission to set it up as a TV movie. Stallone, excited by the prospect, said yes. Winkler goes to the network with the script and they agree to make it, with Winkler producing and starring as Cosmo, and Stallone playing the beefy, simple-minded wrestling brother, Vic.

Everybody's all excited, till ABC decides the script needs a rewrite by somebody other than Stallone. A desperate, heartbroken Sylvester Stallone calls his friend and begs him to blow the deal so no Hollywood hack will fuck up his baby. And a disappointed Winkler cancels the film for a fellow *Lord*.

Actually, at the time, I'd have loved to see Henry Winkler (just once) lean into his black-leather-jacket-wearing persona. All of his non-Fonzie character choices swung wildly in the other direction. And his playing Cosmo Carboni would have given him the opportunity to have done that. But, despite his best efforts, Stallone could never get his wrestling script off the ground. So he put it away and started writing another script for himself to star in.

This time, instead of playing a wrestler, he'd play a boxer.

And the rest is history.

In a blatant act of highway robbery, two producers who had optioned Stallone's *Paradise Alley* script for a penny—because Stallone was starving—John F. Roach and Ronald A. Suppa of Force Ten Productions, sued UA, Chartoff and Winkler, and Stallone, claiming the script for *Rocky* was the same as *Paradise Alley*. Well, any film critic could tell you that's not the case. But since *Paradise Alley* was even closer to Stallone's heart than *Rocky*, the newly christened movie star told Roach and Suppa no problem, I totally intend to make *Paradise Alley*. Except now, he'd be sitting for the first time in the director's chair and playing Cosmo, the role he really wanted all along.

When *Rocky* came out, it became practically my favorite movie of all time. I'm aware I've said that a few times now. But that was the seventies. I was a young enthusiastic movie geek, during a time when movies were fucking incredible. But unless you were there in 1976, it's pretty hard to get across the impact that the film *Rocky* had on audiences.

Everything about *Rocky* took audiences by complete surprise. The unknown guy in the lead, how emotional the film ended up being, that incredibly stirring score by Bill Conti, and one of the most dynamic climaxes most of us had ever experienced in a cinema.

I'd been to movies before where something happened on screen and the audience cheered. But *never*—and I repeat—*never*—like they cheered when Rocky landed that blow in the first round that knocked Apollo Creed to the floor. The entire theatre had been watching the fight with their hearts choking their throats, expecting the worst. Every blow Rocky took seemed to land on you. The smugness of Apollo Creed's superiority over this ham and egg bum seemed like a repudiation of Rocky's humanity. A humanity that both Stallone and the movie had spent the last ninety minutes making us fall in love with. Then suddenly—with one powerful swing—Apollo Creed was knocked to the floor on his back. I saw that film around seven or so times at the theatres, and every single time during that moment the audience practically hit the ceiling. But no time was like that first time. In 1976 I didn't need to be told how involving movies *could* be. I *knew*. In fact I didn't know much else. But until then, I had never been as emotionally invested in a lead character as I was with *Rocky Balboa* and by extension his creator Sylvester Stallone. Now that type of audience innocence would be practically impossible to duplicate for somebody just discovering the movie today. One, they'd have to contend with Stallone's subsequent celebrity and career. And I don't say that as a dig or a snarky comment. But the *Planet Hollywood* Stallone is not the Stallone who sat on Dinah Shore's couch spinning witty stories about his hungry years.

You can't pretend we don't live in a world with eight movies featuring the character of *Rocky*, and five movies featuring Stallone's other franchise character *Rambo*, sit on the shelves of long-ago boarded up video stores alongside cassettes for *Cobra* and *Over the Top*. But the real reason that the film *Rocky* could never have the impact it did in 1976 is because to have that same impact, you had to live through the tough, gritty, downbeat, pessimistic films of the early seventies to be floored by the feel-good catharsis of

Rocky. You had to live in a world where a movie like *Papillon* was a Hollywood blockbuster.

When even crowd-pleasing comedies like *The Longest Yard* included the brutal death of characters.

In a Hollywood that had forsaken the Old Hollywood happy ending as bullshit propaganda from *"the Man"*.

When the senseless death of your hero at the climax was the vogue (*Easy Rider, The New Centurions, Electra Glide in Blue, Hustle*). When even popular audience movies like *Three Days of the Condor* counted on a certain amount of cynicism and paranoia from the popcorn eaters.

The closest thing to a feel-good movie in the early seventies was revenge films.

The closest I came to an audience cheering like we did in *Rocky* was George Kennedy and William Devane blowing the fuck out of the killers that murdered their families in *The "Human" Factor* and *Rolling Thunder.* I remember, before seeing Stallone's film, being at some neighborhood kid's house and the TV spot for *Rocky* came on. The kid wondered out loud, *"What's that?"* And his mother glanced at the TV screen and said dismissively, *"Oh, just another movie about some guy and his problems."* Today it's very easy to romanticize that cynical seventies era—especially since it's long gone—seemingly never to return. But from 1970 to at least 1977, every other movie that came out *did* seem like it was about *"some guy and his problems."* Part of the elation tied to the audience's response to the climactic fight in *Rocky* was after five years of seventies cinema, we didn't really expect things to work out for Balboa. And I don't mean we didn't expect him to win the heavyweight championship of the world. He was never going to fucking *win!* We just hoped he didn't look like a fucking joke. That's why the ending was so surprisingly moving and cathartic. That's why when he knocked Apollo Creed flat on his back we hit the roof. Because from that point on, no matter whatever else happened, Rocky proved he wasn't a joke. But by the time you get to the last round—and Rocky has Apollo Creed on the ropes—hitting him with a left and a right and a left and a right and the crowd in the boxing arena was chanting; "Roc-ky . . . Roc-ky. . . ." *Oh my fucking god!*

There had simply never been anything like it.

Then at the Academy Awards the film duplicates its miraculous win in real life? From that point on cynicism in seventies cinema was dead on arrival.

Needless to say, as a young boy at that time, I LOVED SYLVESTER STALLONE. I loved everything about him. I loved *Rocky*, I loved him in *Rocky*, I loved his story about how he *wrote Rocky* (easily the most inspirational Hollywood story I had ever heard). I loved the way he looked, the way he sounded. I loved his witty and forthright interviews in magazines. He did all the talk shows of the day, numerous times, and was incredibly charming.

Mike Douglas shot an entire episode of his show from the set of *F.I.S.T.*

On *Dinah!* he sang the theme song to *Paradise Alley*!

So to say I was rooting for Stallone to prove himself more than a "Sylvester-come-lately" (as *Los Angeles Magazine* called him), would be an understatement.

His follow-up movie after *Rocky* was a bland epic about the teamsters, where he played a fictional version of Jimmy Hoffa, titled *F.I.S.T.*, directed by Hollywood heavyweight Norman Jewison (as Roger Avary declares him, *"The greatest Canadian filmmaker to ever live!"*). The film wants to be to the trucking union what *The Godfather* was to the Mafia. What it plays like is a truncated seventies television miniseries. In fact, there *was* a television miniseries made to rip-off *F.I.S.T.* called *Power* that featured Joe Don Baker playing another fictionalized Jimmy Hoffa character. Now Stallone didn't embarrass himself in *F.I.S.T.*, but neither did he rise to the occasion of headlining a Hollywood epic. Not that I can imagine anybody else necessarily doing a better job with that movie and that script.

The scenes at the beginning when he flirts with Melinda Dillon, who eventually becomes the character's wife, which Stallone wrote (it's fucking obvious), are the only moments when the witty sparkle of Stallone on talk shows reveals itself (even Pauline Kael, who liked Stallone in *Rocky*, then dedicated herself to his mockery for the rest of her writing career, mentioned this about *F.I.S.T.* in her savage takedown of *Paradise Alley*).

All these years later, the only thing memorable about *F.I.S.T.* is when Stallone's playing the older Hoffa (i.e., *Johnny Kovac*) how much he looks like the supposedly older Rock Hudson in *Giant*.

For his *Rocky* follow-up, there were three offers on the table, the Norman Jewison epic, Jon Voight's Academy Award–winning role in *Coming Home* (don't judge Sly too harshly for turning that down, by all accounts the script of that film was dreadful), and the title role in Walter Hill's Melville-like car chase masterpiece, *The Driver*. Which is definitely a better movie than *F.I.S.T.*, but not necessarily a better fit for Sylvester. It was Stallone's personality that made him a star, the point of *The Driver* is the character hasn't any personality. An aspect that the film's lead, Ryan O'Neal, conveyed superbly. So Stallone's real follow-up to *Rocky* would be his directorial debut of his original passion project, *Paradise Alley*.

Now as you can have guessed, judging from my enthusiasm for all things Sylvester Stallone at that time, I loved *Paradise Alley*! Who knows how many times I saw it in the cinemas when it came out. I also read the very entertaining novelization written by Stallone himself, and later bought the film on video back when MCA home video cassettes were crazy expensive. I even had the *Paradise Alley* poster up on my bedroom wall for a while. Not to mention I owned the soundtrack (which was a really good soundtrack album and it introduced me to Tom Waits). I loved it so much one of the first scripts I ever tried writing was a straight-up rip-off of Stallone's epic titled *Brooklyn B.R.* (don't ask what *B.R.* stood for, like *Reservoir Dogs*, it didn't mean anything, it just sounded good).

It followed the adventures of three Italian brothers in thirties Brooklyn named *the De Vito Brothers* (no relation to Danny). Dominick, Scotty, and Dario (like Stallone, I wrote it to play Dominick—the Cosmo one). I never finished that script, but since I ripped off the entire story from Mr. Stallone, that was the screenplay I got furthest along than any other, before eventually abandoning it.

But if you were a *Paradise Alley* fan, the most important thing wasn't liking it, it was defending it against all comers. And when it came to defending *Paradise Alley*, I dare say I did a damn sight better job than Stallone. My biggest claim was, "*Paradise Alley was one of the greatest directorial debuts of the seventies! And the greatest actor-director directorial debuts [*along with Orson Welles*] of all time!*" Fuck John Cassavetes, fuck Charles Laughton, fuck Charlie Chaplin, it's *Paradise* fucking *Alley*!

Okay, but how do I feel about it now?

Well, maybe it isn't "*one of the greatest directorial debuts of all time!*" But it is a very good debut of a filmmaker with both obvious talent and vision (dare I say Stallone is the best director Sylvester has ever worked with). And in its own way, it's the purest expression of the particular vision that the actor had back in those days. In a way the relative reality of *Rocky* somewhat hemmed in Stallone's movie-movie hot house vision. What Stallone replaces it with in *Rocky* was finding a personal equivalent in his own life to the screenplay he was writing. The way Rocky Balboa was a "*ham and egger*" (the movie's parlance) club fighter, is how Stallone thought of himself as an actor (though Stallone was far more successful an actor before *Rocky* than he presented himself afterwards). And

Rocky's shot at the heavyweight title mirrors exactly Stallone's shot of headlining a United Artist studio motion picture produced by the super producer team of Chartoff and Winkler. This personal expression, filtered through the life of *Rocky*, would become a hallmark of the series and the writer's best work.

Stallone's best movie as a director-writer-actor was *Rocky II* (I even prefer it to the first one). In the sequel, Rocky's triumphant contest with Apollo Creed is at first celebrated, but then eventually discounted as a fluke. His achievement is dismissed by sportswriters, sports fans, and the general public at large as not talent, not skill, but luck. And by mid-movie he's pretty much written off as a flash in the pan (*"Sylvester-Come-Lately"*). Even his rematch with Apollo Creed is dubbed by the sports community as a desperate attempt to both cash in and remain relevant, just like the announcement in the trades that Stallone was making *Rocky II*. One of the things that makes *Rocky II* extremely powerful is the lead character's money worries. At the end of the day, he accepts the rematch because he fucking needs the cash.

And yet again, life imitated art. The way Rocky's rematch with Apollo Creed redeemed the fighter to the world, Stallone's sequel, after the failure of *F.I.S.T.* and *Paradise Alley*, redeemed Sylvester.

As an actor, haters could still speculate out loud whether or not Stallone was able to play anything but a dim-witted boxer. But he did prove, beyond a shadow of a doubt, that the movie-going audience's affection for the character of Rocky Balboa was no fluke. People loved the character in the second movie even more than the first film (the humiliation he suffers in the middle section of the picture is truly hard to watch). And Stallone proved he could direct a good movie. If you *liked* the movie *Rocky*, you probably think the first movie is better. But if you *loved* the character of Rocky, you definitely think the second movie is best.

But the reason, beyond just its effectiveness, that I feel *Rocky II* is superior to the first film is an added layer of depth and perspective that the writer brought to the fairy tale. This time out, Stallone isn't identifying with just Rocky Balboa. This time, Stallone *is* also Apollo Creed.

Rocky made Sylvester Stallone one of the biggest celebrities in the world. And Sylvester Stallone, like many before him, soon realized all that glitters isn't gold.

Rocky is wounded by all the slings and arrows thrown his way by the media.

Apollo Creed, on the other hand, is spitting mad.

Carl Weathers spends the entire movie fucking furious at his perception in the media. Creed stomping around his giant house—angrily reading hate mail—probably mirrors Stallone stomping around his giant house reading Pauline Kael's review of *Paradise Alley.*

In the press, Stallone went from "aww shucks" nice guy to challenging movie reviewers to fights (*"I'd like to see him say that to my face!"*). He had the money, he had the fame, he had the house, he had the wardrobe, he had the cars. But putting pen to paper on the manuscript for *Rocky II,* he knew something he never could have known when he wrote the first movie. To possess those things there's a price to be paid. And yeah, people can say, fuck you—no biggie. I'm sure that's what Stallone would have said before *Rocky.* But those are people who *have never* and *will never* pay that price.

And Stallone didn't handle it well.

And neither does Apollo Creed.

In fact one of the most remarkable things about *Rocky II* is despite all the fucked up shit that Apollo Creed does in the film, we never really hate him. Because we understand he's in pain and he's not himself. He's a howling giant screaming at the moon for shining.

We don't hate him.

We feel sorry for him and wait for him to come to his senses.

Well, *Paradise Alley* isn't as good as either *Rocky* or *Rocky II*, but it's unlikely *Rocky II* would be as good as it is without Stallone making *Paradise Alley* first. And it's much better than either *Rocky III* or *IV*. *Rocky* and *Rocky II* are real movies. *Rocky III* and *Rocky IV* are single issue comic books, with Rocky fighting super villains in films that resemble trailers more than actual movies—like *Superman vs. Muhammad Ali*.

I know a lot of boys who came of age in the eighties love those movies. And I'm not saying they're not effective—for what they are. It's what they are that bugs me. To me, *Rocky* wasn't a comic book. And his opponents weren't villains who could have been created by Jack Kirby.

I always took *Rocky* too seriously to fully endorse the unreal direction that Stallone took the series. Messy though it is, *Paradise Alley is* a real movie.

It's clear Stallone had a vision in his head for the picture, and he killed himself trying to get that vision out of his head, and up on the screen. It's also clear it's the work of a talented young writer in love with his own words and the milieu he's creating at the expense of everything else. In fact this script goes to show how much Stallone learned about screenwriting by the time he penned *Rocky*. The script for *Rocky* works slow and precise, moving steadily forward towards its bring-the-house-down climax. But the structure that works so well in *Rocky* is completely absent from *Paradise Alley*. As opposed to the slow and steady build of the boxing movie, his script for the wrestling movie is all over the place. It invests time in strange subplots that don't go anywhere. The film's whole first act seems to center on Cosmo's Herculean efforts to get his hands on an organ grinder's monkey ("*I could make a fortune with that monkey*"). Which admittedly leads to the film's best sequence, an arm wrestling match between Vic and the local wrestling champion *Frankie the Thumper* (Terry Funk), who looks like a living breathing Chester Gould creation (he out-gargoyles Robert Tessier in Walter Hill's *Hard Times*).

It's the film's best scene, and the scene that proves beyond a doubt that Stallone is a director. Cosmo gets the monkey, but his money-making plans go bust. But then, we never see or hear from the monkey again. What the fuck happened to it? Did the Carbonis eat it?

Other intriguing subplots are brought up yet frustratingly never elaborated on. Like sweet Vic's relationship with *Susan*, a Chinese girl from the neighborhood played by the always adorable Aimee Eccles (from *Pretty Maids All in a Row*). And the film's big dramatic character shift, when crass Cosmo and sensible Lenny switch personalities, isn't earned dramatically. They just all of a sudden switch personalities like they've been struck by some *Freaky Friday*–like curse. And while the final wrestling match between Vic and Frankie the Thumper is cinematic as all get out—a storm breaks out on fight night, leaking water into the fleapit joint that collects in a big puddle in the middle of the ring—it's never dramatic because Vic's victorious outcome seems preordained. Both Canalito and Funk do a great job and it's choreographed well (as is a really powerful wrestling montage earlier in the film that's cut to some terrific Bill Conti music), but because of the kind of movie it is, of course Vic's going to win. True, the outcome of eighty-five percent of all sports movies are preordained. Nevertheless, there's still usually *some* suspense. The final match in *Paradise Alley* is fun to watch with all the splashing water, but it provides zero suspense. The final boxing match in *Rocky IV* is more suspenseful, and that film's one-sheet shows Rocky in the ring, post-fight, wrapped in an American flag, with his gloves raised high in the air in a victory pose. Today it may be hard to remember, but in the first film Rocky's victory was *not* a foregone conclusion. And sure enough—he didn't win. But it *was* excruciatingly suspenseful and emotionally wrenching. The reason it affected audiences so potently was the way the film, slowly, despite Rocky's punchiness, made you take him seriously. More serious than any other on-screen character, including Adrian. Rocky isn't just underestimated, he's a joke. And any serious ambitions on his part is the punch line. In the first film, Rocky Balboa wasn't about winning the heavyweight title from Apollo Creed, he was about proving he deserved to even put the gloves on in the first place.

Nothing that deep happens in *Paradise Alley*. It's all surface. But with cinematographer Laszlo Kovacs providing the eye-popping cinematic sizzle, what a surface (I've watched it on TV with the color turned off in black and white and it looks even better).

This film is Stallone's vision and aesthetic, unfiltered, undiluted, and delivered full bore in your face. Sly's good ear for writing funny dialogue, his collection of larger than life Damon Runyon type characters (especially his rogues' gallery of villains), his Irish-like face-on-the-barroom-floor sentimentality, the film's mean streets milieu and its stylized poetic flourishes set against fire escapes and garbage cans, all amount to a passionate artist's vision, who if he doesn't really have anything to say, for sure has something to express. Without that limiting, demanding structure that *Rocky* forced him to adhere to, Stallone can do everything he always *wanted* to do.

Racing across tenement rooftops (with fellow *Lord* Paul Mace), a big tear-jerking death scene for over the hill black wrestler *Big Glory* (Frank McRae, who should have been nominated for an Oscar), Big Vic who, like a Hell's Kitchen Steve Reeves, carries huge blocks of ice up floor after floor of tenement stairs, Stallone performing one whole section of the movie in a Santa Claus suit, the final wrestling match with the sweaty behemoths splashing in the water.

And his cast is great. You can tell they all enjoyed wearing the costumes and spouting Sly's witty lines. And as the three Carboni brothers, Stallone, Canalito, and Assante are terrific.

Especially Canalito, who plays his cliched part with a poignant depth the other two don't quite match.*

Assante is cast as sort of a poor man's Pacino, and since this movie the actor enjoyed a twenty-five year career as . . . well . . . a poor man's Pacino.

And Stallone—who's never looked better in any film than in *Alley*—plays Cosmo as a one-note obnoxious loudmouth.

But he's an obnoxious loudmouth with really funny lines. Colorful smart-ass dialogue he frustratingly couldn't put in the mouth of dim-witted Rocky, he spouts nonstop as Cosmo. And until he gets all soft and mushy at the end, I think he's a fucking scream. But I think the whole movie is a scream. Is it messy? Yeah of course. But above all *Paradise Alley* is funny.

Because of its genre and setting, its cast of pros, its passionate vision fulfillment, and its actor/director architecture, as Myron Meisel pointed out in *the LA Reader*, the film's reminiscent of another ego epic, Jack Webb's *Pete Kelly's Blues*.

And I would say, as well as Eddie Murphy's much maligned in the white press—but beloved in the hood—gangster fantasia, *Harlem Nights*.

Stallone, Webb, and Murphy share similar visions and similar

---

*Unfortunately, Lee Canalito never made another film. He *almost* did. He was originally cast by John Derek as Tarzan in his Jane-centric, *Tarzan the Ape Man*, starring Derek's wife, Bo Derek. But he was fired because— allegedly—he ate so much he started busting out of his loincloth.

passions behind those visions. As well as similar targets on their foreheads.

It would be amazing to see Stallone direct another movie with the passion he had when he made *Paradise Alley*. It would be amazing to see Stallone *love* something again the way he loved *Paradise Alley*.★

★Maybe his long talked about Edgar Allan Poe biopic?

Escape from Alcatraz

(1979)

E*scape from Alcatraz*, a film I didn't like when it came out—
I'm sure it was just too dry for the seventeen-year-old me—
proved a revelation on a re-view a few years ago. Cinematically
speaking, it's Don Siegel's most expressive film. During his days
in New Hollywood Siegel shot some terrific action scenes: The final fatal shootout for Richard Widmark's *Madigan*. The pool hall
fight (a real showstopper) in *Coogan's Bluff*. The entire school bus
sequence in *Dirty Harry*, as well as that film's action introduction
of hot dog Harry vs. the Black Panthers (the scene suffers a little
now due to its obvious backlot quality. Are they in San Francisco
or Hazzard County?). The machine gun shootout in *The Black
Windmill* (explosions of muzzle flash, bullet casings, and splintered
wood). The actual action part of the bank robbery in *Charley Varrick*. The attack of Harry Bascom of Bascom Auto Repair (Siegel
regular John Mitchum), the first of the sleeper agents that Donald
Pleasence wakes up in *Telefon*.

Yet unlike Leone, Peckinpah, (Peter) Hyams, and De Palma,
Siegel never engaged in cinematic set pieces, until the beautiful,
practically wordless opening sequence of *Escape from Alcatraz*.

The sequence not only takes its time, but it also seems to go
back in time. On one hand, it feels like the no-nonsense fifties

Siegel of *Baby Face Nelson* & *Private Hell 36*—though tellingly, not like the docu-style of *Riot in Cell Block 11*. But on the other hand, never before and never again would Siegel engage in this type of cinematic bravura.

From Eastwood's first appearance as *Frank Morris*, being led off the ferry in the pouring rain onto the isolated island in his raincoat. To the older but still virile Eastwood (who looks as if he's been chipped from granite rock as much as the penitentiary) being walked into processing in his old-school gray suit (back in the day when people went to prison in suits and it wasn't a statement), being made to strip while the prison doctor examines his mouth like livestock. To being marched naked through the cell block (brilliant), the sound of his bare feet slapping out a rhythm against the cold concrete floor that echoes against the stone walls of the Rock. To the final moment when Morris is placed in his cage, the cell door is slammed shut, and the guard says the first real line in the film, "*Welcome to Alcatraz*," punctuated by a Mario Bava–like thunderclap and lightning bolt. "*Bravo!*"

Siegel's next film after the critical and financial success of the Eastwood prison picture would be his Burt Reynolds' caper comedy *Rough Cut*. On that film Siegel would end up getting fired by the producers and replaced, for a few days anyway, by Bond director Peter Hunt, and writer Larry (TV's *M*A*S*H*) Gelbart would have his name removed from the credits.★

In Burt Reynolds' autobiography, he mentions the elderly Siegel spent half the movie asleep in his chair. And when you see *Rough Cut*, you can believe it (that may be the reason he was fired).

But as the opening sequence in the Eastwood picture proved,

★If only Siegel had retired after *Escape from Alcatraz*, he would have ended his career on an iconic high note. The way Phil Karlson did his last film, *Framed*.

not only was the old man wide awake on *Escape*, but fully engaged and inspired to test his craftsmanship and technique.

I suspect the reason for Siegel's full engagement on the Clint Eastwood *Alcatraz* picture—as opposed to the Charles Bronson espionage picture *Telefon* before it, and the Burt Reynolds caper comedy *Rough Cut* after it—was on Clint's film, the director had something to lose.

What do I mean by that? We'll get into that in a minute, but first, leaving *Escape from Alcatraz* for a moment, let's discuss the Charles Bronson spy film Siegel made before the Eastwood prison drama.

For most of the seventies, the two action stars that ruled the globe were Clint Eastwood and Charles Bronson. (After *The Towering Inferno*, Steve McQueen abdicated his throne to drink beer and get fat with Ali MacGraw in Malibu.) In America, the third was Burt Reynolds, who, for a time eclipsed both Clint and Charlie. So much so, both Clint and Charlie tried to do their own version of a comedic Burt Reynolds–like action flick. *Breakout* for Bronson (good), and *Every Which Way but Loose* for Clint (abysmal, but successful). But Burt's films, while they did great in the States—and killed in the South—never traveled as well to Europe, Asia, Latin America, and Africa as the Eastwood and Bronson pictures did.

In Europe that third spot would go to either Franco Nero or Alain Delon, depending on the year.

In Japan it would be Takakura Ken.

Even Christopher Mitchum was a big noise in Spain due to his pretty decent Spanish Revengeamatic *Summertime Killer*, directed by Spaniard action maestro Antonio Isasi.

The only really serious threat to Bronson and Eastwood's worldwide dominance came from Hong Kong's Bruce Lee. But the actor's untimely death would stop the competition before it ever really got started.

However, Charles Bronson, by the end of the seventies, was

looking a little long in the tooth—little did we know then that Bronson still had more than a decade of action films in front of him. So by the time he did his best picture during his tenure at Cannon Pictures, J. Lee Thompson's delightfully lurid *Kinjite* (the movie where Charlie shoves a dildo up a guy's ass in the first scene), it looks like an action picture starring a *Terror*-era Boris Karloff.

During the same period when Burt Reynolds was kicking ass with *Gator, Smokey and the Bandit,* and *Hooper,* and Eastwood was laying waste with *The Outlaw Josey Wales, The Enforcer,* and *The Gauntlet,* Bronson was getting passe with mediocre efforts like *St. Ives, Breakheart Pass,* and *The White Buffalo.*

In an effort on the studio's part to keep Bronson from getting marginalized, they wisely deduced that it wasn't Bronson's age that was sapping his energy—considering how old he was, he looked remarkably good back then—it was his habit of working with tired old hacks like J. Lee Thompson (I love Thompson and Bronson's Cannon Pictures of the eighties, but their seventies movies are lackluster) and Tom Gries (how did Ted Post miss the call?).

The last Bronson films to make any real noise were his excellent turn in future action auteur Walter Hill's first film, *Hard Times,* and the very good—offbeat—Frank D. Gilroy comedy *From Noon Till Three,* which provided Bronson's wife Jill Ireland with easily her best role. Most of the roles in her husband's films were marked by her miscasting. But, for once, she was perfectly cast in the comedy. In fact, she's better cast than he is, though he's quite funny, and at the finale, quite poignant. The whole enterprise is even romantic, because it's obvious the only reason Bronson did the movie was to provide Jill with that role.

At some point Bronson being comfortable on the set became more important than the movie, hence working time and time again with helmers like J. Lee & Gries. So in an effort to resuscitate Bronson's waning career in the mainstream of commercial

Hollywood filmmaking, action master and Eastwood mentor Don Siegel was brought in to pump some life into *"the ugly one"* (one of Charlie's nicknames in Italy).

Unfortunately, it sorta worked the other way around.

In his autobiography Siegel recounted his *Telefon* experience with Bronson was prickly and the script was stupid. Which reveals all you need to know about the take-the-money-and-run aspect of the endeavor. The wacky *Manchurian Candidate*–like story tells the tale that during the Cold War fifties, Russia planted a bunch of deep-cover sleeper agents in America near important military installations. The sleeper agents don't know who they are, they've been brainwashed into believing they're Americans. But when a certain Robert Frost poem is recited to them, it triggers their assignment, and they suicidally sabotage military targets. The plan was ultimately abandoned by the Russians, and the sleeper agents are left where they were to live out the rest of their lives as Americans.

Until thirty years later when an evil rogue Russian mastermind named *Dalchimsky* (played by Donald Pleasence), with a hard-on for the world, has a list of names and starts calling the sleeper agents on the telephone (hence the title) and setting them off. Bronson plays KGB agent *Grigori Borzov* and Lee Remick plays a CIA agent who joins forces with Bronson to assist him in killing Dalchimsky (the only reason that Pleasence doesn't just call all the agents in one hour, is that if he did, there'd be no movie).

As I said, the idea is wacky.

In fact the Zucker brothers did a takeoff on it in one of the Leslie Nielsen *Naked Gun* movies and didn't bother to add any jokes.

But just because the premise is nutty doesn't mean it's bad.

In fact, it's far out enough that in the right hands, it could have been a stone gas. But those right hands definitely didn't belong to old fart Siegel, who blew the picture's chance for success by de-emphasizing the kooky elements and emphasizing the dull ones.

Siegel not only wasted his time, he wasted the Stirling Silliphant and Peter Hyams (who should have directed) script.

The scenes where the sleeper agents are activated are a blast (almost all Siegel regulars: Mitchum, Sheree North, and Roy Jenson).

And Donald Pleasence, as he is in all of his pictures for Siegel, is a theatrical beast. Not to mention his reading of the Robert Frost trigger poem, once heard, is never forgotten.

> ### DALCHIMSKY
>
> The woods are lovely, dark and deep,
> but I have promises to keep,
> and miles to go before I sleep.
> *Remember Nikolai, miles to go before you sleep.*

But in his autobiography, Siegel admits to finding the plot dumb, so naturally he decided not to feature it. I always wondered why the film starts out such fun, only to turn into such a snooze once Bronson and Remick enter the picture. So MGM's idea of bringing in a big director gun to keep Bronson vital was a bust.

After this film Bronson would forever be banished to second tier status.

So while Siegel took the money and ran on *Telefon*, and took the money and slept on *Rough Cut*, *Escape from Alcatraz* gave him one last artistic erection. The difference between Siegel on the Eastwood film, and the other two films with Bronson and Reynolds, was on this prison film Siegel had something to lose. . . . his reputation.

With Richard Tuggle's taut, minimalist script, he had the best material for a cracking good picture in some time. Siegel was also returning to the playing fields of two of his biggest past triumphs, the prison picture and a Clint Eastwood picture.

The old lion always made it very clear he considered his docu-style prison fifties muckraker *Riot in Cell Block 11* as his first real (good) movie. In regard to a picture whose technique and intensity rises to the top of its field—be it prison pictures, fifties crime films, or old movies playing late at night on local television—*Riot in Cell Block 11* is hard to beat. With *Riot in Cell Block 11*, not only did the Don Siegel "*B movie maestro*" reputation begin, so did his penchant for violence and brutality, and his talent for (when left to his own devices) excellent casting.

Scary Neville Brand, and even scarier Leo Gordon, have as much to do with *Riot in Cell Block 11*'s success as Eastwood does with *Escape from Alcatraz.*

But, finally, the reason for *Riot in Cell Block 11*'s reputation was simple: it was the best prison movie ever made.

In his autobiography, Siegel speaks of *Escape from Alcatraz*'s scribe Richard Tuggle telling him that *Riot in Cell Block 11* was his favorite prison film.

But *Alcatraz* was also his first collaboration with Eastwood since their phenomenal success with *Dirty Harry* (it would also be their last).

Magnum Force was written for Siegel (Ted Post did it), and Eastwood offered Don *Every Which Way but Loose*, which Siegel said he turned down because he didn't think Clint could pull it off (it turned out to be Eastwood's biggest hit up to that time. . . . *Ugh*).

But after a few films with other stars, Matthau, Michael Caine, Bronson, and John Wayne, this was a return to the kind of picture the old man did best, with the actor he did it best with.

There would be no sleeping in the chair on this movie.

A bad movie from this script would not only signal the old dog was washed up, but it would tarnish both the memory of *Riot in Cell Block 11 and Dirty Harry and* Siegel's privileged place as the man who understood Eastwood. Not to mention by this time, as much as Clint respected Don, if Siegel fell asleep in his chair on the *Alcatraz* set, he'd probably wake up to find Eastwood directing the picture.

Eastwood, from the very beginning, always had a clear understanding of his own iconic persona and so did Siegel. No other director, including Leone—judging by the harsh, insulting remarks Sergio made at Clint's expense during the publicity for *Once Upon a Time in America*—understood Eastwood better. And Eastwood didn't trust anybody with his carefully crafted persona the way he trusted Don Siegel.

Siegel and Eastwood were always in clever cahoots with how they exploited Clint's iconic image.

First as a handsome young stud in *Coogan's Bluff* and *The Beguiled*, then away from westerns into urban crime dramas with *Dirty Harry.*

With Harry Callahan, Eastwood was brought up to date, and the only true western heir to John Wayne was turned into the quintessential cop of the seventies, the decade when cops replaced cowboys as the action film heroes of choice.

And in *Escape from Alcatraz*, yet again, Siegel and Eastwood had a new plateau to break through.

An older, middle-age Eastwood.

And, as was their way, they exploited the hell out of it.

Eastwood's naked walk through the corridors of Alcatraz is simply a thing of cinematic beauty. But it's highly doubtful Eastwood would have trusted this type of imagery with the other directors he was working with at the time, James Fargo and Buddy Van Horn.

And while I don't know this for a fact, my guess is Eastwood might have been too self-conscious (i.e., embarrassed) to direct himself in a scene like that.

By this time in their collaboration, many of the creative decisions are the joint decisions of two simpatico minds. I can imagine Eastwood and Siegel in a script meeting discussing how long can they go in the picture before Frank Morris says his first line.

Then how few lines can he speak after that. How few lines can all the characters speak, except for Patrick McGoohan's loquacious and sadistic warden. And speaking of iconic persona manipulation, McGoohan tweaks his own. The former *Prisoner* (Number Six) trapped on an island prison, is now in control of the most famous island prison since Devil's Island. Only this time McGoohan gets to play "Number Two."

And his opening speech to Eastwood's prisoner, "*We don't make good citizens in Alcatraz, but we do make good prisoners*," echoes the speech Patrick Cargill's Number Two gives McGoohan in episode 14, "*Hammer into Anvil.*"

What's so intriguing about the way Siegel opens the picture is that as bravura as it is, it also has a starkness—I'd describe it as a *cool boil*—that seems appropriate for the film's period setting.

A genuine stylistic prison film precursor to *Escape from Alcatraz* is the first of the fourteen films in the Japanese action film series *Abashiri Bangaichi* (1965) starring Japan's answer to Eastwood, Takakura Ken, and directed by Ken's Siegel, Teruo Ishii. This stark stylistic black and white snow-set prison escape adventure is a perfect companion piece to the Siegel and Eastwood endeavor (it's highly unlikely Siegel would have ever seen *Abashiri Bangaichi*, but not unthinkable that Eastwood may have viewed it for its possible remake potential).

Escape from Alcatraz concerns the, *supposedly*, true story of armed robber and prison escape artist Frank Morris' arrival to the prison in the early sixties. Almost everything about the movie seems a throwback to another time. The way Eastwood seemed not like his normal self, but like a fifties tough-guy actor. Yet in trying to think of an appropriate fifties equivalent, I couldn't. The most hard-boiled badasses of that Eisenhower era, like Ralph Meeker and Charles Bronson, and laconic tough guys like Robert Mitchum, Brian Keith, and John Garfield all talked a blue streak.

Among those fifties tough guys, only Alan Ladd knew how to

keep his mouth shut. But the diminutive Ladd could never compare as a camera subject with the massive Rodin-chiseled Eastwood.

Where the throwback quality is most profoundly felt is in the very genre of prison films itself. Starting with Harvey Hart's (underrated director) very filmic adaptation of John Herbert's play *Fortune and Men's Eyes*, starring Wendell (*The Sterile Cuckoo*) Burton and Zooey (*I Dismember Mama*) Hall in 1971, the subject of male domination by homosexual rape was introduced into the genre.

The subject was timidly touched on again in the TV movie *Truman Capote's The Glass House*. But the true reality of the racial implications of prison rage rape against the machine wasn't dealt with forthrightly until ex-convict Miguel Pinero's play and later movie adaptation *Short Eyes* changed the prison film genre forever—the resulting Robert Young–directed film was also rereleased as an exploitation film, retitled *Slammer* (which I saw at the Carson Twin Cinema, on a double bill with Richard Pryor's *Which Way Is Up?*).

And this reality at the time was compounded by the landmark television docu-special *Scared Straight!*

Post-*Scared Straight!*, not only every story about prison had to deal with the threat of homosexual rape, any thoughts *you* might think about prison had to deal with it as well.

The only reason Jamaa Fanaka's shoddy prison pic *Penitentiary*, made the same year as the Siegel film, was a surprise hit was the *"bustin' the new bronc"* cell fight, an exciting, compelling, and seemingly realistic new addition to the genre.

Escape from Alcatraz represents—at the height of that awareness—the last time a convincing prison story could be told that didn't dwell on those male-rape aspects. And even this film couldn't completely ignore it.

The film's most unconvincing scene is a ludicrous attempt by some barrel-built prick to bust Morris in the shower. As if *anybody* would earmark the forty-five-year-old Clint Eastwood for homosexual subjugation. So instead of the sexually violent and racially motivated survival of the fittest warped society of desperate felons, Siegel's picture, maybe for the last time (without being a thirties period piece), could dwell on old-school prison genre concerns.

In the first half, the brutal isolation, monotonous regimented routines, numbered privileges, and that character that had all (except for *women-in-prison* films) but disappeared from the genre, the cruel sadistic warden, are depicted. In the second half, the film deals with something else that had been all but ignored by the genre in the last decade, a masterly crafted, minutiae-filled escape plan.

Most movie prison breaks are exciting high-flying affairs, milked for every second of nail-biting suspense. Oliver Reed and Ian McShane's prison escape at the beginning of British action maestro Douglas Hickox's crime film *Sitting Target* is a perfect example.

But Morris' constant chipping away at the Rock with a pair of nail clippers at first seems futile, then impressive, then finally heroic. Almost everything about the escape strikes you as unique.

Morris' first revelation that maybe he's found a way off the Rock isn't presented the way we've become accustomed to. We don't see Morris moseying along the corridor, suddenly spotting a flaw in the stone fortress that only he can recognize. Morris doesn't have one big eureka idea.

One tiny reveal reveals another minutia of opportunity.

All the step-by-step moments of the escape become intriguing, and by the time you've put together a clear picture of the plan, you're fascinated.

The constant chipping away of the Rock, the collecting of the clothes for their moonlight swim (the faultiest part of the plan, and what surely killed them in real life), the paper-mache heads they painstakingly paint and sculpt (the image Siegel uses for the closing credits), the jerry-rigged welding gun they build to cut the cell bars.

The plan takes such talent and intelligence that if they hadn't died, you can't help but think it could have won them parole.

By the same token, all the qualities involved in the escape attempt–discipline, skill, intelligence, talent, daring–could equally apply to Siegel's technique in depicting the escape.

In the same way that Morris chips away at the Rock, Siegel chips away at Tuggle's scenario.

As simpatico as Siegel and Eastwood were as artists, Siegel and Morris were as simpatico in methodology.

Morris uses lifelong learned methods of ingenuity, practicality, and experience to dig through that rock wall.

Siegel takes lifelong learned lessons of ingenuity, practicality, experience, and skill and applies them to his use of montage. Siegel is almost as silent as Morris, preferring to illustrate via montage than explain through expositional dialogue.

After beginning his career in the film business creating montages for other director's movies (*Casablanca* & *The Roaring Twenties*, among many others), the first really significant montage he ever used in his own work belongs to this late-in-life masterwork.

Did Morris and his compatriots escape? I'm sure they were dead ducks nineteen minutes after they hit the water.

But the real true-life escape is Siegel escaped letting his pal Eastwood down. These two men shared an artistic collaboration between great star and great director that will stand aside the greatest of all time. A big part of that collaboration is both men owed the other more than they could ever repay.

With Siegel, Eastwood had escaped flash-in-the-pan status inside the Hollywood studio system (as opposed to staying in Italy, like Lee Van Cleef, and cranking out pasta-land potboilers).

With Eastwood, Siegel had escaped anonymity, becoming a major A-list Hollywood filmmaker fairly late in life.

And when these two old compadres, with a friendship based on mutual respect, admiration, masculinity, and love, did the impossible—*escaped from Alcatraz*—they slammed the iron door behind them.

Hardcore

(1979)

After *Who's That Knocking at My Door* and *Boxcar Bertha* and *Mean Streets* and *Taxi Driver*, Scorsese finally got John Ford and *The Searchers* out of his system.

But Paul Schrader didn't.

Before the seventies were out, he still had one more thematic *Searchers* remake to go.

His second film as a director, 1979's *Hardcore*.

In the Schrader film, John Wayne's Civil War veteran—Comanche hating bastard—*Ethan Edwards* is replaced by George C. Scott's Michigan-based Dutch Calvinist man of strong moral fiber—*Jacob Van Dorn* (Schrader based the character on his own father). The way *Ethan Edwards* searches for his niece *Debbie* (Natalie Wood) among the Comanche tribes for years is how *Jacob Van Dorn* comes to Los Angeles to "*search*" for his underage daughter, who's lost in the bit-part world of the adult film industry.

Normally, films that deal with this type of subject matter are exploitation flicks (*Trackdown, Angel, Avenging Angel, Vice Squad, Kinjite*) or TV movie exposés (*Little Ladies of the Night, Dawn: Portrait of a Teenaged Runaway, Off the Minnesota Strip, Girls of the White Orchid*). *Hardcore* tells the same old story, but tells it differently, and to different effect. In the above films it's laughably easy for young girl runways to fall prey to street hustlers. In *Trackdown*, *Little Ladies of the Night*, and *Kinjite*, the pimps have the bus station staked out and can approach a scared young white girl within twenty minutes of her stepping off the bus. And in all of them the young girls are tricked, drugged, or seduced into the prostitution racket. But the mostly told off-screen story of Jacob's daughter *Kristen Van Dorn* (Ilah Davis) in Schrader's script isn't the same old cautionary tale.

When we first meet sixteen- or seventeen-year-old Kristen at a Grand Rapids Christmas church party, she looks like a runaway even in her own home. One look at her and you can tell she's either going to be a junkie, a child prostitute, or a suicide victim. So this daughter of Scott's respected deacon of the church goes to Los Angeles on a church group field trip, and just never returns. Van Dorn hires a private detective, played by Peter Boyle, to find some information about his lost little girl. The detective invites the worried father to a closed movie theatre, and screens for him a degrading 8mm sex film loop of his daughter having a three-way with a couple of skeezy guys titled: *Slave of Love.*

"*Turn it off!*" Scott screams as he watches his daughter's grainy degradation. Columbia Pictures based their whole print campaign on that scene, with the tag line: "*OH MY GOD, THAT'S MY DAUGHTER!*"

Columbia Pictures cut a dynamite trailer for the picture that featured all the sex-for-sale bright red lights of the milieu, Jack Nitzsche's terrific hellish electronic theme, George C. Scott's intense anguished face, and female costar Season Hubley's cherry-red messy lips pouting around in her silver satin pants.

The trailer's not only good, it's *too* good. You just kind of get the sense that no fucking way is the finished film gonna deliver the way the trailer does.

But Schrader's film does have a few can't-miss elements.

He's got a compelling premise that can't be denied (a father searching for his daughter in the world of Triple XXX cinema), and a perfect lead for this type of story (Scott). *Hardcore* is a handsome-looking studio drama that's meant, for the price of a movie ticket, to take the viewer on a tourist tour of the porn world of Los Angeles in the late seventies. It's supposed to possess the class of a studio picture, but simultaneously appeal to cinema of sensation viewers. And for the film's first hour Schrader makes a compelling movie with undeniable power.

For one thing, Schrader completely breaks ranks with those other films by not featuring the degradation of the innocent. The dramatization of the young girl falling prey to flesh peddlers is half the reason they usually made these fucking movies in the first place. No matter how tawdry or obvious as these movies can be, the degradation of the innocent sequence is the one part that's always effective.

Because it's impossible not to feel sorry for the poor girl (and often the poor actress).

But Paul Schrader's *Hardcore* has different fish to fry. Like he did with Travis Bickle, he makes us see the world from Jake Van Dorn's perspective. We never see *exactly* what happened that led his daughter to miss the bus to Michigan and stay in Hollywood. But as the movie goes on, little by little, you start getting a pretty good idea. Which the movie never officially confirms, but insinuates nevertheless. What, in the first half, gives the film weight is that while Van Dorn wants to punish somebody for his daughter being in this world, there is no *Sport* or *Acuna Boys* or any other exploitation movie villains to punish. His daughter's decision to not show up for the bus back to Grand Rapids was just that—*a decision.*

Obviously, the first chance she got, she ran away from Van Dorn's strict grotesque Grand Rapids upbringing. She may have been seduced by somebody, but we aren't given the impression that she was drugged or kidnapped, or held against her will, like Karen Lamm in *Trackdown.*

But since we watch the movie from Van Dorn's perspective, we only know what Van Dorn knows, and we learn information about his daughter the same time he does, though we probably come to different conclusions about the information we become privy to.

Also Schrader presents an avenger that is vastly different than in the above movies. In the other runaway movies, the guy who's working hard to get the girl off the street, no matter how ridiculous he looks (David Soul in *Little Ladies of the Night*), you're obviously meant to root for them. In *Trackdown*, you really want Jim Mitchum to find poor Karen Lamm, and when she dies (without them even getting another scene together) it's tragic. Everything Mitchum does from that point on is justified.

But we feel different about Scott's Jake Van Dorn. As he walks the porno district seething, you don't want him to find Kristen. You want him to just go home.

Schrader wastes no time invoking *The Searchers* by opening up the film with a—well done—Ford-like sequence of community ritual. The Christmas celebration of a Dutch Calvinist church group in Grand Rapids. With George C. Scott's Van Dorn acting as one of the church elders (he leads the saying of grace before Christmas dinner, and he doesn't forget to put in a word for the missionaries spreading the word of God in far-off lands).

There's a great line in the opening scene that Schrader says comes from one of his uncles. The children at the Christmas party are gathered around the television watching a show, when one of the grumpy elders bitches at them, "*Do you know who makes television? All the kids who couldn't get along here go out to Hollywood and make TV and they send it back here. Well, I didn't like them when they were here and I don't like them now they're there.*"

Schrader presents Scott's Van Dorn, in his snow-covered Michigan cocoon, as a decent man almost comically repressed. When he meets with his interior decorator for his family's furniture warehouse business, he objects to the shade of blue she uses for his sign, deeming it *"overpowering."* But pretty soon afterwards the same man is prowling the streets of Hollywood, filled with their Triple XXX cinema marquees, and their signs for sex-for-sale clubs that are pink, red, and a blue bolder than the one he rejected back in Grand Rapids. He's repulsed by the openness and explicitness of the sex and material he's forced to confront in this industry, and sick with grief over the fate of his daughter. And that repulsion turns the decent church deacon into a man of brutal violence. He brutalizes the people he comes across in the porno world the way Ethan Edwards shoots buffalos in *The Searchers*, out of impotent rage.

Historically, the film offers an interesting glimpse of the adult film industry of 1979. Schrader was given carte blanche by William Margold, sort of the ambassador to the adult film world of the late seventies, who gave Schrader the grand tour and provided him and his production shooting access similar to what Harvey Bernhard and Michael Campus were able to acquire from the Ward brothers on *The Mack*.

But all the adult entertainment movers and shakers that Schrader met along the way were crying bloody murder when the film came out.

They rightly felt that the adult entertainment film industry was just as legitimate a film industry as the Hollywood film industry (they employed many people, they paid a lot of money in California state taxes, they rented their equipment from the same facilities, they processed their film at the same labs). Yet *corrupt* Hollywood had no qualms about pointing a finger at them, no qualms demonizing them, and no qualms slandering them to make their point. And frankly, the slander part is what makes Schrader's film, at the end of the day, a phony-baloney moralistic con job. Despite his self-righteous moralizing, without a shred of conscience, Schrader squeezed in a *snuff film* subplot. *Snuff films* weren't a reality, they were an urban myth (like the mythological *white pimp*) that the squares used to marginalize the legitimate adult film industry. And at the end of the day Paul Schrader and Columbia Pictures were no different than the Moral Majority when it came to lying to make their negative case.

So all the people who opened their doors to Schrader felt *justifiably* betrayed.

But in 1979 what wasn't apparent was that the industry depicted in *Hardcore* was going to go through a seismic change in the next couple of years that would make the events portrayed in Schrader's movie seem like a relic from a lost era. At the end of the seventies *some* people had video recorders (mostly *Beta*), but not many. The VHS video revolution wouldn't really get going till 1981–82. At the point when this movie takes place, if you wanted to see a new adult film, you still had to leave the house and go to an adult movie theatre to watch a feature length film that included explicit sex. But the average suburban Dick and Jane had long since stopped seeing dirty movies in dirty movie theatres.

But the video revolution opened up a whole new audience for porno movies. Now you could just rent them from your mom-and-pop video shop (the reason most mom-and-pop video stores could compete with the chains like Blockbuster—for a while—was that they rented XXX tapes, which Blockbuster didn't).

XXX-rated motion pictures and porn stars were about to go mainstream. This seems a decade away from the tale told in *Hardcore*. Even though Schrader uses many real (now defunct) sex districts, storefronts, and massage parlors, his depiction of the adult entertainment industry of the seventies never strikes the viewer as completely *authentic*. Because Schrader's moralizing of the landscape seems phony, and when he throws *snuff movies* into the mix it's downright insulting. Schrader's tour of the porno world can't hold a flickering birthday candle next to Friedkin's tour of the New York all-male S&M leather bars in that same year's *Cruising* (which also contains a terrific Jack Nitzsche score). Friedkin's film not only strikes the viewer as authentic, it's also a sexy/scary phantasmagorical sensory experience like no other in cinema (not even seventies all-male porn). Nevertheless, like I said, the first half of the film has an undeniable power, and George C. Scott, an actor whose stock in trade was volcanic eruption, makes Van Dorn's journey compelling. And while at first this journey produces only frustration in the Michigan tourist, towards the end of the film's first hour, both Van Dorn and Schrader come up with a clever idea.

In order to "*Trackdown*" his daughter, he tries to locate one of the actors that appeared with her in the sex loop. And to that end he gets the bright idea to stage auditions for his own adult film. The montage of different actors coming in for their casting sessions with Van Dorn (who disguises himself as his idea of a porno producer, phony hair piece, fake mustache, and tie-dyed T-shirt) is the film's best sequence, and the comedy inherent within is the film's only relief from its own disgust with itself. Hal Williams, the drill sergeant from Goldie Hawn's *Private Benjamin*, brings down the house as irate porn stud *Big Dick Blaque*.

Then . . . skinny, skeevy Keith Carradine look-alike Will Walker (the actor who we saw fuck Scott's daughter in *Slave of Love*) walks in the room, accompanied by Jack Nitzsche's score sting (its most effective use in the film), and we in the audience notice this an instant before Van Dorn does, making us straighten up in our seat and lean closer to the screen. And it's at this point *Hardcore* becomes the movie it wants to be, and the movie the fantastic Columbia Pictures trailer sold.

This scene is where the whole movie has been heading and now we've finally arrived. And playing a bit part adult film actor who goes by the moniker *Jism Jim*, Will Walker is the best casting in the film.

Walker was a weird, skinny, shaggy blond-haired, almost handsome (but not quite) actor who suddenly appeared in the late seventies in a few films, *The Driver* and *Deathsport*, and then just as quickly disappeared. Jake Van Dorn is *searching* for his daughter, but he's also *searching* for somebody to punish. Somebody to punish for his daughter leaving Grand Rapids, for being in that 8mm sex loop, and for making him descend to this hell on earth. And when he finally comes face-to-face with a tangible connection to her degradation, a man he actually *saw* shove his dick inside his daughter (from behind, no less), both the film and Van Dorn boil over.

Yet, like Harvey Keitel's *Sport* in *Taxi Driver*, Will Walker's budding explicit bit player *Jism Jim* may be creepy, but he isn't entirely loathsome. At first he treats Van Dorn's ridiculous-looking porn producer with audience-impressing savvy skepticism.

But when Scott's character recognizes him, and tells Jim he's seen his work, Walker's reaction is sort of charming. After his initial arrogance, he transforms into an excited budding actor, "*Yeah, I've done a lot of good work, ya know. Shorts, features—no major roles yet, but it's all been really good stuff.*"

His genuine excitement for a few moments at being considered for a real film—and not just a loop—is slightly infectious. It's also the only time Schrader drops his moralizing and presents the adult film industry for what it really is.

Not a criminal enterprise.

Not the fourth rung of hell.

But a legal, tax-paying film industry catering to explicit entertainment for adults.

Jism Jim even mentions the guys who made the 8mm sex loop with his daughter were a couple of college kids and they were paid twenty dollars. In other words, Kristen is hardly poor Karen Lamm in *Trackdown*, she *wanted* to be in *Slave of Love*. The reason Kristen is wearing silver pants and fucking on film in Hollywood, as opposed to baking cupcakes for a church bake sale in Grand Rapids, isn't because of Jism Jim or those college kids who made the loop, or any of the other phony villains Schrader yanks out of his ass in the film's last half hour. She's there because of Van Dorn. She *chose* this life over *his* strict upbringing.

After Jake experiences a momentary shock of recognition once Jim enters the room, he recovers and keeps his cool for a few moments. Van Dorn brings up he saw the loop *Slave of Love*, and he inquires about the actress Jim appeared with, mentioning he'd like to track her down for his film. Walker's Jim complains that girl was a *"freaky bitch"* and that his prick was sore for a week afterwards. That's when Jake explodes, attacking the poor kid, beating him till he extracts information in the form of a name so Jake can continue his *search* and Schrader can continue telling his story. This is Schrader's most daring move, because when George C. Scott's impotent rage explodes in the face of this hapless little creep, we're not on Scott's side. We even believe what Jim said about his daughter. She probably *was* a *"freaky bitch,"* and his prick *was* probably sore for a week. Unfortunately, after this scene, the film has nowhere else to go, and the rest of the movie takes a turn towards the ludicrous.

Because after Van Dorn vents his spleen on the one tangible face he can blame, and realizes his daughter *wasn't* abducted or *forced* to be in the loop (she did it for twenty bucks), in real life Van Dorn would have probably gone home. But since it's a movie, Van Dorn goes on *searching.* And to keep the movie going Schrader throws in a shopping list of unconvincing movie plot contrivances that rob the film of whatever integrity it had in the first part.

Paul Schrader is a magnificent screenwriter, with one gigantic glaring weakness. He can't write genre films. And either out of inattention or a deep-seated contempt for genre, all of his self-penned genre scripts contain absurd plot contrivances in order to get the story rolling and keep it rolling on their contrived tracks.

At the beginning of *Hardcore* it's utterly unbelievable that—with the little information he had—Peter Boyle's detective was able to track down that particular 8mm sex loop featuring his daughter (forget the absurdity that some random movie theatre in Grand Rapids would have 8mm projection capabilities). How Boyle was able to accomplish this is never even remotely dealt with, even though the entire plot hinges on it. I guess Peter Boyle's character is just the greatest detective in the world (boy, you coulda fooled me).

In *American Gigolo*, *Julian Kaye*'s (Richard Gere) innocence in the murder investigation at its center is obvious. But in order to entwine him into the investigation, Schrader has the police detective on the case (Hector Elizondo), minus any logic, suspect Julian as his number one suspect.

When he tells Julian, "*I think you're guilty as hell*," you wait for Julian to ask him *why*, but he doesn't because the only conceivable answer is Schrader's need to put Gere in jeopardy and turn this character study of a lifestyle into some sort of half-ass murder mystery. Now, there is another reason that is suggested to the audience for Elizondo's suspicion of Gere, jealousy. But are we really supposed to believe that Elizondo's police detective is *so* corrupt he would frame an innocent man for a murder just because he envied his prowess with women? Nothing else we see of his character even remotely suggests this.

But none of his other films pile up the plot contrivances like the last half of *Hardcore*.

Of course you don't buy that Walker would have any real information to impart to Scott. But because it's a movie, and Schrader has to keep the story moving, *of course* he does.

Then there's the off-topic detour into snuff films (that strikes me as a more cynical form of exploitation than the type Schrader spends the movie condemning).

Then towards the end—and this is where Schrader's screenwriting is really the pits—a couple of puny minor characters, *Tod* (Gary Graham) and *Ratan* (Marc Alaimo), are unconvincingly beefed up to full villain status in order for Scott's father and Boyle's detective to have somebody to combat in the climax (what was good about the film is it didn't offer up easy villains). Boyle even shoots Ratan dead on a crowded San Francisco street, and *of course* there's no repercussions for this out and out murder (when film-maker Schrader makes these absurd decisions, you wonder where film critic Schrader went).

All of these hackneyed devices turn the last half of *Hardcore* into a vastly inferior version of Richard Heffron's similarly themed *Trackdown*, which was released only a few months after *Taxi Driver*. The two films not only tell similar stories, they also share similar tag lines.

HARDCORE
OH MY GOD, THAT'S MY DAUGHTER!

TRACKDOWN
WHAT WOULD YOU DO IF IT WAS YOUR SISTER?

The big difference between the two is, while the first half of the nuanced *Hardcore* is undoubtedly better than the obviously exploitation minded *Trackdown*, the last half of *Hardcore* is a mess, while *Trackdown* is a pretty effective Revengeamatic. Also *Trackdown* just happens to be written by Ivan Nagy—who according to Nick Broomfield in his documentary *Hollywood Madam*—was Heidi Fleiss's pimp (*finally* a real-life *white pimp*! And he doesn't look anything like Harvey Keitel, or David Soul, or Wings Hauser. Nor does he hang around on street corners like his black counterparts. Instead he directs episodes of *Starsky and Hutch!*). In *Trackdown*, a slumming Anne Archer basically plays a young Heidi. Consequently, the prostitution organization depicted in *Trackdown* is slightly more credible than the other exploitation pictures with similar subjects (*Vice Squad, Angel, Avenging Angel, Streetwalkin', Kinjite, Little Ladies of the Night*, and *They Call Her One-Eye*).

And, in a telling way, the villains who run the prostitution racket in *Trackdown* are *slightly* less villainous than the above titles (when James Mitchum's sister dies, it's due to a psycho John, not their doing. And Anne Archer is shown to be distraught at Karen Lamm's death).

Hardcore's troubled second half also introduces a female surrogate for Jeffrey Hunter's *Martin Pawley* character in the guise of *Niki* (Season Hubley), a porn actress with a heart of gold that Jake befriends and pays to help him *Trackdown* his daughter Kristen. Like *The Searchers'* Martin Pawley, Niki is a creature of the culture that Van Dorn despises. In the film's first half, Scott's character only has one thing on his mind, finding Kristen. And while Peter Boyle's scummy private detective who (sorta) helps Scott out and Dick (*Bewitched*) Sargent as a church friend who tries to lure Van Dorn back from the dark side, are both good in their on-the-nose roles, their only real function is to facilitate (Boyle) and illustrate (Sargent) Van Dorn's savage character arc.

Every actor or extra Scott comes across in the film's sleazy sideshow of *Hollyweird* exists only to frustrate, repulse, or enrage this wounded warrior of moral superiority.

That is until *Niki* enters the picture.

Niki talks like a movie character, is allowed a few whimsical lines (she's an astrology nut), and is allowed to be more than just a human representative of societal decay. Not only that, Van Dorn (rather quickly) actually likes her, allowing Scott to play more than just the one note he's been hammering all picture long.

Now, through no fault of Hubley's, Niki is never really a convincing character. She's the late seventies sex-worker version of the late sixties kooky hippie screwballs that Goldie Hawn used to play. Nor does she have the depth that Jodie Foster brought to *Iris* and Linda Haynes brought to *Linda Forchet*. Schrader had wanted to cast Diana Scarwid, who had just popped from her Academy Award–nominated turn in Richard Donner's *Inside Moves*. But, according to Schrader, Columbia Pictures' head Dan Melnick (more on him later) "*put his foot down*" and told the director "*I don't want to cast someone I don't want to fuck.*" So Schrader was forced to uncast Scarwid and find Season Hubley, commenting "*Hubley, too cute for me but perfect for Danny.*"

Nevertheless, Hubley's Niki does lighten up the proceedings a bit, and she introduces an intriguing new thematic element to Schrader's paraphrased remake of *The Searchers*.

While Van Dorn *searches* for his real daughter, *Kristen*, little by little *Niki* functions as his surrogate daughter. She puts a human face that he can't despise on a world and a culture he *does* despise. And he puts a human face on a world that she's never known. Like we in the audience (and Paul Schrader), she finds his Dutch Calvinist beliefs ridiculous, but she respects that he believes in things. And when she tells him at one point, "*We'll find her in a couple of days,*" for the first time in the picture somebody offers this poor hopeless bastard some credible semblance of hope.

The scene in the hotel room when Van Dorn tries to explain to Niki the beliefs of his antiquated religious order is the only time in the film when actor Scott is allowed to show any hint of charm, or sense of humor. When he hears his gospel through Niki's ears, even Van Dorn sort of recognizes its absurdity. Both characters feel the other is completely lost, yet they sympathize and care for the other anyway.

Like *Taxi Driver*, *Hardcore* builds to an ending that has been thematically set up all through the film.

In Schrader's original conception, the script was sort of a cross between *The Searchers* and *Chinatown*. After searching the whole movie for his daughter, Van Dorn learns she died in a car accident unrelated to porn. That's when Peter Boyle delivers the *"it's China-town, Jake"* news, and Van Dorn returns to Grand Rapids.

However this doesn't play so tragic.

Because by this time the audience has fallen in love with Jake's sex worker sidekick Niki, and he takes Niki with him. Though twisted, it is emotionally satisfying. Van Dorn replaces one daughter with another. One he can't save, for one he can. What's not emotionally satisfying is the end of the movie Paul Schrader directed. In Schrader's movie, he finds his daughter, and we wait for her to reject him and send him back to Grand Rapids, when unconvincingly (*understatement!*) she changes her mind at the last minute. And Van Dorn says his version of *The Searchers* line, *"Kristen, take me home."*

Boo!

When I saw *Hardcore* on opening night at the United Artists Del Amo Mall theatre, the entire (packed) audience rejected the daughter's final decision as an unconvincing and contrived conclusion to the story (there were *literal* boos).

So Van Dorn returns to Michigan with his dishrag daughter leaving the lovable Niki to her own devices and ultimate fate. The very next year Season Hubley starred as another Hollywood sex-for-sale worker (this time a prostitute), in another tour of the *Holly-weird* jungle in the exploitation cult favorite *Vice Squad* (which features yet another of these only-in-the-movies white pimp unicorns). Due to how close the release of both *Hardcore* and *Vice Squad* were to each other, the latter movie can't help but play like the final act of *Niki's* arc.

In the book *Schrader on Schrader & Other Writings*, in his DVD commentary, and in an email exchange with me, Schrader blames Columbia Pictures' head honcho Daniel Melnick for the change to his script's original ending.

Schrader told me, *"Dan Melnick insisted that Van Dorn rescue his daughter.*" One of the reasons for the audience's boos at the opening night screening was not only the picture's contrived ending, but the unconvincing performance by Ilah Davis as Kristen. I don't buy Debbie wanting to go home in *The Searchers* either. But Natalie Wood was a good enough actress to sell the contrived conceit. Ilah Davis isn't. In fact, she's fucking awful. Schrader explained that Davis wasn't an actress, she was cast because of her porn experience. He really only needed her to deliver in the *Slave of Love* loop, because in his intended third act, she died offscreen. But once Melnick forced this change on him, that required much more of Davis than she could deliver. He recounted, "*I had to get Ilah acting lessons and throw this frightened, frail creature in the cage with the notorious drunk, George C. Scott.*"

Schrader's *Melnick made me* excuse is not backed up by the film's executive producer John Milius. Three years after *Hardcore*'s original release, I asked Milius about the production. He described it then as "*A wonderful script turned into a lousy movie*," and he laid the blame on Schrader's direction. When I asked Milius about Schrader's studio interference excuse, Big John told me, "*Nobody made him change anything, he did exactly what he wanted.*"

Then, I believed Milius. But today I believe Schrader. I do believe that the head of the studio made him turn his "*wonderful script*" into "*a lousy movie.*"

But I still blame Schrader.

I blame him for giving the same spineless excuse a lot of directors of fiascos claim after the fact, *the big bad studio made me.*

As if they couldn't say *no.*

Well, then they wouldn't have made it.

Good.

Who wants to spend three months making a fucked-up version of their movie? Then spend the rest of their lives making excuses for it, or cringing whenever they watch it, like Schrader does on the DVD commentary?

When I reached out to Schrader, I warned him that, while I liked the film's first half, I'm very rough on it and him in the second half.

He wrote back, "*I don't think you could be harsher than I am on the second half of the film.*"

The Funhouse

(1981)

In the sweltering hot Texas summer of '73, on a threadbare budget in four weeks, with a crew of Texas locals, filmmaker Tobe Hooper fucked around and made one of the greatest movies of all time, *The Texas Chainsaw Massacre*.

To me, *The Texas Chainsaw Massacre* is one of the few perfect movies ever made. There are very few *perfect* movies. This is okay, since in the pursuit of cinematic art, *perfection* shouldn't be the goal. Nevertheless, when it's accomplished (even by accident), it's an achievement.

I didn't see *TCM* when it was first released in 1974. Then, I was still dependent on an adult to take me to see something like that. It wasn't like my mother forbade me to see it. It's just she wasn't interested in going out and seeing something called *The Texas Chainsaw Massacre* (she wouldn't take me to auditoriums where they held wrestling matches either. So, no Jimmy *Superfly* Snuka and Porkchop for me). I did see it about two years later, once *New Line Cinema* acquired the rights and rereleased it on a double feature with Sergio Martino's terrific Italian giallo *Torso*.

Rather than a tumble down the rabbit hole of *TCM*'s perfection, I want to discuss some of Mr. Hooper's subsequent work.

TCM was such a one-of-a-kind beast, there really wouldn't be any way for him to satisfyingly follow it up.

So it isn't surprising that Hooper's next film, *Eaten Alive* (starring Neville Brand and a hungry crocodile), was initially considered a disappointment. But as more people started seeing it on home video in the eighties, its reputation among genre aficionados started improving. It's no *Texas Chainsaw Massacre*, but it's effectively sleazy and spooky. Most of the film takes place in one location, a shanty hotel located at the lip of a swamp. And Hooper does a tremendous job with the cheap but effective set. Neville Brand is a hoot as the batshit maniac *Judd* who runs the *Starlight Hotel*. The establishment's main attraction is a huge crocodile that Judd's got penned up for the tourists. But it would appear the hotel owner's main forte is murdering his guests, especially sexy young females (though why any female would choose to stay at this dump is the picture's biggest leap of faith), then disposing of the bodies by feeding them to his croc. The plot thickens when a weird married couple and their seven-year-old daughter check in to the *Starlight* as guests (*Chainsaw*'s Marilyn Burns and *Phantom of the Paradise*'s William Finley, giving unglued performances that wouldn't be out of place in a John Waters feature). The croc ends up eating both the little girl's dog and her daddy. Judd ends up capturing and terrorizing the mother. The little girl gets away, and the raving lunatic's efforts to catch her lead to Judd's inevitable final resting place inside the crocodile's belly.

The film has an entertaining combination of genuinely spooky and eerie ambiance, a sexual sleaze factor that makes it resemble an early seventies *roughie*, and high-pitched camp performances played by a tired-out cast of familiar puffy faces.

Any fans of actress Carolyn Jones (who was one of the coolest females in fifties films) will be shocked to see how terrible she looks in this. Yet her characterization of a bayou whorehouse madam is surprisingly specific and convincingly authentic.

Roberta Collins, one of my favorite *New World Pictures* starlets (*The Big Doll House, Caged Heat,* and Matilda the Hun in *Death Race 2000*), plays her opening reel role as one of Jones' prostitutes and Judd's first victim surprisingly serious (it's the film's most effective reel).

And a young, full of gage Robert Englund is just flat out sensational.

As opposed to George Romero's *Creepshow* and the *Tales from the Crypt* TV series, which killed themselves trying to capture the look and the aesthetic of the *E.C. Horror Comics,* Hooper's flick captures the humorously mean-spirited repulsion of the lurid magazine without seemingly trying.

I saw *Eaten Alive* before I saw *Texas Chainsaw Massacre,* during the week it played in Los Angeles (naturally at *the Carson Twin Cinema*) on a double feature with a mondo documentary about the occult called *Journey into the Beyond,* narrated by John Carradine. It supposedly contained footage of a real exorcism (I didn't buy that, but it looked pretty good). Because of the newspaper movie ad, I was aware this crocodile movie was directed by the same guy who did *The Texas Chainsaw Massacre.*

I went to the film that night with the thirty-seven-year-old fellow that rented an empty room in my mom's house named *Floyd.*★

Floyd and I loved *Eaten Alive.*

Not because either of us thought it was a great movie. We both felt, for a cheap horror flick, it wasn't bad. And a few moments were better than that. We liked the actors. We liked the sleaziness. We especially appreciated the effective (*Jaws*-like) jump scare—when the crocodile suddenly busts through the railing and snatches William Finley from behind. But most of all we loved Robert Englund as the butt-fucking, shit-talking, white trash *Buck.*

As soon as the movie begins—right off the bat—it starts with a shot of a tentative Roberta Collins, shot through the V frame of Buck's Levi clad pant legs, as he says off-screen:

"My name's Buck, and I'm here to fuck."

Floyd turned to me and asked incredulously, *"What did he say?"*

I repeated, *"My name's Buck, and I'm here to fuck."*

At the repeating of that line, Floyd burst out laughing. And when Floyd got the giggles it was impossible not to laugh with him. So the two of us started laughing. And then, right at the beginning of the movie, we got into the single biggest case of the giggles I ever fell into during a movie. And then when Buck tried to fuck Roberta Collins in the ass, we fell out again. We laughed about that *Buck/fuck* line for the first whole twenty minutes of the movie (the most serious part of the film). Just as soon as one of us would calm down and start trying to reclaim their shit, the other one would laugh again, and that would set both of us off for another four minutes.

At the world premiere of *Once Upon a Time . . . in Hollywood* at the Cannes Film Festival, Gael García Bernal told me the same thing happened to him and Diego Luna when Brad Pitt said the line in the *Musso and Frank* parking lot, *"Don't cry in front of the Mexicans."*

He said they laughed so hard and so long, Gael's girlfriend started getting mad at them.

In a normal theatre (i.e., not a grindhouse) other patrons might have been annoyed by Floyd and me. But there was always a general malaise and apathy to sparsely populated grindhouse audiences (packed grindhouse audiences, with good action movies, were the exact opposite).

Eventually, we got our shit back together and settled down and watched the movie. But we waited impatiently for Buck's return. And about forty minutes later, he did. The minute we saw Robert Englund's face, we burst out laughing again. We weren't trying to be silly, we just couldn't help it. Consequently, we didn't love the movie, but we loved *watching* the movie. And on the drive home, we laughed ourselves silly about the *Buck/fuck* line all over again.

Soon after, I started noticing Robert Englund showing up in

other movies (this was years before *Nightmare on Elm Street*). *A Star Is Born*, *Big Wednesday*, and my favorite post-*Eaten Alive* appearance, Robert Mulligan's *Bloodbrothers.*

I'd tell Floyd, "*Hey man, I just saw Buck in another movie [*Floyd never knew his real name, he was just always *Buck]*."

Needless to say, I have very fond memories of watching *Eaten Alive* during its one-week Los Angeles engagement in 1976.

Then Tobe Hooper did the two-part/two-night TV movie adaption of Stephen King's *Salem's Lot,* which received some of the best reviews of any TV movie made up to that time. Judith Crist in *TV Guide* gave it a rave, as well as the TV critic for *the Los Angeles Times* who said it was one of the best filmed vampire tales of all time!

I missed the movie when it first aired because I was performing in a play at that time (this was a good five years before I had a VHS recorder). I not only read those good reviews, but I read the extensive coverage of the film in the reigning horror magazine of its day, *Fangoria.*

George Romero said in the pages of that magazine that *Salem's Lot* was his favorite King adaptation. He added, "*Yeah, Carrie was good but not as good as the book.*" (I don't agree. And neither does King.) Actress Marie Windsor, who was in both Hooper's *Salem's Lot* and Stanley Kubrick's *The Killing*, said Hooper was the best young director she'd worked with since Kubrick. She called him "*Another Stanley.*"

Bob Martin, the editor of *Fangoria*, wrote, "*Hooper's adaptation showed much more understanding of King's work and the horror genre than was displayed in Kubrick's The Shining*" (this was back when the horror press completely took King's side in his beef with Kubrick).

So when I finally saw it, I was prepared for something great.

And man was I disappointed.

To me, it just seemed like a stretched-out TV movie done in a very TV style (and I like TV movies). Even in terms of two-night TV-movie events based on classic horror novels featuring James Mason, Jack Smight's *Frankenstein: The True Story* was *way* better.

I tried to watch it again a couple of years ago and it was just too dull. I turned it off after about twenty-five minutes.

The only thing that held up for me was David Soul's performance. It reminded me of what an intense actor he was back in those days (the pilot TV movie for *Starsky and Hutch* is another good reminder). To put that in perspective, David Soul's performance was the one negative *Fangoria* had about Hooper's adaptation.

So after the success of *Salem's Lot*, Tobe Hooper landed his first studio feature film deal when Universal Pictures hired him to helm their horror quickie *The Funhouse*.

For the readers of *Fangoria*, along with John Carpenter, George Romero, David Cronenberg, and later Joe Dante (he gave the best interviews), Tobe Hooper was a superstar. The main readership of the magazine were boys thirteen to twenty-three (of which I was one).

It's kind of cool to think back on a magazine that encouraged its adolescent readership to subscribe so fully to Andrew Sarris' *Auteur theory*. In the eighties, inside the pages of *Fangoria* magazine, it was horror film movie directors that were its readers' heroes, along with special effect makeup artists (Tom Savini, Rick Baker, and Rob Bottin). This was a drastic difference when compared to Forrest Ackerman's *Famous Monsters of Filmland* magazine, the leading horror movie mag of adolescents ten years before. They may have, from time to time, featured an interview with the director of a current horror flick, but they weren't the mag's name attractions. That spot was reserved for the *Universal monsters (the Frankenstein Monster, the Wolf Man, the Mummy, and the Creature from the Black La-*

goon). As well as the reigning horror movie stars—both old (Boris Karloff, Lon Chaney Jr.) and current (Vincent Price, Christopher Lee, Peter Cushing).

So naturally, Tobe Hooper's first studio feature received big coverage in *Fangoria*, including in the February 1981 issue #11, the cover featuring makeup artist Rick Baker's creature design for the film's deformed, pathetic antagonist.

Even sister mag *Cinefantastique* (which dealt in horror but leaned more towards science fiction) featured a nice piece on the making of *The Funhouse* including a cool photograph of the director.

So for readers of the magazine, *The Funhouse* wasn't just another new horror film ad in the movie section of your local newspaper, appearing suddenly out of nowhere. We were well aware of it, had been following reports of its production, and were awaiting its release.

The biggest horror movie boom in cinema history occurred from 1979 through 1982. The *slasher film* cycle was in full swing with a seemingly endless string of titles. But also monster movies, animal attack movies, *Jaws* rip-offs, *Alien* rip-offs, *Omen* rip-offs, *Carrie* rip-offs, haunted house movies, ghost stories, vampire films, science fiction terror, as well as the last gasp of theatrically released Italian horror and New World Pictures fright fests like *Humanoids from the Deep*.

In 1981 it seemed every two weeks another horror title was *playing at a theatre or drive-in near you*. And it was amid this horror movie glut when—in its opening week—I went to see *The Funhouse* at the UA Del Amo Mall cinemas.

My verdict?

I enjoyed it, well enough, but considered it a touch on the mediocre side.

Then sometime in 2011, I went on a *slasher film* kick. I rewatched all the slasher films I had seen before, and caught all the ones I had missed or ignored. And after my rewatch of *The Funhouse* I was a little surprised. I found myself much, much more impressed with Hooper's direction (the staging of scenes, his dynamic coverage, and the cynical, tawdry, and downright nasty tone he carries throughout the picture), cinematographer Andrew Laszlo's photography—his towering crane shots—and his imaginative focus pulls, but especially production designer Mort Rabinowitz's creepy carnival and his immensely effective funhouse set.

But the big surprise was Larry Block's screenplay.

At first view, it may appear simple and obvious, but on the second go-round, it revealed both a level of depth and even sophistication that forced me to reconsider the whole film.

While movies have had no problem depicting life with a traveling circus (Chaplin's *The Circus*, *The Greatest Show on Earth*, *Circus World*, *Toby Tyler*, *Big Top Pee-wee*), carnival stories have been further and farther between.

Of course, the two indisputable classics in the genre are Tod Browning's *Freaks* and Edmund Goulding's *Nightmare Alley*. *Freaks* is rightly recognized as a towering classic of cinema's golden age, which once seen is never forgotten (what the fuck is that Pinhead girl?).

And while *Nightmare Alley* is also rightly considered a classic, I *still* think it's underrated. To me *Nightmare Alley* is as good as studio filmmaking ever gets. Tyrone Power (who I've never been fond of) is fucking sensational in the movie. And the script adaptation by Jules Furthman (one of my handful of nominees for greatest Hollywood screenwriter of all time) is excellent (it could have never been made in the fifties). Power doesn't say Furthman's dialogue, he *sings* it. *Nightmare Alley* feels every inch like an Italian neorealism movie from the same era. The film could swap casts with *Bitter Rice*, Tyrone Power/Vittorio Gassman, Doris Dowling/Joan

Blondell, Silvana Mangano/Coleen Gray, and both films would still hold their same place of pride in film history.

I'm also fond of Roger Corman's *Carnival Rock*, which plays like a Roger Corman directed Josef von Sternberg film. It hits its *Pagliacci* imagery a little too on the nose. But the card game showdown between David J. Stewart and future director Brian Hutton is one of my favorite Corman-directed scenes.

Growing up, my favorite carnival film was Elvis' superior vehicle, *Roustabout*. In that era of *"Elvis Presley movies"* (Elvis movies weren't *real* movies, they were *"Elvis Presley movies"*) it was a pretty entertaining little picture chock-full of cool elements, Elvis entering the movie on a motorcycle—dressed head to toe in black leather (in what looks like the same outfit he'll later make iconic in the '69 comeback special), a strong *Big Valley* era Barbara Stanwyck as his colead, a one-line bit at the beginning by Raquel Welch, the best soundtrack of any of Elvis' color films, including a rarity for the King on film—Elvis singing a cover of somebody else's hit, the Coasters' *Little Egypt*, and the only film where Elvis gets to demonstrate his Ed Parker-taught karate moves.

Only a year before *The Funhouse*, Lorimar released Robert Kaylor's *Carny* starring Gary Busey, Jodie Foster, and Robbie Robertson. *Carny* was written by Thomas Baum, a very talented screenwriter who also wrote the compelling horror film *The Sender*. But it's directed by a very untalented director, Robert Kaylor—if you can even call what he does in the film directing. Baum's script and his self-penned (superior) novelization shows the seedy realistic side of carny life, concentrating more on the grifting Carny games, which lure *marks* to the midway and fleece them of their hard-earned cash. The film wants to do for life on the midway what Ron Shelton's *Bull Durham* later did for minor league baseball: take you on a tour of a world you never really knew anything about, and by the time the picture's over you leave an expert, even speaking the lingo with confidence.

And to a certain degree, *Carny* is successful in that endeavor. Nevertheless, the missed and fumbled opportunities add up to, ultimately, an unsatisfying experience.

If *Carny* has an authorial voice, it isn't due to anyone behind the camera, it's due to the unique combination of manic energy and beyond-the-beyond naturalism that Gary Busey displays in front of the camera. *Carny* was the actor's follow-up to his break-out Oscar nominated turn as Buddy Holly in *The Buddy Holly Story*. The film positioned Busey, after a decade of character actor work, as an exciting leading man (at one time he was attached to Jim McBride's superlative remake of *Breathless* as *Jesse Lujack aka Jesse Burns aka Jesse Lee Burns*, the character that Richard Gere ultimately essayed).

Believe it or not, the manic hee-hawing buffoon of reality television was (pre-motorcycle accident), one of the seventies' greatest actors. Not just a talented journeyman character actor, but an acting giant. Just ask other acting giants that performed with him, like Dustin Hoffman (*Straight Time*), Martin Sheen (*The Execution of Private Slovick*), and Jeff Bridges (*The Last American Hero*).

Busey had a gift for a highly theatrical version of naturalism that was unlike any of his peers. Naturally, it was unlike anybody else, because it sprang from his soul. Gary Busey had such a deeply felt way of saying lines, you couldn't believe *anyone* wrote his dialogue. It just always sounded like it sprang fully formed out of him. The only other actor of his era that shared the same combination of naturalism and dynamic intensity was Robert Blake. What most actors pass off as naturalism is just *aw-shucks* mumbling. It reminds me what Uma Thurman once said about actors improvising: "*What most actors call improvising is just stammering and swearing. But another word for improvising is writing. And that's not what you pay actors to do.*"

Busey's unaffected line readings were documentary-real, but

backed by a dramatic storytelling drive that most naturalistic actors don't possess.

Tobe Hooper's *The Funhouse*, like Brian De Palma's *Blow Out* of the same year, starts with a parody of both the then-popular *slasher film* genre and the shower scene from *Psycho*.

The film's opening shot (like *Blow Out*, the POV of a killer with a knife) looks around the bedroom of a young boy obsessed with monster movies. Posters of Karloff's *Frankenstein* and Lugosi's *Dracula* line his walls (one of the benefits of the film being produced by *Universal*). As well as a wall collage of Halloween masks, which the unseen POV perspective character slips on his face (like in the opening of *Halloween*). As well, a section of the bedroom wall is covered in a collection of medieval weapons (you can imagine a mother letting her son pin up a *Frankenstein* movie poster, but a collection of weapons?).

Meanwhile, the movie crosscuts with the sixteen- or seventeen-year-old *Amy* (Elizabeth Berridge, who would later play Mozart's wife in *Amadeus*), who will end up being the film's requisite *Final Girl*, as she enters her bathroom and strips off her clothes to take a shower.

The *Coed Frenzy* fake-out opening of *Blow Out* fooled a lot of viewers (*not me*), but the fake-out opening of *The Funhouse*, while fun, doesn't fool anybody. Even though the only character we've physically seen is Amy, we know from the style of the little boy's bedroom, this is her horror freak little brother trying to scare the shit out of her.

Then, years before Gus Van Sant, Hooper repeats a series of shots from Hitchcock's classic shower set piece as the knife-wielding intruder enters the bathroom, rips open the shower curtain, and stabs at the screaming young girl. Then Hooper reveals the knife is bendable plastic, Amy rips off the attacker's mask, and we see it's her laughing ten-year-old asshole little brother *Joey* (Shawn Carson).

We're not supposed to take any of this seriously, it would appear, but the sequence does illustrate a repellent quality that almost all the film's characters demonstrate. As well as a cynical and disturbing undertone that pulsates throughout the picture.

Joey's vicious attack isn't that of a mischievous little scamp. He's a bona fide little creep with an obvious tendency towards sexual violence. For a younger brother to walk into an older sister's room and catch her stark naked is enough to make any teenage girl hit the roof. But to rip open the shower curtain and attack her naked body with a phony butcher knife?

That sounds like, "*we need to have a discussion about Joey.*"

Yet, Amy's reaction seems similarly disturbed. She throws on a bathrobe, chases him down the hall, grabs him by the front of his shirt, throwing the boy around, screaming at him in a violent rage, "*I'm gonna make you pay for this Joey! I'm gonna get you Joey, if it's the last thing I ever do!*"

And when she says it, it doesn't sound like a cliche or she's just saying an overused expression. It sounds like she's going to *fuck him up*! She'd like to fuck him up now, but she's got a date coming over and she has to finish getting ready.

Really?

Why not just tell your mother what this little asshole did? Telling mom and dad *should* suggest a harsher comeuppance.

Instead, the scene suggests that Amy and Joey are perpetrating a violent and sadistic private war against each other. A war they keep secret from their parents (throughout the film it's demonstrated that Amy and Joey never tell their parents anything).

Now you can take the scene at face value, and come to the conclusion we're not meant to invest in the realistic implications of this opening. It's just a Hitchcock homage put in to start this horror film off with a bang. It's a goof, it's a joke, nothing more.

But the scene *does* affect the viewer. Nor does screenwriter Block present this opening as just a phony scare scene that we're supposed to forget then move on to the real movie. Amy's words ("*I'm gonna make you pay for this Joey! I'm gonna get you if it's the last thing I ever do!*") play back much later in the film and affect the entire outcome of the storyline. And when it doubles back into the story again, it suggests that the antagonism between Joey and Amy isn't mere sibling rivalry, but a true callous animosity that exists between the youngsters. As opposed to the screenplay's other (mostly stock) characters, Joey is an interesting deviation from type. In the early eighties, the monster movie aficionado little boy whose room is covered in horror film posters and Frankenstein busts was a new age horror trope. They were usually meant to be a stand-in for a young version of either the screenwriter or the director or the grown horror fans in the audience (they always seemed to be a ten-year-old Joe Dante). And, *normally*, they're the most lovable character in the whole fucking movie (i.e., Corey Feldman in *Friday the 13th Part 4: The Final Chapter*). And in this group of children, Joey stands alone. Block gives the boy an entire B storyline that sets up how Joey is going to save the day and rescue his sister. Only to deliciously flip the script and have the malevolent little boy consciously doom his sibling to her ultimate fate.

Larry Block's deceptively thin screenplay tells the tale of four teenagers on a double date, who visit a seedy traveling carnival passing through town (we've already learned from Amy's father that two girls in a nearby municipality were found dead after visiting the same carnival last year).

Each of the four teens is a remarkably unappealing representation of the stock teenage characters in a slasher film.

Cooper Huckabee is *Buzz*, the insensitive, muscle-headed, muscle-car driving, hunky jerk jock who's Amy's date.

Miles Chapin, an actor I've always been allergic to, is as annoying as usual as *Richie*, the wimpy-creepy-bespectacled best friend of Buzz. Chapin goes through the whole film with a sweater tied around his neck (which in those days was egregious enough for me to hate him on sight).

Richie's date is the blond-haired slightly slutty *Liz*, played by the bizarrely named Largo Woodruff, who waltzes through the entire picture in tight, tomato-red pants (*a nice touch*).

From the moment Berridge's Amy climbs into Buzz's muscle car, she starts transforming into the uptight final girl archetype. Yet after that weird opening scene, we never really *like* her. She's not as *unlikable* as the repellent group of fuck faces she attends the carnival with. But for a slasher film final girl, she's singularly unsympathetic. And our feelings about her don't change.

We never *like* her.

We just *dislike* her less than Buzz, Richie, and Liz.

While the carny lingo and description of the crooked games on the midway in Robert Kaylor's *Carny* strike the viewer as authentic, the seedy, shitty carnival of Hooper's *The Funhouse* is both more compelling and entertaining. *Carny* focuses more on the shady midway games and how their crooked operators manipulate both the games and the marks. But, for the most part, it ignores the sordid attractions and performers (the exception is one of the film's best moments when the carnival fat man sings a blues version of Fats Domino's *The Fat Man*).

This is not a mistake Hooper makes. The kids take in *the Freak Show*, and we in the audience get a gander at some real animal oddities (a two-headed cow and a bovine with a cleft palate). The freak show barker's spiel (*"Alive, alive, alive! These are all creatures of God, ladies and gentlemen, not man"*) stays in your head and haunts the rest of the film like a subtextual narrator.

The three dancers in the hoochie-coochie tent seem as real as a gas station toilet. And the film's three older actors, Kevin Conway,

William Finley, and Sylvia Miles all give entertaining guest star turns as the carnival's featured performers.

De Palma regular William Finley (who was also in Hooper's *Eaten Alive*) as a derelict, flask-sipping magician (*Marko the Magnificent*) performs an especially inspired bit.

It's Chapin's sneaky, troublemaking Richie who gets the bright idea that it would be a gas for the four of them to spend the night in the funhouse. And naturally the other three idiots go along with the stupid plan. But before the quarrelsome quartet sneak into the funhouse, setting the film's rigid slasher structure in motion, Hooper takes the viewer on a vivid tour of the sordid pleasures found in this bottom feeding rung of entertainment. Made all the more vivid by cinematographer Andrew Laszlo's nighttime photography and the flashing and blinking colored lights of the trashy enterprise. And as the director guides our perspective we start noticing little things. The three featured barkers (for the freak show, the hoochie-coochie tent, and the funhouse) are all played by the same actor, Broadway's Kevin Conway.

And, little by little, due to his slightly haunted demeanor, we start noticing the stumbling worker of the funhouse ride, with the oversized Frankenstein mask he wears over his head. And since it's a *Universal* picture, Hooper can use the classic Jack Pierce flatheaded Frankenstein's Monster design. And the historic Karloff monster design, put to such a tawdry use, has an iconic power (like Mickey Mouse redrawn as a rat). We also take notice that while our four leads are off-putting, this figure in the Frankenstein mask is immediately sympathetic. The character never loses our sympathy, but once he removes the mask and we see the deformed cleft-headed face underneath, he's never as poignant as he was. Mostly because the creature design by Rick Baker (the best special effects makeup artist in the business) is surprisingly bad; ironically, it's the character's *supposedly* real face that looks like the monster mask. Also, behind the mask is a San Francisco mime named

Wayne Doba, who's really effective before his Rick Baker freak face is revealed. Once he loses the Frankenstein mask, out goes Doba's previously finely crafted performance and he spends the rest of the movie jumping around and screaming. Plus the slender and small Doba (who looks about the size of Joel Grey) nowhere near fits the description of the character in the script, where he's supposed to be powerfully built, and eight feet tall! Yet, in an ass-backward way, it's one of the reasons we never lose our sympathy for this character.

Now while I enjoyed the movie in 1981, one of the big reasons I wasn't more impressed after my first viewing was its similarity to another slasher film that came out the same year, former gay porn director Tom DeSimone's Linda Blair-led effort, *Hell Night*. Even though the story and setup of both films were practically identical, in terms of script, dialogue, performances, and characters, *Hell Night* was far superior to *The Funhouse*.

The one area that Hooper's film has it over the Linda Blair picture is in production designer Morton Rabinowitz's impressively eerie funhouse set (*Hell Night* is set in an abandoned mansion). Assisted by Jose Duarte's art direction and Tom Coll's set decoration, Rabinowitz's creepy set manages to balance the difficult combination of being the showcase funhouse set that a movie titled *The Funhouse* requires, yet is still believable as part of this low rent truck and van carnival. The ghoulish faces and the rickety movements of the authentic, paint chipped, herky-jerky animatronic funhouse dolls are the film's real stars. That's why Hooper features them during the opening credits (we remember them from the opening and look forward to spotting them later).

Another reason (back in '81) I didn't like the film more was how little I gave a fuck about the lead kids. That doesn't mean the leads are bad actors. Berridge could be better, and Largo Woodruff is no Suki Goodwin, but while I've never liked Miles Chapin, you can't deny he is perfectly cast as shit-heel Richie. And Cooper Huckabee, like John Travolta's Billy Nolan in *Carrie*, has a bit of scumbag pizzaz (in her review of *Carrie*, Pauline Kael said Travolta's Billy Nolan could be *"Warren Beatty's low life younger brother."* Huckabee could be Harrison Ford's).

Except for the poor guy in the Frankenstein mask, nobody in the movie is sympathetic. But now I see that as part of the film's subtextual strategy. Doba's character is listed in the credits as *"The Monster."* Which—considering he's clearly presented as a man with a horrible birth defect—is remarkably insensitive (*"These are creatures of God, ladies and gentlemen, not man!"*). Even Rick Baker, in his *Fangoria* interview, mentioned this aspect of the character gave him trepidation. Baker said, *"It's a birth-defect type monster. After I started thinking about it for a while, I felt real guilty about making that deformity a monster. It's so easy to take horror straight from nature, because there are some pretty horrifying real things. I just didn't feel right about making it a straight freak, so I added a little more to it. I hope it comes across that way, because it still has a lot of the birth defect aspect to it."*

Easily the film's best scene is when the pitiful, naive, and confused young man, hiding inside his Frankenstein mask, tries to buy sex from the Carnival's phony Gypsy fortune teller (Sylvia Miles). The teens hiding in the funhouse peep and giggle at this poor pathetic wretch as he gets a handjob from the mean and far more monstrous than he is Sylvia Miles. *"The Monster*'s" inability to control himself leads to him having an *episode* (remember those two dead girls from the nearby town?) that the snickering jerks witness. Soon it's revealed that Kevin Conway, the scary funhouse barker, is the boy's father. And it's *he* who insists the boy kill the teenagers (*"Ain't as if I'm asking you to do something you ain't never done before. . . . Them two little half-pint Girl Scouts in Memphis."*).

Significantly, Kevin Conway originated the role of the freak show barker in the original production of the theatrical version of *The Elephant Man*. And for a while, *The Funhouse* resembles a slasher film version of that story. Except, compared to this poor thing, John Merrick had it good. He gets Anne Bancroft reading *Juliet* to his *Romeo.*

The best this poor bastard can do is a hateful handjob from Sylvia Miles!

*Floyd Footnote

So who exactly was this Floyd character I was referring to earlier?

His name was *Floyd Ray Wilson* and he was a black guy of about thirty-seven, who for about a year and a half in the late seventies lived in my house. He used to date my mom's best friend Jackie and he hung around in their circle. Years earlier, from time to time, he would visit the apartment my mom and I shared with her roommates Jackie and Lillian. And every time he came by it was exciting, because I thought Floyd was really cool and I could talk movies with him. And since he was a hip guy who saw a lot of shit, he could keep up (at least compared to the adults I knew). He especially knew all the action movies and the Blaxploitation films. I remember when Jackie introduced us (I was ten), she said, "*Quentin, Floyd's who you should talk to about movies. He knows as much as you.*"

So I—a ten-year-old white boy—started testing this grown-ass black man on his knowledge of black movies.

"*Do you know who Brenda Sykes is?*" I tested.

"*Of course I do,*" he said.

I told him, "*I think she's the prettiest black actress in movies.*"

"*You damn right she is,*" he answered.

"*Do you know who James A. Watson is?*" I asked.

"*Yes,*" he said.

Wow, that's pretty good, I thought, *he mostly does TV.*

"*What's your favorite Jim Kelly movie?*" Again a test.

If he answered *Enter the Dragon*, he's just like everybody else.

"*Three the Hard Way, obviously,*" he answered correctly.

Lillian just stared at the two of us and said to the room, "*I don't know who any of these people are.*"

So from that moment on, whenever Floyd visited the apartment, it was practically like a holiday for me. Because finally, I was going to be able to talk to somebody about movies who knew what the fuck I was talking about. So when Floyd would come over I'd attach myself to him like a tick. But also during this time, I realized the hard way that Floyd was a flakey guy who couldn't be counted on. On at least two occasions when Floyd was visiting, he played the big man and told me he'd come over next Saturday and take me to the movies.

Oh boy, I thought, *not just talking about movies with Floyd, but actually going to the movies with Floyd.*

But when Saturday came, no Floyd.

No call.

No, I'm sorry.

No excuse.

Just, no show.

He either forgot or he just didn't give a shit.

I was *so* excited too.

If Floyd visiting the apartment was a holiday, *this* was going to be Christmas. And as the hours passed, and I waited, and waited for the buzzer to buzz on the intercom of our apartment, and it got later and later, I finally realized he wasn't coming.

I wasn't mad. I was heartbroken. I also realized Floyd wasn't as great a guy as I thought he was. I didn't even think of myself as a *kid*, but even *I* knew you didn't do that to a *kid*. But I forgave Floyd and played it cool next time he came by.

And a few visits later, he promised to take me out again. I said, "*yeah sure.*" And without mentioning the last time, I made sure when he left that he remembered that we had plans, and I'd be waiting for him. He said, "*Of course, no problem. See you Saturday.*"

And the fucking guy did it to me again. But this time, I wasn't heartbroken. I felt lousy, but not crushed. It was just now I knew who Floyd really was. And when he came over again, I didn't confront him with his—bordering on cruel—behavior. I didn't bring it up, and we still had great conversations, and I still really dug talking to him. I just knew not to try and make plans with him. Because he was an adult I couldn't count on (I also promised myself—when I grew up—I'd never do that to a kid).

CUT TO 1978.

I'm fifteen going on sixteen.

My mom's work is requiring her to spend more and more time away from the house, or she *wanted to*, and that was a good *excuse*, so she ran with it. Which happened to coincide with the age I started getting in trouble a lot (fights in school, ditching, and staying out later and later). There wasn't necessarily a correlation between these two events, I was just a young wise guy who thought he was tough.

So mom rented Floyd a spare room in our house with the proviso that he keep an eye on her sixteen-year-old son. Which worked for me, because I still thought Floyd was the coolest. Yeah, years ago he stood me up. But since that time, I had gone through the whole trauma of being sent to Tennessee and put in the care of hillbilly alcoholics. So by that time, Floyd being a flake was easy to forgive. But it equipped me with two pieces of information that would prove valuable as our relationship moved forward.

One, I couldn't count on Floyd. And if I ever did, be aware he'd probably let me down. And two, I cared more for Floyd than Floyd cared for me.

Knowing how much I dug Floyd, I'm sure my mom thought she came up with the perfect solution for the *"What to do with Quentin?" problem.*

At the time, I don't think she was as aware of (though I think

Jackie knew) what a shady cat Floyd really was. Nor did she consider the ramifications of having her *very* impressionable young son spend so much time around such a sketchy dude. It was sorta like moving Sam Jackson's character in *Jackie Brown* (Ordell Robbie) into your home and having him look after your sixteen-year-old boy for over a year.

Not that *I* had any problem with it. Floyd could be mercurial and he could get irritated easily but I dug him. He lived an interesting vagabond life, he told great stories, he was funny as hell and I drank in all his hustler/male-centric/streetwise wisdom.

Floyd grew up in the fifties in Catahoula, Louisiana, and it was interesting listening to him recount pop culture history from *his* perspective.

He told me about being a little boy and going to the Saturday matinee and seeing the cowboys for a nickel. His favorite was the man in black *Lash LaRue*. Lash LaRue was extremely popular in the South. Like Johnny Cash he dressed all in black but he also carried a bullwhip and wasn't shy about using it. In the book about the Gower Gulch matinee cowboy stars, *The Sunset Corral*, it described LaRue as looking like a cowboy Bogart. His sidekick was a very funny Gabby Hayes type, with a face full of whiskers called *Fuzzy St. John.*

And Floyd told me about going to see a Lash LaRue picture when he was nine and both Lash and Fuzzy made a personal appearance at his neighborhood cinema. This was back when the movie theatres were segregated and the black kids had to sit up in the balcony.

"*But those are the best seats?*" I said.

And he said, "*That's what we thought! But if these dumb motherfuckers think they're gonna put us down by givin' us the best seats in the house? Fine by me.*"

He said that Lash and Fuzzy were on stage, talking about all the kids in the audience. Pointing out at the white boys on the bottom level, in his cantankerous accent, Fuzzy said, "*We got some real tough looking cowpokes in the audience today.*"

Then, pointing out the girls in attendance, Lash added, "*And some mighty pretty does.*"

Then Fuzzy pointed up at the balcony and said with a twinkle, "*And them the bucks.*"

Floyd said the whole place laughed, but for different reasons. The white kids thought Fuzzy was making fun of the black kids, but the black kids knew Fuzzy was calling them badasses.

Floyd was still a kid the first time he saw Elvis when he was on *The Tommy Dorsey Show*. And he said the next day at school everybody was talking about it, "*Didja see that wild white boy on TV last night?*"

Once I asked him what was he doing when he was my age.

He said, "*Walking around trying to look as much like Elvis Presley as I could.*" His other favorite at the time was *Jackie Wilson*. He'd act out seeing Jackie, when he was a teenager, on stage singing *Lonely Teardrops*. Floyd told me Elvis said, "*If Jackie Wilson was white, he'd be twice as big as me.*" Now I don't know if Elvis ever really said that. But Floyd said he did.

There was a rumor going around in the black community that back in the fifties somebody asked Elvis what he thought of colored folks.

And Elvis said, "*All they can do is shine my shoes and buy my records.*"

Floyd didn't buy that shit at all. "*Elvis never said that shit.*"

Then I said, "*But so-an-so said she heard him say it?*"

"*So-an-so never heard that shit,*" he came back, "*So-an-so's a fuckin' liar!*"

I was all ears about this firsthand rock 'n' roll history, because I wasn't into seventies white-boy rock. I didn't give a fuck about *Kiss*, I didn't give a fuck about *Aerosmith*, I didn't give a fuck about *Alice Cooper* or *Black Sabbath* or *Jethro Tull*. I didn't own *Frampton*

Comes Alive. I openly rejected that entire culture. At sixteen, I think I heard of *Bruce Springsteen*, but I'd never *heard* Bruce Springsteen.

I was into fifties rock 'n' roll.

Not sixties.

Not *The Beatles.*

Not *Jimi Hendrix.*

Not *Bob Dylan* (that would come later).

But fifties rock 'n' roll . . . *and* . . . seventies soul music.

Elvis and Stevie Wonder.

Eddie Cochran and Bootsy Collins.

Gene Vincent and Parliament.

The Five Satins and Rufus.

Jackie Wilson and Rick James.

The Coasters and the Commodores.

Chuck Berry and Barry White.

Brenda Lee and Teena Marie.

Curtis Mayfield *in* the Impressions *and* the Curtis Mayfield that did the *Super Fly* soundtrack.

Well, that just happened to be Floyd's wheelhouse too.

It was great watching something like Floyd Mutrux's *American Hot Wax* with Floyd. One, he explained to me who *Screamin' Jay Hawkins* was and he laughed at the fellow who was supposed to be *Dee Clark.* And he remarked about Tim McIntire (who was playing disc jockey Alan Freed), "*Alan Freed didn't look nothin' like that motherfucker.*"

He liked *American Hot Wax*, but he didn't like *The Buddy Holly Story.*

"*They tried to make Buddy Holly bigger than he was. Nobody gave a fuck when Buddy Holly died. Now Ritchie Valens and the Big Bopper, that was a loss.*"

I remember when I told him after Buddy Holly, Ritchie Valens, and the Big Bopper died they replaced them with *Bobby Vee* on the remaining concert dates. Floyd smiled and said, "*Man, those musta been some real disappointed people."* And we both burst out laughing.

He introduced me to *Howlin' Wolf.* In fact as I'm proofreading this page right now I'm listening to Howlin' Wolf and thinking about Floyd.

He introduced me to *George Thorogood* and played his second album *Move It on Over* all the time.

He liked *Johnny Cash*, but he used to joke, *"I don't listen to Johnny around the brothers."*

He had *one* Bob Dylan album, *Bringing It All Back Home*, but he only listened to *one* song, *Gates of Eden*. But he listened to it all the time.

He taught me who the abolitionist *John Brown* was. John Brown was his favorite American, he knew a lot about him, and over the year we were together he told me John Brown's whole story. And made it damn entertaining. His two favorite historical characters were John Brown and Gen. George Patton. And he quoted the both of them a lot.

He served in the army with *Frankie Lymon.*

Back in the day he dated *Joey Heatherton* for a while.

And he used to know Bobby Poole, the screenwriter of *The Mack.*

He said, incredulously, *"That ugly motherfucker wanted to play Goldie. Ain't nobody with good sense making a movie with that motherfucker as The Mack!"*

He saw all the Blaxploitation movies when they came out.

Floyd on *The Spook Who Sat by the Door:*

"That movie was way too heavy for Hollywood. They had to shut that shit down."

Floyd on *The Mack:*

"If Max Julien were white, after The Mack, he'd be the biggest motherfucker in Hollywood."

Floyd on Jim Brown:

"People say Jim Brown can't act. I say I don't go to Jim Brown movies to see good acting. If I want to see good acting I'll go watch Marlon Brando. I go to see Jim Brown movies to see Jim throw a motherfucker outta window."

Floyd on *100 Rifles:*

"You went to that movie to see Jim Brown fuck Raquel Welch. But Burt Reynolds stole that motherfuckin' movie."

Floyd on Sidney Poitier:

"Sidney Poitier is a good actor. But he played them nice guy 'Patch of Blue' roles too long. Now I understand it. He had to play those roles, so other motherfuckers could play other parts. But he done it too long. So when he's in Buck and the Preacher you're like, so what, now you're this dude now? Naw man, you done played that other shit too long. I can't buy you in this Jim Brown shit, you ain't that guy. You're the motherfucker from Guess Who's Coming to Dinner."

Floyd on Bill Cosby:

"Bill Cosby ain't been a good actor since I Spy. And on I Spy, Cosby wasn't shit next to Culp."

Floyd on Charles Bronson:

"I'll see any movie starring Charles Bronson 'cause I know Bronson's gonna be good."

Floyd's Five Favorite Actors

1. Marlon Brando
2. George C. Scott
3. Peter O'Toole
4. Charles Bronson
5. William Marshall

Floyd on William Marshall:

"Greatest Shakespearean actor in America. Marshall's voice was so magnificent, they'd use him to dub white dudes. He's the guy who played Blacula. Now don't get me wrong, he's good in Blacula—that movie wouldn't be shit without him. But he's better than motherfucking Blacula. He had to do that shit to get a name."

Later, when I'd watch William Marshall play the King of Cartoons on *Pee-wee's Playhouse*, I'd always think of Floyd.

Floyd liked Richard Pryor in movies, but he didn't consider him an actor. *"He's a comedian. He ain't no actor. For a comedian, he's a good actor, but he ain't no actor."*

But Harry Belafonte he took serious as an actor. Especially in his character roles, like *Buck and the Preacher, Uptown Saturday Night,* and *The Angel Levine,* which he was a big fan of.

His five favorite movies starred three of his favorite actors (in fact they're why they were his favorite movies).

Floyd's Top Five Movies
1. *The Godfather* (hands down, top of the list)
2. *The Lion in Winter*
3. *Patton*
4. *Pandora and the Flying Dutchman*
5. *Cluny Brown* (yes, a Lubitsch movie made it on Floyd's top five. Though I'm positive he never knew Lubitsch by name. Which I think Ernst might appreciate even more than if he did).

During the year (1978, some of 1979) Floyd and I saw a lot of movies together. Both at the theatres and on *On-TV* (pay movie channel).

The movies I can remember, *Eaten Alive* (especially the parts with Robert Englund as *Buck*), *American Hot Wax, Bloodbrothers* (he especially loved the part when Robert Englund fucks Kristen DeBell on the couch), *Journey into the Beyond, Paradise Alley,*

Animal House, Fingers (he loved the head clunking scene), *The Boys in Company C, Go Tell the Spartans, Days of Heaven, Invasion of the Body Snatchers* (Kaufman version), *Dawn of the Dead* (he was blown away), *The Private Files of J. Edgar Hoover* (he thought Michael Parks was a *great* Bobby Kennedy), *Death on the Nile, Blue Collar, Eyeball, Autopsy, The Boys from Brazil, Brass Target* (he saw it because George Kennedy played Patton in it), *Who'll Stop the Rain, Thank God It's Friday, Rocky II, Time After Time, The Wanderers,* and *Apocalypse Now.*

We also devotedly watched the miniseries *Centennial* and he loved, loved, loved Robert Conrad's French fur trapper character *Pasquinel.* (*"Best thing that motherfucker ever did."*)

And we watched Franco Zeffirelli's miniseries *Jesus of Nazareth* and he thought Rod Steiger stole the show as Pontius Pilate.

But of all the movies we saw together, his number one favorite was:

The Deer Hunter ("Now that was a great movie").

Floyd dug all the big comedians of the day, Richard Pryor, George Carlin, Flip Wilson, Redd Foxx, but he thought Steve Martin was silly.

Nor could Floyd wrap his head around the fact that Rudy Ray Moore was starring in kung fu movies. When Rudy came out with *The Human Tornado,* I asked him did he know who this kung fu star Rudy Ray Moore was? Floyd looked at me as if I'd lost my goddamn mind. *"I know who Rudy Ray Moore is. But the Rudy I know ain't starring in no damn kung fu movies."*

But there were two comedic actors I saw break Floyd down laughing more than anybody else.

One was *Willie Best.*

If you don't know who Willie Best is, it's because for the last thirty years he's been effectively erased from film history. He was a young skinny black comedy actor, from mostly the forties, that started getting some big roles in comedies opposite some big-name farceurs. The reason you might not be familiar with Best is because his comedic character, *the black man that's scared of his own shadow*, has—to say the least—gone out of favor. And if you just look at the names of some of the characters he performed (Sambo, Algernon, Woodrow, Sunshine, Chattanooga Brown), they don't bode well for his filmography.

Best *did* do his share of insulting, slow witted, mush mouthed black caricatures (especially in *High Sierra*). But not all Willie Best performances were created equal. Best was a very skilled comedian and was very popular with black Americans in the forties and even into the fifties. Yes, his comedic persona was that of the shaking-like-a-leaf coward, but stick that character in a haunted house, like they did opposite Bob Hope in *The Ghost Breakers* or Eddie Bracken in *Hold That Blonde!*, now you got just a funny guy. Is Best really any different from Jerry Lewis in *Scared Stiff* or Lou Costello in *Hold That Ghost*?

Yes, he's *a little* different, but not by much. And many times the black audiences of the forties and fifties appreciated the difference.

When black folks watched Hollywood movies in those days, they were used to seeing a world that hadn't any relation to their lives. But Willie Best, partly because he was so young, would make cool hip references, which sailed over the head of the floor-level white audiences, but made direct hits in the balcony (white audiences always found it disconcerting when the black folks in the balcony laughed at something they didn't get). This was Mantan Moreland's specialty too. As he was goofing around next to Charlie Chan, he was also creating a private dialogue with black audiences.

Floyd was very pragmatic about the black performers from that time.

"They did what they had to do."

I once put down Stepin Fetchit.

He asked me, *"Have you ever seen Stepin Fetchit?"*

"No," I answered.

"I didn't think so," he said.

"Don't be so quick to make judgments about people stuck in situations you can never understand. I got no problem with Stepin Fetchit. Those were the only roles he could get, so he did 'em. And by doing those roles became the wealthiest black man in America. Fuck those motherfuckers say he shuffled. Yeah, he shuffled his black ass all the way to the motherfuckin' bank!"

Floyd didn't understand why they didn't air *The Amos 'n' Andy Show* on reruns like they did other shows he grew up with from the fifties. *"That was a funny show! How is Amos 'n' Andy degrading? How is Kingfish degrading? When I was a kid I thought he was the baddest motherfucker on the box! They lived well. They dressed nice. Kingfish had his own business. And they didn't walk around callin' each other nigger. What's the problem?"*

But it was watching the George Marshall comedy *Hold That Blonde!* late one night, on KTLA Channel 5, starring Eddie Bracken, Veronica Lake, and Willie Best that I saw Floyd laugh like I never saw him laugh before. Willie Best played Eddie Bracken's manservant *Willie.* And Willie's antics cracked Floyd up the whole movie. But the whole climax—when Eddie and Willie go to investigate a supposedly haunted house—that's the sequence that physically doubled Floyd up on the couch in hysterics. By that point every single thing Willie did cracked Floyd up. It's a really funny movie. George Marshall was a terrific comedy director and movies with haunted house set pieces were sort of his forte. And personally *Hold That Blonde!* is my favorite.

But Floyd's favorite comedy actor . . . *Don Knotts.*

Floyd would watch an episode of *The Andy Griffith Show* and howl with laughter at everything Don Knotts as *Barney Fife* did.

I remember Floyd both describing and acting out for me the Don Knotts haunted house comedy, *The Ghost and Mr. Chicken,* with the same enthusiasm that Peter Bogdanovich had for Buster Keaton or François Truffaut had for Jerry Lewis.

"*Don Knotts just tickles me,*" is what Floyd would say.

Once Floyd and I were in a pizza parlor. A gay nineties joint. Sawdust on the floor. Player piano in the corner playing a jaunty piano roll.

And they were projecting a series of Charlie Chaplin shorts on the wall from a 16mm projector. Floyd poured a glass of beer from a pitcher, glanced over at the image of *the Little Tramp* projected on the wall, and sneered, "*That motherfucker's never made me laugh. Folks say that nigger's a comic genius. Not to me he ain't. Just look at that shit . . . it ain't funny. Now you wanna know who's a comic GENIUS?*

"*Don Knotts is a motherfuckin' comic genius! Don Knotts make ya laugh!*

"*Don Knotts might be the funniest motherfucker in the whole wide world!*

"*Compared to Don Knotts, Charlie Chaplin ain't shit!*"

And it was from watching Willie Best and Don Knotts from Floyd's perspective that made me realize how similar to each other their comedic personas were. Is the shaking scared black man a stereotype of an earlier time? Yes it was. It's also an attribute of many white comedians of the time (Jerry Lewis, Bob Hope, Danny Kaye, Lou Costello). And none more so than Don Knotts. When Knotts did a remake of Bob Hope's *The Paleface*, it was titled *The Shakiest Gun in the West*. Meanwhile Don Knotts is respected as one of the most beloved comedians in the history of television, whereas Willie Best doesn't get any respect.

Naturally, it's a question of context. Even in Willie Best's most legit studio film outings, his shaky subordinate was (usually) the only black character on display. While Don Knotts shared the screen with a cast of able white characters and he *still* ended up the hero and got the girl. Even as a *fish*!

Nevertheless, the almost identical nature of their two comedic personas brings up two questions.

If Don Knotts were black, he *couldn't* be Don Knotts?

And if Willie Best were white, would he still be a disgrace . . . or a legend?

During this time the only family I had around me was my mom. But to us her close circle of friends *were* our family. Her best friend *Jackie* was like my second *mom*. Her friend *Lillian* was like my aunt. Jackie's brother *Don* was like my uncle. Jackie's daughter *Nikki* was like my sister. And they all looked out for me. Floyd, in his own way, looked out for me too. The difference between Floyd and them was, while *they* loved me, Floyd didn't give a shit about me. Don't get me wrong, Floyd *liked* me. We had a good time together. He liked telling his stories to me, he liked being admired by a young boy, and he liked handing out his sage wisdom to open ears.

You see, a guy like Floyd could *like* you, and simultaneously not *give a fuck whether you lived or died.*

One doesn't contradict the other . . . *if* you're a guy like Floyd.

Not to say Floyd didn't have affection for me, but he was always looking out for number one. And that wasn't me.

And it wasn't the worst thing in the world to hang around an adult who didn't treat you with kid gloves. Who told it to you like it is, without too much concern for your feelings.

For one thing Floyd never lied to me. Yeah, maybe about some of the shit he *said* he did in his past (like that Joey Heatherton shit).

But he never *lied* to me about *me*. He didn't care enough *about me* to lie to me.

Obviously, sometimes that hurt my feelings. But through Floyd I received an authentic glimpse of the impression I was making on others.

Once, Floyd and I went to the Del Amo Mall with a young girl I was dating, and while there we caught a movie. Later, Floyd told me, "*When you take a woman to the movies, don't buy all that candy shit. It makes you look childish.*"

Well, on the one hand, I was childish. On the other, I wanted to grow up. And Floyd gave me some unvarnished masculine advice.

Not all of it was correct.

On account of Floyd it took me a few years before I broke down and ate pussy ("*No man has to do that shit!*").

But that was for me to work out for myself.

Now when Floyd moved out in 1979, my initial memory is I never saw him again. But that can't be correct, because I remember seeing the movie *American Gigolo* with Floyd, and that didn't come out till 1980. So I guess we kept in touch somewhat. Enough to go to a movie together. But when Floyd moved out, for the most part, he was gone, never to be seen or heard from again.

And that was the story of Floyd.

I didn't hold it against Floyd for not keeping in touch. By that time I knew what kind of a guy Floyd was, so I didn't expect anything else. Also, I'm sure he'd had enough of *me*. And by that time, he had done things to disenchant everybody in our circle. He was persona non grata with my mom due to some jewelry and a pawn shop, and I'm sure other things I wasn't aware of. Jackie was done with him. And her daughter Nikki hated him and ran him down all the time.

Nevertheless, Floyd Ray Wilson left a lasting impression on the fifteen- and sixteen-year-old boy he mentored in the year of 1978, as well as a bit of a legacy he never could have imagined.

What *exactly* Floyd did for a living all these years was open to wild speculation. He never had a *career*. He just moved from one situation to another—some more lucrative than others—for most of his life. Like everybody I've ever met like him, he always had stories of the days when he was living the high life, dating Joey Heatherton and driving a yellow *Stingray*.

If he's thirty-seven years old, moving into his old girlfriend's best friend's spare room, and made to keep a lookout on her teenage son, he wasn't doing so well (but you'd never know it to look at or talk to him).

Floyd didn't have any serious bad habits. He didn't take drugs, he didn't even smoke weed as far as I could tell. Nor did he have a drinking habit. I don't just mean he wasn't a drunk. I mean, he didn't need a drink or a couple of glasses of wine to unwind at the end of the day. But he wasn't a recovering alcoholic either. He drank a beer, or a glass of whiskey when he was out. Not that any of those things are serious *bad habits*. But it's a little unusual he didn't develop a recreational reliance on at least one of them.

He did have a job when we lived together. He worked the night shift at the post office. Which was a pretty good job for a vagabond type guy, as anyone who's read Charles Bukowski's novel *Post Office* can tell you. Floyd was a very personable guy, yet he never had friends from the old days visit him. Which I can't say rang any bells back then. But now, I think it's due to the fact he didn't *have* any old friends. People were in Floyd's life for a while, then they weren't. Usually it was probably a burnt bridge situation, or he just disappeared one day, leaving nothing but a memory.

He did have friends who came to the house every once in a while and hung out. But they were work buddies from the post office. And they were good guys who I liked and remember fondly. Nickleberry and Toulivert (in early attempts at script writing their names would find their way in). Nickleberry looked a bit like Montel Williams and Toulivert looked a lot like Sonny Liston (Floyd called me Quint, but he always called them by their last names).

Floyd might have been a vagabond, and a scrounger, and an opportunist, but he did have an ambition.

He wanted to be a screenwriter.

By the time he moved into my house he had written two screenplays and one novel. And we spent many hours discussing his screenplays during the year he lived with me. The novel, which

I never read, was a romance set in Roman times, featuring two black characters titled *Demetrius & Desiree* (which Nikki claimed was plagiarized. *"I saw that goddamn book in the store once. I just laughed, that fakey motherfucker."*).

Floyd's two screenplays were the first two screenplays I ever read.

One was a horror film titled *The Mysterious Mr. Black*.

The Mysterious Mr. Black, Floyd admitted, was inspired by the Sidney Poitier movie *Brother John* (about the second coming of Christ, but as a black man in Mississippi). But *Mr. Black* wasn't Christ. He was the vengeful spirit of a former slave, out to punish the descendants of the white slave owners who performed some ghoulish experiment on him a hundred years earlier. The suit clad *Mr. Black*, distinguished by his dignified manner and his mastery of languages, suddenly showed up in town one day and integrated himself in the highest echelons of upper New Orleans high society. Meeting and targeting the wealthy and powerful descendants of the family whose fortunes were built on the pain and suffering of black flesh. And then, *Omen*-style, causing their death in grand glorious set pieces.

Okay, I'm making this screenplay sound a little better than it was. I only read it once, about forty-five years ago, so I'm not sure how much is memory and how much is me filling in to complete the picture (I remember it being a little dry). But that was the basic idea—and no doubt—*Mr. Black* was a damn cool character. Floyd's choice for *Mr. Black* . . . Harry Belafonte.

But the script I loved, and was the first script I ever read, was Floyd's *epic* western saga, *Billy Spencer*.

Floyd was a big fan of westerns and his mammoth screenplay was basically every moment he loved from his favorite westerns, all rolled up into one story, and featuring an incredibly cool black cowboy named Billy Spencer.

In the script, which was similar to a *Marvel Comic* I liked called

Gunhawks, the Spencers—owners of the most powerful ranch in the territory—find the baby of a runaway slave in the desert. They decide to keep the child and raise it as their own son. A few years later Mrs. Spencer has a son, *Tracy* (yeah, I know, Spencer Tracy. But I didn't put that together back then). And *Billy* and *Tracy* grow up together, the best of friends, and a dynamic duo. The script didn't really have one story, just a lot of different adventures for Billy and Tracy and the Spencer clan. Mother Spencer and the tough father were great characters, and there was never even a hint of ambiguity when it came to their love and devotion for Billy or his for them (the mother and the father made no distinction between Tracy and Billy). And as long as the screenplay was, Floyd wasn't finished yet. He kept coming up with different adventures and situations to stick into the script. I remember when we watched the Muhammad Ali and Kris Kristofferson miniseries *Freedom Road,* Floyd thinking maybe *Billy Spencer* should be a miniseries. He felt Charlton Heston or Burt Lancaster should be old man Spencer and he thought Peter Fonda should be Tracy. But he strongly felt Billy Spencer should be an unknown (when I read it I always saw the actor Thomas Carter).

I don't remember the villains, but at some point a range war develops and, in a scene taken from *Public Enemy,* Tracy is murdered by the bad guys and his fucked-up, dead carcass is dropped off at the Spencers' front door. The scene was genuinely powerful, and Floyd would act it out so I got the full effect, and I did. After reading the massive screenplay, you did fall in love with the Tracy Spencer character and his death was devastating. Especially the detail that it was his mother who opened the door to find the mutilated corpse of her son. Floyd would act this out to maximum effect (of course, he'd seen *Public Enemy*). Once the bad guys murder his brother, Billy knows it's time to leave the safety of the Spencer ranch behind and kill every single member of the bad guys' gang.

So donning a poncho, which represents his now solitary existence, he rains hell on the bad guy camp with a bow and arrow and dynamite, and his lightning fast pistol.

Riding off, never able to return back to his home, to wherever the trail takes him.

Sound familiar?

Okay, not a single scene, situation, idea, or image that was in *that* screenplay was in *my* script for *Django Unchained.*

Yet . . . the essence of what Floyd was trying to accomplish in that script, an epic western with a black heroic cowboy at its center, *was* the very heart of what I was trying to accomplish with *Django Unchained.*

But even more influential than any one script was having a man trying to be a screenwriter living in my house. Him writing, him talking about his script, me reading it, made me consider for the first time writing movies. The reason I knew how to even format a screenplay was from reading Floyd's screenplays. It would be a long road—from that year of 1978 to me completing my first feature length screenplay—*True Romance*—in September 1987.

But due to Floyd's inspiration I *tried* writing screenplays. I usually never got that far. I think page thirty was by far the furthest I ever got. But I tried. And eventually I succeeded.

What happened to the script for *Billy Spencer*?

Nothing.

I doubt any really serious entity has ever read it.

And I'm fairly positive not a single copy of it exists anymore.

I'm sure at the time of his death Floyd was the only one who still had a copy of it. And whenever he died, wherever he was, it was disposed of with the rest of his meager possessions (the fate of most vagabonds).

And whatever trash can it was tossed into was the final resting place of Floyd Ray Wilson's dream of a black cowboy hero named *Billy Spencer.*

My dream of a black cowboy hero, *Django Unchained,* was not only read, it was made, by me, into a worldwide smash. A smash that resulted in me winning the Academy Award for Best Original Screenplay.

By the time I walked up to that podium and accepted that little gold man, with Dustin Hoffman and Charlize Theron standing behind me, Floyd was long since dead.

I don't know how he died, where he died, or where he's buried.

But I do know I should've thanked him.

Index

ng is below.

About the Author

QUENTIN TARANTINO was born in 1963 in Knoxville, Tennessee. He is the writer-director of nine feature films, the winner of two Academy Awards for Best Original Screenplay, and the author of the novel *Once Upon a Time in Hollywood*. He lives in Los Angeles and Tel Aviv.